THE CRISIS OF 1830–1842 IN CANADIAN-AMERICAN RELATIONS

THE RELATIONS OF
CANADA AND THE UNITED STATES

———

A SERIES OF STUDIES
PREPARED UNDER THE DIRECTION OF THE
CARNEGIE ENDOWMENT FOR INTERNATIONAL PEACE
DIVISION OF ECONOMICS AND HISTORY

JAMES T. SHOTWELL, *Director*

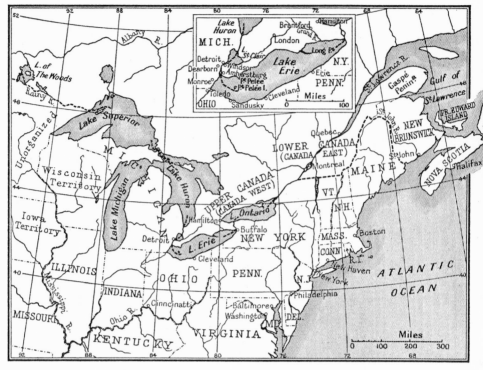

Northeastern North America in the 1830's

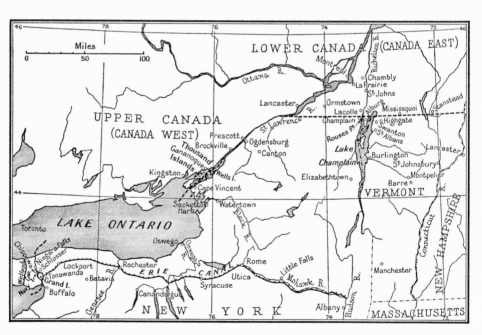

Lake Ontario to Lake Champlain

THE CRISIS OF 1830-1842 IN CANADIAN-AMERICAN RELATIONS

BY

ALBERT B. COREY

THE ST. LAWRENCE UNIVERSITY

NEW YORK / RUSSELL & RUSSELL

FIRST PUBLISHED IN 1941
REISSUED, 1970, BY RUSSELL & RUSSELL
A DIVISION OF ATHENEUM PUBLISHERS, INC.
BY ARRANGEMENT WITH
THE CARNEGIE ENDOWMENT FOR INTERNATIONAL PEACE
L. C. CATALOG CARD NO: 77-102483
PRINTED IN THE UNITED STATES OF AMERICA

TO
INEZ McCALLUM COREY

INTRODUCTION

This volume is one of the most important in the series on Canadian-American relations, though it is a small book and one largely confined to but five years of the history of those relations a hundred years ago. In the first place, it is important for the corrective which it offers to that superficial reading of Canadian-American history which over-emphasizes the "unarmed frontier" as the guarantee of peace between the two nations. This myth which has been so often exploited by those who think of disarmament as a prime cause of peace does not stand the test of history. The real achievement, as narratives like this remind us, lies in the development of trust and confidence in the good will of nations. That confidence, now so thoroughly established between Canada and the United States as to seem almost like a law of nature, was by no means their constant possession throughout the history of the last century and a quarter, since the Rush Bagot agreement set the program for disarmament on the joint waterways of the two countries, with the corollary of extension across the continent. It was a development that grew out of the success of peaceful settlements of a whole series of difficult crises. The War of 1812 had not settled some of the most serious sources of contention between the United States and Canada, and the flame of conflict was fanned at different times and places on both sides of the border, from Maine to Oregon. It was but natural, therefore, and in line with this ominous trend of history, that when rebellion broke out in Canada in 1837, and the expressed aims seemed so much like those of the American Revolution, the disorders consequent upon it should extend far across the border. How near to war this brought the Government of the United States and Great Britain will surprise many a reader of the pages that follow. Incident after incident gave the hotheads and the jingoes in each country their chance to stir latent antagonisms. Under such circumstances the provision for disarmament along the border was of little effect. Fearing attack, the British Government strengthened its military establishment in Canada until it definitely outranked that of the United States available for action. What ultimately saved the peace of the American continent in that crisis was not the mechanical device of disarmament but statesmanship which arose above contentions, and a public opinion which turned away from the cruder methods of pioneer days to a realization of common interests in a common North American community of nations, each intent upon the achievement of its own destiny in terms of freedom.

Of the statesmen of the period, the three who stand out above all the rest are Lord Durham, Daniel Webster, and Lord Ashburton. The other American whose name should be added in this connection is that of a soldier, General Winfield Scott. Of these, the one whose place is assured in Canadian-American history beyond all chance of international differences of opinion is Lord Durham. In the record as presented here, taken for the most part from original sources, we see the man who first drew the blueprints for the structure of the British Commonwealth of Nations pointing the way to fundamental principles of peace between Canada and the United States. It was no sentimentalist who set about undoing the irritation caused among Americans by the irresponsible jingoism of the English-Canadian press, for while consciously cultivating good will by presenting the "sight of the two flags united in one common effort to put an end to this unnatural excitement on the frontiers," he was firm in his assertion of Canadian rights, and backed them by the show of force. It is a strange fact that the appreciation by Americans of Durham's statesmanship should have been almost completely lost sight of in the years that followed. One wonders what might have happened if a Durham had been sent to the American colonies in 1775!

The story of the Webster-Ashburton Treaty is approached here from a different background from that common in the schoolbook histories. The narrative presents the dangers of the policy of "muddling through" when unsettled objects of contention accumulate in an atmosphere of mutual distrust and growing hostility. The rights and wrongs of the contestants become less capable of adjustment the longer this situation lasts. The situation with which Webster and Ashburton grappled was in its way not unlike that of the frontier problems in Europe at the end of the World War, when the claims of neighbor nations were so fundamentally opposed that no settlement could be found that both sides would regard as just. But decisions have to be taken, and the only ultimate solution is to achieve conditions of international amity and mutual confidence so that the question of exactly where a boundary line shall run will be of less and less importance with the development of the international neighborhood.

Finally there is the contribution of the soldier, intent, as in this instance, not on making war but on preventing it. When General Winfield Scott was sent to take command on the border, he found that it was his fellow Americans who were making much of the trouble. Yet that did not swerve him from his duty, and with the little military force at his command he policed the frontier, using, as he afterward explained, "rhetoric and diplomacy" as his chief weapons, and having "countrymen and friends" as his chief enemies! Fortunately the British commander of the Canadian forces, Sir John Colborne, that good veteran of the Peninsular War, had a similar conception of the soldier's duty. With such effective restraint upon the hotheads and the troublemakers, it was possible for the statesmen to come to terms. Who now remembers even the name of the man McLeod, for whom the British Government raised the question of national honor almost to the point of threatening war. These are now "old, far off, forgotten things" and it is well that it should be so. In the world crisis of today the one important thing for both the United States and Canada is that they have each in its own way preserved to the full and cherished with patriotic devotion their common heritage of liberty.

JAMES T. SHOTWELL

PREFACE

THE decade of the 1830's has been regarded in the history of British North America as chiefly one in which the conflict over self-government came to a head. The Canadian rebellions have been explained therefore in terms almost exclusively of domestic and imperial problems in the Canadas. As between British North America and the United States the 1830's have been regarded mainly in terms of the troublesome Northeastern boundary dispute between Maine and New Brunswick. Actually these two approaches present a limited picture of Canadian history and throw out of perspective the consequences of the Canadian rebellions in British-American and Canadian-American relations. It is the purpose of this book to provide a perspective which accords more nearly with the actual importance of this period. Hence the title, "The Crisis of 1830–1842 in Canadian-American Relations."

My obligations to others for assistance, encouragement, and advice are very great. The most helpful of all has been my wife. To her this book is dedicated in gratitude for her patience and devotion to the cause of scholarship. I have leaned with varying degrees of weight upon Professors H. Donaldson Jordan of Clark University, Allan Nevins of Columbia University, Charles P. Stacey of Princeton University, and my colleagues Howard William Crocker, Clarence Hurd Gaines, Richard Lyle Power, and Henry Reiff at St. Lawrence. I am grateful for the courteous assistance given me by Dr. Gustav Lanctot and Mr. Norman Fee of the Public Archives of Canada, and by the staffs of the Archives of the Department of State, the Manuscript Room of the Library of Congress, and the American Antiquarian Society. I am particularly indebted to Professor Reginald G. Trotter of Queen's University for aid in more directions than he is ever likely to realize, and to Professor J. Bartlet Brebner of Columbia University whose advice and counsel have been as gladly received as they were generously given. Every page bears evidence of the painstaking effort of Mr. Arthur E. McFarlane of the Carnegie Endowment for International Peace. And finally, I am glad to express a deep sense of obligation to Dr. James T. Shotwell for many kindnesses, not the least of which has been his assistance in making possible the completion of this book.

ALBERT B. COREY

Canton, N. Y.
    March, 1941.

CONTENTS

MAPS

ABBREVIATIONS

A.S.P.—American State Papers.

C—Public Archives of Canada, C Series (Military Papers, originals).

D.S. Br. Legation, Notes from—Archives of the Department of State: Notes from the British Legation.

D.S. Br. Legation, Notes to—Archives of the Department of State: Notes to the British Legation.

D.S. Dom. Letters—Archives of the Department of State, Domestic Letters (Letters in answer to those received from territorial United States).

D.S. Misc. Letters—Archives of the Department of State, Miscellaneous Letters (Letters from territorial United States).

G—Public Archives of Canada, G Series (Dispatches from the Colonial Office to the governments of Upper and Lower Canada, and the United Province of Canada, originals).

G.B., Dispatches from—Archives of the Department of State: Dispatches from the United States Minister in London.

G.B., Instructions—Archives of the Department of State: Instructions to the United States Minister in London.

M—Public Archives of Canada, M Series (Miscellaneous Letters).

Q—Public Archives of Canada, Q Series (Correspondence of the Colonial Office with the governments of Upper and Lower Canada, Transcripts from the Public Record Office).

Com. Adv.—New York Commercial Advertiser.

Jour. of Com.—New York Journal of Commerce.

Nat. Int.—Daily National Intelligencer, Washington, D.C.

N. Am. Rev.—North American Review.

Niles—Niles' Weekly Register, Baltimore.

THE CRISIS OF 1830–1842 IN CANADIAN-AMERICAN RELATIONS

CHAPTER I

THE SETTING: COUNTRIES AND PEOPLES

In 1830 that portion of British North America known as the Canadas extended from the mouth of the St. Lawrence to the Detroit River, a distance of about 1,200 miles. In area this territory covered some 350,000 square miles. Geographically and geologically it is anything but a single unit.[1] The most easterly portion, the Gaspé peninsula, points out into the ocean, a rock-bound, mountainous coast whose northern shore along the St. Lawrence is well-nigh uninhabitable. Only along its southern shore did this projection of the Appalachian system provide low-lying agricultural lands. Here lived a hardy people composed of French, Scotch, and English settlers. Far removed from the centers of political strife and agitation these people quietly followed their several callings as fishermen, farmers, and lumberjacks. Scarcely ever did they see the political agitator; nor did they give him more than a feeble and cautious welcome when he came among them. To live quietly, to work undisturbed, to exchange their fish for the merchandise of their provincial and American neighbors—these were the main interests in their existence. The Bay of Chaleur was their highway in summer, the frozen trails their highway in winter. They were a segregated and secluded people. So it is that they never loomed large in the political and economic squabbles of the 1830's or were forced to take measures to defend themselves from the proposed aggression of filibusters from the United States.

To the west, along the south shore of the St. Lawrence, lay a fertile valley which widened and contracted and widened again until it reached the city of Montreal itself. Here dwelt a people French in origin, customs, and manner of living, holding lands under seigneurial tenure, guided by a dominating if benignant church, simple in

1. Cf. W. N. Thayer, "The Northward Extension of the Physiographic Divisions of the United States," *The Journal of Geology*, XXVI (February–March, April–May, 1918), 161–185, 237–254.

their interests and in their standard of living, for the most part ignorant of the rudiments of the three R's, and subject to the dominance of the three authorities, the curé, the seigneur, and the prothonotary. Both east and west of the city of Quebec these French Canadians were a hard-working peasantry who like their kinsmen in Gaspé desired above all else as little interference as possible with their time-honored ways of living, working, and worshiping. Nor can it be said that they were disappointed, for they did enjoy comparative tranquillity.

In the vicinity of Quebec and Montreal, and the towns in between, discordant elements had nevertheless begun to appear as soon as New France had been occupied by the British. In the towns and cities an Anglo-Saxon trading class began to establish itself and to demand privileges and power out of all proportion to its numbers. Fortunately for the French various judgments, acts, and ordinances established for them those privileges which had been hinted at in the Treaty of Paris of 1763 and which had been legally destroyed by the proclamation of that year.[2] The Constitutional Act of 1791 once again safeguarded their interests and gave evidence of the opinion then in the ascendant that, paradoxical as it might seem, the way to keep French Canada British was to allow it to remain French in culture and law. Yet it was not clearly apparent after 1791 that the French were to be left to themselves, for into those areas not occupied by the French there came, between 1784 and 1830, a large number of English and Scotch settlers.[3] By the latter year schemes were afoot to organize land companies, and in 1833 the British American Land Company was chartered. It took as its special preserve the area south and east of Montreal which came to be known as the Eastern Townships.

Despite the advent of this alien population there was no evident line of cleavage at first between the two racial groups in the country districts. That was because, while contiguous, the English and French lands were not coextensive. English and French did not mix.

2. For example, Lord Mansfield's judgment in Campbell v. Hall, 1774; the Quebec Act, 1774, 14 Geo. III, c. 83; and Carleton's Ordinance for Establishing Civil Courts, February 25, 1777.

3. Helen I. Cowan, *British Emigration to British North America, 1783–1837* (Toronto, 1928).

So long as they remained apart clashes due to racial antipathies were not likely to arise.

It soon became evident, however, that, though separated in the countryside, divergent interests brought the two races sharply into conflict in the towns and cities. Living side by side and competing in commerce and industry there now was ample opportunity for clashes of opinion and of interest. This condition was aggravated by the ease and the frequency with which French political agitators aroused the French working population in town and country round about. The center of greatest agitation was Montreal, although Three Rivers, St. Charles, St. Denis, and Quebec were no strangers to demagoguery and violent criticism of government.

In the large it may be said that so far as Canadian and American relations are concerned, the area which will engage our attention extends from Quebec to Montreal, southward to the border, but to the north of the river not at all except where, in the vicinity of Montreal, the city itself blended with and was transformed into the countryside. Even within this area Canadian activities as they were related to the United States grew less and less as one approached Quebec. Politically, all of Lower Canada was affected in its relations with the United States. Nevertheless but a small area was directly and immediately involved.

To the west of Lower Canada and separated from it by the Ottawa River lay Upper Canada, with an area of approximately one hundred thousand square miles. Except for the rim of settlement along the St. Lawrence this area was largely a wilderness. Settlement was not easy north of the fertile plain which bounded the river, for one soon ran into the great "Canadian shield" whose underlying formation of pre-Cambrian rocks was covered with soil too scanty to permit of the pursuit of agriculture on an extended scale.

In the settled portions of Upper Canada; that is, in the fertile belts north of the St. Lawrence River and Lakes Ontario and Erie, there were in 1830 three distinct types of people. The United Empire Loyalists had been the first to come. Many of them had previously been engaged in agriculture; most were skeptical of the nascent republicanism and democracy of their neighbors to the south, and all were unwilling to give up their connections with Great Britain for the more dubious privileges which they thought American citizenship conferred. The second group was made up of emigrants from the British Isles. Though they came from the Highlands and Lowlands of Scotland, the farms of Ireland, and the villages of England, they all displayed certain characteristics in common. They "all had been more uniformly influenced by the conditions that *drove* them from the home land than by those which attracted them to the colonies."[4] For the most part they felt the need of economic freedom and opportunity. From among their numbers came the agitators who demanded more democratic forms of government; but it was from their ranks and from the United Empire Loyalists that were drawn the most steadfast adherents of the Crown. The third group was composed of non-Loyalist American settlers who found it both convenient and profitable to take up the good lands around the Great Lakes. As numerous perhaps in 1830 as the other two groups put together,[5] they made good farmers, were generally law-abiding, and by degrees became accustomed to the new political scene. Many naturally remained sympathetic toward the American form of government and toward American institutions, with the consequence that they were accused oftentimes of intriguing to unite Upper Canada with the United States or of attempting to introduce republicanism and democracy of the American type into the British provinces.

Upper Canada was dependent primarily upon agriculture for its existence. There were a few towns like Kingston, York (later Toronto), Hamilton, London, and Sandwich, but they were of far less importance as manufacturing centers than as trading marts, as places where the law courts were situated, and as centers of social and military life. The largest of these in 1834 was Toronto with a population of 9,174.[6] The other towns ranged in population from 4,196 in the case of Kingston to 1,406 in Niagara.[7] No one town, it

4. *Ibid.*, p. 2.

5. This balance was sharply altered when immigration to Upper Canada from Great Britain increased rapidly during the 1830's, and especially during the 1840's.

6. R. Montgomery Martin, *History of Upper and Lower Canada* (London, 1836), p. 63.

7. *Ibid.*, pp. 224, 230.

may be said, had the prominence which distinguished Montreal or Quebec. Yet, provincial as they were, it was their citizens who led the fight for a more democratic form of government.

The area in the United States which lay adjacent to that just described extended from Vermont in the east to Michigan in the west. Occasional towns which proudly called themselves cities dotted the landscape, such as Detroit, Buffalo, Rochester, Syracuse, and Burlington. There were villages too, like Swanton, St. Albans, and Danville in Vermont, Ogdensburg, Watertown, Oswego, and Lockport in New York, Cleveland in Ohio, and Monroe in Michigan.

Along the whole of this frontier lived a farming population, taking its livelihood from the raised river plain of the St. Lawrence Basin. But what gave farming a fillip was the large immigration of New Englanders who came from Connecticut by way of Vermont. Such a movement was significant also because it gave evidence of and helped to create a spirit of adventure and a toughness of physique so characteristic of a farming frontier. It bred a type of "rugged individualism" and intolerance in these New Englanders which was strongly accentuated by the fetish of Jacksonian democracy. This, in turn, evoked a warm sympathy for those who were said to be oppressed by tyrannical rulers.

What gave western New York its peculiar distinction was not its farming population, many of whom were immigrants from Europe, but the fact that it was the center of the most interesting and fanatical religious experiments of the time. This "burnt over" district was justly renowned for the number of its religious revivals and for the beginnings of quixotic religious faiths. Such enthusiasm was carried far and wide. It made martyrs and it made adventurers and filibusters.[8]

If frontier life was characteristic of the northern tier of counties of New York, it was even more characteristic of the new West, the new land of promise, from Ohio to Michigan, where good land could easily be acquired. Not only did a considerable proportion of the new immigration of the 1820's and 1830's find its way directly from American ports to these new lands, but possibly half the immigrants

8. W. W. Sweet, *The Story of Religions in America* (New York, 1930), chap. xvii.

arriving at Quebec found their way to western New York, and thence to Ohio, Indiana, and Michigan.[9]

Before the rise of the great cities which now stand as sentinels of conflicting commercial interests, the people of this northern border area had a singularly uniform outlook on economic and political affairs. They gave to the area an atmosphere and an appearance of homogeneity. It was and remained until the 1850's a unit as much as the solid South or the North.

Elsewhere, to the south, there was far less uniformity of life or of outlook. The new industrialism was beginning to make headway along the eastern seaboard and came into conflict with the agricultural interests of the hinterland and the new West. Slavery held sway in the South. The balancing of free and slave states was looming as an increasingly significant issue. Already there was dangerous talk of the dissolution of the Union.

9. Cowan, *op. cit.;* W. F. Adams, *Ireland and Irish Emigration to the New World from 1815 to the Famine* (New Haven, 1923).

CHAPTER II

BEFORE THE REBELLIONS

CROSS-BORDER OPINIONS

EXCEPT when their interests were directly and immediately affected Americans gave relatively little thought to the Canadas between 1815 and 1830. Their government, to be sure, concerned itself about armaments on the Great Lakes, the acquisition of control over the frontier forts which British soldiers continued to occupy for some time after the Treaty of Ghent, the Indian question along the northern frontier, and the delimitation of the boundary between the United States and British North America.[1] Freedom of commerce and the carrying trade between British-American possessions and the United States provided the elements of a controversy with Great Britain.[2] All of these matters were dealt with officially. Only those who were in the vicinity where disputes arose or whose commercial interests were involved seem to have been much concerned about the so-called aggressive policy of Britain in North America.

There was, nevertheless, to be found in the United States a considerable amount of well-formed opinion which was expressed in books of travel, newspapers, and correspondence. Certainly much of this was based upon hearsay or prejudice or upon observations drawn from a hurried visit to the Canadas rather than upon a sound knowledge and deep understanding of the country. But this opinion is significant because it was characteristic of the educated classes; for it was from the writings and public utterances of these classes that the inarticulate mass of American society derived its ideas of and its attitudes toward Canadians.

Among the few books[3] which, prior to 1840, were written by

1. David R. Moore, *Canada and the United States, 1815–1830* (Chicago, 1910); J. M. Callahan, *The Neutrality of the American Lakes and Anglo-American Relations,* "Johns Hopkins University Studies in Historical and Political Science," Ser. XVI, Nos. 1–4 (Baltimore, 1898), chap. iv.

2. F. Lee Benns, *The American Struggle for the British West India Carrying Trade, 1815–1830,* "Indiana University Studies," No. 56, Vol. X (1923).

3. Seven books on Canada appear to have been published by American

Americans on their travels in Canada, one by Joseph Sansom of Philadelphia, a member of the American Philosophical Society, enjoyed a considerable vogue during the ten years following 1818. Sansom had spent one month during the summer of 1817 in Lower Canada and spoke with the assurance of a lifelong resident. He deprecated the lack of information upon which Americans could rely concerning "the sentiments of the People, or the comparative situation, and future prospects of that Country."[4] In attempting to describe Canada he succeeded merely in freezing some of the grotesque ideas then current about the French Canadians, a situation which Benjamin Silliman of Yale vainly attempted to modify in a book written in 1820.[5] Sansom called Lower Canada a country "in a state of ignorance" little better than that of the Indians, "and of poverty little removed from a state of absolute want." It was the "Siberia of Britain." Yet he found the French were entirely content with their lot.[6] All this was corroborated in 1828 by the Duke of Saxe-Weimar whose book of travels received a tremendous ovation in the American press. According to the Duke, Canadian towns were very poor because of the oppressiveness of the feudal system, "which opposes all prosperity." Because of it the more affluent immigrants proceeded to the United States where, in comparison with Lower Canada, "nobody is oppressed; on the contrary, . . . all laws are in their favor."[7]

During these years occasional correctives were published by *Niles' Weekly Register* and the *New York Journal of Commerce*, as well as by Benjamin Silliman who claimed that by 1820 "a more correct

travelers between 1799 and 1830. The majority of these were more concerned with Lower than with Upper Canada.

4. Joseph Sansom, *Sketches of Lower Canada, historical and descriptive; with the author's recollections of the soil, and aspect; the morals, habits, and religious institutions of that isolated country; during a tour to Quebec in the month of July, 1817* (New York, 1817), p. 6.

5. Benjamin Silliman, *Remarks, made on a Short Tour, between Hartford and Quebec, in the Autumn of 1819* (New Haven, 1820).

6. Sansom, *op. cit.*, pp. 236, 237, 300.

7. His Highness Bernhard, Duke of Saxe-Weimar-Eisenach, *Travels through North America, during the years 1825 and 1826* (Philadelphia, 1828), I, 96. These ideas were quoted with approval in the *North American Review*, XXVIII (October, 1828), 236. Hereafter referred to as *N. Am. Rev.*

knowledge of Canada, is now fast diffusing itself through the American States." Few Americans could visit Canada "without returning more favourably impressed, respecting it than they expected to be."[8] A decade later *Niles* found that Canada was "rapidly improving" though, by comparison, New York and Ohio were developing at a faster rate.[9] In 1833 the *Journal of Commerce* came out with the surprising statement that the prosperity of Upper Canada seemed to be "as great as our own," for property values had doubled during the past four years while the population of Upper Canada towns had grown enormously—for example, that of York which had increased from 2,500 in 1820 to 8,731 on July 1, 1833.[10] This was indeed a roseate picture of the good times of the early 1830's.

During the decade from 1825 to 1835 the almost universal acceptance of the more unfavorable opinion was, however, far more characteristic. Of all the journals, the *North American Review*, the most influential and the keenest in its analysis, was the most stubborn in its insinuations. The chief reason for backwardness in Lower Canada it found to be the existence of large areas of uncultivated land in the seigneuries, and this despite the circumstance that the burdens of the seigneurial system were light and that land could be obtained for nothing.[11] It was, it said, "the natural indolence of the French inhabitants" due to their disregard of "what we call comforts, from education and habits, and from their religious tenets," which accounted for this lack of agricultural progress. Moreover, it continued, "the state of society in Canada . . . is a very primitive one. . . . Wealth has not there the same attraction as, for instance, in the superlatively artificial society of England." Furthermore, "the Catholic religion is essentially inimical to wealth. On a people of primitive character that cause acts very powerfully."

The writer in this instance based his conclusions on something more than hearsay or personal predilection. He had before him the "Report of the Select Committee of the House of Assembly, 1821, on

8. Silliman, *op. cit.*, p. 369.

9. *Niles' Weekly Register*, XXXIX, 328 (January 9, 1830). Hereafter referred to as *Niles*.

10. Quoted in the *Daily National Intelligencer* (Washington), November 14, 1833. Hereafter referred to as *Nat. Int.*

11. *N. Am. Rev.*, XXVII (July, 1828), 1–30.

the Settlement of Crown Lands." From this he drew twelve conclusions or, rather, in it he found twelve specific reasons for the lack of settlement and progress in Lower Canada. The main reasons for backwardness he held to be the lack of means of communication— that is, roads, bridges, and canals; the paralyzing effect of large land grants in earlier years; the preference shown for settling in towns and villages, due to the desire of Roman Catholics to receive instruction and to have the protection of judicial processes; the expensiveness of acquiring lands in free socage; the reservation of lands for the Crown and the clergy which had proved to be a marked impediment to settlement; the scarcity of currency; the poor soil in some districts; the severity of the climate; and, in some sections, the insecurity of land titles.

Of these many drawbacks to the extension of settlement and the advance of agriculture, one, the "Clergy Reserves," was of particular interest. In commenting upon this the writer fell into the very obvious attitude of many Americans at the time, an attitude which was colored by the nativistic and anti-Catholic sentiment[12] which was soon to become such a force in American politics and which had colored American relations with French Canada since 1774. The Clergy Reserves were defended on the twin grounds of expediency and right. They were made imperative because of the religious and civil privileges which the Roman Catholic clergy enjoyed. Owning large domains they (the Roman Catholic clergy) exercised "probably a greater influence over the minds of the people than the Catholic clergy exercise in any other country."[13] For that reason it would obviously be foolish for Great Britain to disregard the security of supremacy in Lower and Upper Canada by refusing to provide endowments for the Anglican church, upon whose shoulders rested to a considerable extent the burden of maintaining British supremacy in Canada. In view of this it was incomprehensible that the average Canadian should object vehemently, as he did, to the setting aside of land for the Protestant clergy. From every point of view the Clergy

12. Cf. J. B. McMaster, *A History of the People of the United States from the Revolution to the Civil War* (New York, 1883–1913), VI, 84–85. Also Edward Channing, *A History of the United States* (New York, 1905–25), V, 217.

13. *N. Am. Rev.,* XXVII (July, 1828), 18.

Reserves were a hindrance to the advance of settlement, but to the Protestant-American mind it seemed more important to offset the influence of Roman Catholicism than to extend the cultivation of the soil.

The seigneurial system, so much discussed among those of Anglo-Saxon descent, received modified commendation. The system was not recommended for persons of English parentage. On the contrary, those who were prone to condemn it out of court were advised to hesitate before condemning it "on no other ground than the effects which other institutions, distinguished by the same names, have produced elsewhere." The seigneurs were a fine lot of men, most of whom were "mixed with the rest of the landholders, and destitute of all peculiar distinctions and prerogatives." The system was not a harsh one. Even if the tenant did not own his own land, his dues and obligations were not at all onerous and he was to all intents and purposes a free man. The seigneurial system was beneficent even if it was patriarchal as well.

Americans knew far less of Upper Canada than of Lower Canada. The latter had a glamour and a history which the former did not possess. Its history was entwined with the romance of French settlement, with the struggle for supremacy in the fur trade, and with the clash of arms. Legends sprang up around this country peopled by the French, giving rise to curiosity and to travel. What was more, French Canada stood at the entrance to "the commercial empire of the St. Lawrence,"[14] guarding and controlling the river highway to the sea, and forming a formidable competitor for the trade of the West. Thus it was that economic competition and the existence of a curious novelty formed the twin bases upon which American interest in Lower Canada rested. But Americans could by no means dismiss the upper province from their attention by a mere flash of the magician's wand. Everywhere to the north there spread the shadow if not the substance of the British lion, clearly not a welcome beast while the eagle was still sprouting feathers and growing talons. In Lower Canada the lion's presence frequently seemed unreal in the midst of a seigneurial society, but that was not so in Upper Canada where Loyalists and recent immigrants from Britain were not averse to

14. D. G. Creighton, *The Commercial Empire of the St. Lawrence, 1760–1850* (Toronto and New Haven, 1937).

hurling epithets at Americans in a language they were able to understand.

Interest in Annexation

With the fall of Quebec and with the treaty which followed in 1763, the stage was set for the dominion of a single state from the Rio Grande to the Arctic. Within twenty years this territory was to be cut in two by the recognition of American independence, while it was only by the most fortuitous circumstances that Quebec was not forced by the revolting colonies to join them in secession from the mother country. For many decades after 1783 the beacon of annexation glowed, at times at white heat, at times very dimly, but it was never completely snuffed out; for despite lulls in American expansionist sentiment, there continued until the 1840's to be a widespread belief in the United States that some day by war a settlement of all outstanding disputes with Great Britain would eventuate in the acquisition of all of British North America.

Quite aside from annexation there lingered the belief that the colonies would eventually, of their own volition, break away from the mother country, and that they must thereafter, by the very nature of their location and association with the United States, be forced willingly or unwillingly to join that country. This break with Great Britain would depend, in the first place, upon the progressive decline of royal authority within the colonies. Nor could the decline be prevented. It was as inevitable as the rise to preëminence of republican and democratic over monarchical institutions in the New World. Monarchy simply could not thrive in North America. Some day its very weaknesses, in comparison with the rugged strength of republicanism, would force its expulsion from the continent. At any rate, should self-government emerge in Canada as a consequence of an insistent and increasing populace, "all the power of Britain" could not delay or prevent separation.[15]

Now that a hundred years have passed, and in view of the change which has taken place in the very spirit of colonial government, we can see that so far as Canada was concerned the panacea for the

15. Sansom, *op. cit.*, pp. 138–146; *Boston Bulletin*, quoted in *Nat. Int.*, July 11, 1828; *N. Am. Rev.*, XXXIV (January, 1832), 46–49.

colonial controls exerted over the second British Empire was not to
be separation, independence, or union with the United States but a
new practice in government which would draw the colonies and the
mother country together into a commonwealth of autonomous units.
But during the years from 1815 to 1837 nothing of this vast change
was envisaged on either side of the Atlantic. Instead it was assumed
that the colonies were destined to become independent. After all, was
it not true that there were two excellent examples of the ripe colonial
fruit falling from the parent tree? And had not both of these come
about through revolution? Americans remembered first of all their
own experience; then they recalled the revolt of the Spanish colonies
in Central and South America. As if this were insufficient Texas likewise provided further proof that insubordination would occur if
grievances remained unredressed, and that despite the existence of a
republican form of government.

— There was a second good reason why Americans expected the
eventual separation of the British colonies from the mother country.
Considerable numbers of them had emigrated to the Canadas, especially to Upper Canada, before 1828. In that year barriers to natu-
ralization were removed in the upper province and American immigration increased. By November, 1831, Sir John Colborne, the lieutenant governor, was so disturbed by this influx from the south and
the consequent acquisition of land "by private purchase in spite of
the law" that he reported to the Colonial Office his concern and alarm
over the prospective Americanization of the province. The laconic
Goderich was, however, content to allow the situation to be handled
by the local government.[16]

At the same time, no immediate danger presented itself in the
lower province where Americans settled largely in Montreal, and
played an important part in commercial and financial, and even political, affairs as members of the dominant merchant group.[17] In Upper Canada, on the other hand, the influx of Americans gave an im-

16. Aileen Dunham, *Political Unrest in Upper Canada, 1815–1836* (London, 1927), p. 78.

17. Adam Shortt, "Founders of Canadian Banking. Horatio Gates, Whole-
sale Merchant, Banker, and Legislator," *Journal of Canadian Bankers' Association*, XXX (October, 1922), 34–47. There was also a substantial American population east and west of the Richelieu.

petus to different types of dissent in politics and religion.[18] One of the complaints of the anti-American party was that the Methodists had taken a firm hold of the religious life of the rural districts and that circuit riders who ministered to the spiritual needs of their flocks came from the United States whence they brought strange ideas about government that were incompatible with the acceptance of colonial dependence upon Great Britain. Fear of this influence remained acute even after the Methodists set up, in 1828, a Canadian branch of the church, known as the Canadian Conference. Colborne claimed in 1829 that four or five newspapers were allied with them and were undermining the patriotism of the people by spreading anti-British ideas.[19] The Reverend Isaac Fidler wrote in 1833 that "most of the Methodist ministers in Canada are from the States and have a double object: they ostensibly minister in sacred offices but secretly and effectively disseminate principles destructive to the present order of affairs. They are concerting schemes for the establishment of republican institutions and plans of government."[20] Opinions similar to these appear to have been held by the majority of the Anglicans and the financial interests in Upper Canada.

It was not alone the peculiar political system, the increase of American population, and the diffusion of American ideas in Canada that gave, in American eyes, promise of separation from Great Britain. The Canadas, and especially Upper Canada, lay athwart that life line, the St. Lawrence River, whose right to continued vitality was being seriously challenged in the 1830's by the Erie Canal and the Hudson River. Upper Canada was coming thus to be peculiarly dependent upon the United States, as it already was upon Lower Canada, for a thoroughfare for its supplies and its products on their way to market.

In fact, the upper province was in a peculiar position with respect

18. M. A. Garland, "Some Frontier and American Influences in Upper Canada prior to 1837," *Transactions* of the London and Middlesex Historical Society, Part XIII (1929), 5–33.

19. Canadian Archives, *Series Q*, CCCLI, 85. Colborne to Hay, March 13, 1829. Hereafter referred to as *Q*.

20. Rev. Isaac Fidler, *Observations on Professions, Literature, Manners and Emigration in the United States and Canada made during a residence there in 1832* (New York, 1833), p. 82.

to trade and commerce. Ever since its establishment in 1791 it had fought with its sister province over the use of the river, over the allocation of import and export duties collected at Montreal, St. John's, and Quebec, and over the prevention of smuggling. This continuing quarrel was matched by one between the two provinces and the mother country over the latter's hesitation to allow free importation of colonial wheat into Great Britain and refusal to relax the trade laws with respect to importation from the United States to Canada. What with increasing dependence of the provinces upon the Republic, increasing clamor for removal of restrictions on trade, and increasing smuggling along the entire border, it did not appear to be a far stretch of the imagination to assume that in time these British provinces must sever their transatlantic connections and throw in their lot with the United States.

For some ten years after the Treaty of Ghent expansionist sentiment in the United States was comparatively dormant, but after 1825 it awoke to new life. The most vigorous exponent of this idea was the *North American Review* which kept recurring to the subject for twenty years. As early as 1830 that journal[21] advocated the union of Canada and the United States as an unmitigated blessing. It would confer privileges on Canada, obviate collisions between the United States and Great Britain, and make a worthy addition to the Republic. Both justice and reason would compel the mother country to give up the colonies if they themselves should desire it.

The following year the *North American Review*[22] made another sortie. Recognizing the principle that in all cases where a change in the current political scene is desired careful planning and preparation are necessary, it reviewed the past relations between the United States and the Canadas and discovered that Americans had either taken insufficient steps to win over the Canadians or had actually alienated them. This had been true after the War of 1812. There was no reasonable doubt that if the British provinces were given an opportunity freely to make a choice they would prefer to become "four States of the American Union, with eight Senators and forty members of Congress." Yet the United States had done nothing constructive to bring this to pass. Now, however, that Great Britain and the

21. *N. Am. Rev.*, XXX (January, 1830), 234–236.
22. *Ibid.*, XXXIII (October, 1831), 454–455.

United States were at peace "honor as well as public policy" forbade
the United States to tamper with British subjects. Nevertheless it
was

a great public duty of the American statesman to look forward,—to con-
template the unfortunate probability of future wars, and the relations
of the colonial possessions of the British Government to the United
States . . . and to guard against all sources of alienation and bitter-
ness between this country and the neighboring and kindred population
beyond the northern boundary. He ought to feel, in all its force, even as
a purely domestic question, the desirableness of an extension of the
United States to the north, to preserve a safe balance of its growth to
the south. For these reasons, the march of events in the Canadas ought
to be carefully watched;—their parties and controversies understood;
—all causes of irritation avoided;—all means of conciliation sought;—
intercourse, commercial, political, and personal, cultivated in every
manner, consistent with the principles of honor toward the Government
of Great Britain, with which we are at peace; and thus a good foundation laid for adopting on the first day of the next war, a provision tan-
tamount to

an eleventh Article of Confederation which would provide for the admission of Canada with all the privileges and "advantages of this
Union." But so great was American ignorance of Canada that the
Review greatly feared that, if a war broke out in the next fifty years
"the most efficient preparation for it in the minds of the people in the
British provinces, will remain unmade." Union if it should come at
all must come at the request of Canada, although the United States
could and should do much to foster a desire for it.

It was all very well to urge union but there still remained the
question: Were the colonies fit to receive their independence and
were they politically advanced enough to join the United States? To
most Americans these questions suggested no doubts at all. It was
universally conceded that wherever Englishmen settled in North
America they were quite capable of governing themselves. This applied to the present British provinces. It followed therefore that they
would make admirable additions to the United States.[23] The problem
of assimilation would not be a difficult one; on the contrary, it would
be relatively simple. Coercion by the mother country would make the

23. *Ibid.,* XXXIV (January, 1832), 47–49.

whole issue easier of solution. The first war between the United States and Great Britain would send the provinces fleeing precipitately into the arms of the United States.

Short of war or rebellion there were still other ways of acquiring Canada. These were by purchase and by exchange. The opposition press, perhaps intent upon worrying the administration of President Jackson and preventing it from carrying on negotiations leading to treaties, recommended that the proposed purchase of Texas, which was at that time being widely discussed in the press, should be offset by the purchase of the British North American possessions. The *Providence Patriot* likewise suggested that Upper Canada and the district around Montreal might be exchanged for the Oregon country.[24] This was too much for the Democratic papers. They rose to the defense of the administration[25] and to attack the policy of purchase or exchange unless the people of Texas or Canada declared their desire to be annexed by the United States. Apparently the hornet's nest had better be left alone.

The acquisition of Canada was clearly associated with the question of securing a balance of free against slave states in the event that Texas should be admitted to the Union. What is one's surprise therefore to find at a time when the slavery question was sharpening domestic politics that the *Lexington* (Kentucky) *Intelligencer*,[26] which certainly represented one portion of the South, was wholeheartedly in favor of acquiring Canada, in case the provinces should declare their independence of Great Britain. The Lexington paper would even pursue an aggressive policy. Should not the people of the United States, it suggested, petition Congress "with one breath to acknowledge her [Canada's] independence, and, with the next, to take her into the union with us as 'another star' or stars, in the bright American constellation of freedom's jewels, to increase our stripes? And would there not be as much of national justice—international faith—sound policy—patriotism, philanthropy and common sense in such a course of proceeding on our part as there was in the . . . partition of Poland?"

24. *Boston Patriot,* quoted in *Nat. Int.,* October 12, 1829; *New York Courier and Enquirer,* quoted in *Northern Sentinel* (Vermont), October 16, 1829.

25. *Ibid.,* October 16, 1829.   26. Quoted in *Nat. Int.,* July 12, 1836.

In spite of this apparently bellicose attitude it seems that Americans were as a whole opposed to governmental interference in Canadian affairs. In the spring of 1829 William Lyon Mackenzie visited the United States.[27] While there he wrote a long and ardent letter on Canadian affairs to the editor of the *National Gazette*. The publication of this letter, Mackenzie's reception by Jackson and Van Buren, and his vivid comparisons of the United States and Canada to the disparagement of the latter gave rise to charges that his visit had been made for treasonable purposes; that is, "to sound out the Government as to the assistance they [Canadians] might expect to receive from the United States in case of rebellion."[28] The Whig press immediately took up the hue and cry. However respectable it might be for the press or for the American people to suggest the acquisition of Canada or to proffer aid to the Canadians against Great Britain it was certainly improper for the government to do so. The *Watch Tower* (Washington) claimed that all that was wanting to start a rebellion in Upper Canada was the sanction of the United States government.[29] Against this policy the *New York Commercial Advertiser* and the *National Intelligencer* were adamant,[30] and they both breathed a sigh of relief when they found the report was erroneous.

The recognition of the independence of Texas by resolution of the House of Representatives in July, 1836, brought a burst of approval and a storm of protest. The latter was particularly significant because of the manner in which the recognition of Canadian independence was currently linked up with that of Texas. The anti-administration papers, led by the *National Intelligencer*,[31] wondered whether the United States did not have certain moral obligations to refrain from interference in the affairs of the countries of North America. Would, for instance, the recognition of the independence

---

27. Charles Lindsey, *The Life and Times of Wm. Lyon Mackenzie. With an account of the Canadian Rebellion of 1837, and the subsequent frontier disturbances, chiefly from unpublished documents* (Toronto, 1862), I, 161.

28. *New York Commercial Advertiser*, hereafter referred to as *Com. Adv.*, quoted in *Nat. Int.*, June 24, 1830. Mackenzie insisted the charges were groundless and finally wrote to Van Buren asking for an official denial. This he received. Cf. the letter in Lindsey, *op. cit.*, I, 164 n.

29. Dunham, *op. cit.*, p. 147.

30. *Nat. Int.*, June 24, and July 20, 1830.

31. July 16, 1836.

of Canada by resolution mean anything more than an assertion of an abstract principle? Would "any wise nation, under the influence of a feeling of sympathy, rush into a policy which the usage of nations condemns"? And this sums up the attitude of a very large body of the American public with respect to official interference in British North American affairs.

AMERICAN VIEWS OF CANADIAN POLITICS

In the 1830's most Americans were frankly puzzled, as many still are, as to why Canadians should willingly remain under the dominion of Great Britain. Although this anomaly could not readily be explained, even in 1830, certain mitigating factors seemed reasonably clear. Some Americans had discovered that despite evidences of paternalism, the Canadas were reasonably well governed and that they enjoyed measurable freedom. Besides, it was well known that there was not overmuch enthusiasm among Englishmen for continuing to hold troublesome colonies like the Canadas; and it was also well known that there was in Britain sentiment in favor of allowing the white colonies to become independent. Americans, like many Englishmen, anticipated the eventual independence of the colonies. They assumed that Canadians were willing to accept domination by Britain for the moment largely because they anticipated and gladly awaited separation from the mother country in the not-too-distant future. Such an opinion—a mere bit of wishful thinking—illustrates only too well the immaturity of American knowledge of Canada.[32]

Much of this lack of understanding may be attributed to two factors. In the first place, this was a period during which Americans were developing an ebullient national self-consciousness and a pride in their own peculiar form of self-government. Gradually making headway in reducing their dependence upon Great Britain in a multitude of ways, they were still confronted and irked by the presence of British authority in North America. In consequence of this, American interest in the Canadas was quite naturally overshadowed

32. In October, 1831, the *North American Review* (XXXIII, 455) complained that the lack of knowledge of Canadian political and economic life was appalling. See also "Democrat" in the *New York Journal of Commerce* (hereafter referred to as *Jour. of Com.*), January 6, 1835, who also spoke of the lack of knowledge and interest in Canadian affairs.

by American interest in Great Britain and British affairs. In the second place, it is clear that there was relatively little understanding in the United States of the manner in which the Canadas were governed. It could not have soothed the feelings of British officialdom in Canada or in Great Britain to find that the blame for all political and economic ills was laid at the door of the British government. It was accused of heaping "taunts and insults" upon the Canadians.[33] It was informed that "a change of policy *must* take place . . ., *or the evil can only be met by the exercise of power.*" Canada would have "its just rights *at any expense.* This ought no longer to be dissimulated."[34] Further to illustrate the policy of Great Britain, *Niles' Register* printed an excerpt to the effect that William Lyon Mackenzie, the editor of the *Colonial Advocate* (York), had above his desk a device of a cock, hens, and chickens over which hovered a hawk about to pounce down. This was "intended as an illustration of that policy which 'covers and devours.' "[35]

While Americans were prone to congratulate themselves upon their own form of government, upon their political sagacity, and upon the reasonableness with which they conducted their political affairs—this in spite of the frequent assertion that the republican experiment could not last and that the United States must inevitably break up into two or more parts—they condemned the lack of "coolness of tempo" with which Canadian politics were conducted.[36] To them the reasons for acts of violence were apparent but the meaning of party strife or of what lay behind such strife was by no means clear. To be sure, party squabbles at election time were not unlike those which accompanied elections in the United States. There was violence and browbeating, obstructing of the polls by ruffians, and contested elections. Yet *Niles' Register* probably voiced the opinion of the majority of Americans when it said, "We do not know what the parties are contending for, but the great division" seemed to be

33. *Albany Argus,* July 3, 1829.
34. *Nat. Int.,* July 7, 1829. "Canada is not to be trifled with, or partially treated as Ireland has so long been; the land of civil and religious freedom is too near to render such an experiment safe." Editorial in the *Boston Bulletin,* quoted in *Nat. Int.,* July 11, 1828.
35. *Niles,* XXXVII, 53 (September 19, 1829).
36. *Albany Argus,* April 29, 1829.

the French on one side and the English, Americans, and Scotch on the other. In fact, social relations between persons in opposite parties appeared to be almost at an end.[37]

Aside from the lack of sound information about Canada much of the misunderstanding of the political scene may be traced to the current confusion in the meaning of the terms "republicanism" and "democracy." In the United States the march of the democratic system of government was to be seen in the extension of the franchise in the several states from the 1820's onward. In England the Reform Bill and the Municipal Corporation Act had, in a halting fashion, kept intact the liberties of the subject and moderately enlarged the suffrage. Since the march toward democracy was more evident in the United States and since that country was a republic, the tendency among literate and illiterate alike was to associate the two ideas and to fuse them into one. The Reform Bill was denounced as a step toward republicanism and as a measure designed to deprive Englishmen of their liberties while the strivings of the Canadians for a more liberal form of government were considered an attempt to extend both democracy and republicanism to British North America. As was to be expected the misunderstanding of and the blending of the two terms so that they represented all the most violent and distasteful elements of American political life did little to allay the fears of the conservative elements in Canada. They became increasingly staunch defenders of the colonial system of government, and therefore defenders of the prerogatives of the Crown and rights of Parliament as a means to preserve, in the traditional English manner, the liberties of Englishmen in America.

This confusion in terms did not obscure the need for the redress of grievances or the possibility of revolt, if remedies were not granted. Members of Parliament like Hume and Roebuck, and the English press, had for some years been attacking the "system of exclusion, favoritism, jobbing, and inadequate representation"[38] in the Canadas, and had been demanding a change in the system of colonial government. Americans were well aware of this. Indeed, as early as 1831, the American press was beginning to discover the likelihood of revolt

---

37. *Niles,* XLVI, 191 (May 17, 1834); XLVII, 262 (December 20, 1834).
38. *Nat. Int.,* July 11, 1828, and November 15, 1828, which quoted excerpts from the *London Morning Chronicle.*

in Canada if grievances remained unredressed.[39] Consequently it was prepared with a ready-made, revolutionary political philosophy for Canada when Elzéar Bédard, the first mayor of the city of Quebec, introduced the famous Ninety-two Resolutions in the Lower Canadian Assembly on February 21, 1834. Although the disjointed character of the Resolutions represented the epitome of ineptitude on the part of Louis Joseph Papineau and his followers, they did at least turn the searchlight on the Canadian desire for popular control of colonial government and a consequent gradual withdrawal of local affairs from long-established imperial control.

In both England and the United States it was the spirit and temper of the Resolutions rather than what they contained that roused public opinion and stimulated comment. Roebuck's considered opinion that "the provinces are in a state nearly approaching open revolt" was echoed by the American press.[40] The *Baltimore American* even went so far as to wonder "how a country can exist under pressure of ninety-two real grievances . . . inflicted by its government," and to agree with Hume's statement that "if the present system of misrule was suffered to continue in the Colonies, the inhabitants would not rest satisfied until the management of their affairs was entrusted to their own hands."[41]

The sympathetic response which the Ninety-two Resolutions inspired would lead one to expect that, in the following year, Mackenzie's Seventh Report on Grievances would elicit equal interest in the United States. On the contrary, there were no reverberations. Even the publication of Lord Glenelg's disparaging dispatch to Sir Francis Bond Head of December 5, 1835, the official reply of the Colonial Office to the Report, caused no immediate ripple south of the line. It was not because American interest had suddenly subsided that there was this conspicuous lull. Rather it was due to the nature of the Report itself and to its sponsors. Though the Seventh Report was the most famous, it was but one of many presented to the Upper Cana-

---

39. "Signs of a Spirit of Liberty in Canada," in *Albany Daily Advertiser*, quoted in *Nat. Int.*, January 20, 1831. Also *ibid.*, March 25, 1831; *Niles*, XLII, 22 (March 10, 1832).

40. *Nat. Int.*, March 6, 1834; *Niles*, XLVI, 35 (March 15, 1834); 191 (May 17, 1834).

41. Quoted in *Nat. Int.*, October 7, 1834.

dian Assembly by select committees. On the other hand, the Ninety-two Resolutions were hurled into the legislature like a bomb and they had the desired explosive effect. The Report contained 553 closely printed pages. Relatively few could become enthusiastic over so long a document. Moreover, according to Head's evidence, the reformers —Mackenzie, Bidwell, and others—were reluctant to concentrate on the grievances mentioned in the Report and insisted upon arguing about inconsequential matters.[42]

Between 1835 and 1837 the Canadian situation became tense. This was noted in many American papers. Revolution, separation from Great Britain, and union with the United States were confidently predicted.[43] Yet some papers noted with relief that attempts at conciliation were being made. The *National Intelligencer* noted on September 12, 1835, that the Earl of Gosford, the new governor of Lower Canada, and the members of his Commission of Inquiry, Sir Charles Grey and Sir George Gipps, had arrived at Quebec on August 23 to inquire into Canadian grievances and to propose remedies. The *New York Commercial Advertiser*[44] hoped that Gosford's attempts at conciliation "would soon be brought to an amiable termination." Two months later its hopes were dashed to the ground when news of the answer to the speech from the throne made it apparent that the reformers in Lower Canada would be satisfied with nothing less than the complete fulfillment of their demands. *Niles' Register* had likewise hoped for the success of the reformers, and was also disappointed.[45]

Up to this time the American press reflected the idea that Canadians were loyal to the Crown, in spite of their display of a headstrong determination to achieve advanced reforms. There appeared to be no inconsistency in a concurrent wholehearted allegiance to political authority and an equally wholehearted demand for a redress of grievances. It was the answer to the address referred to above that gave the first intimation that perhaps in some quarters in Canada allegiance and loyalty had begun to waver or had already given way

42. Sir Francis Bond Head, Bart., *A Narrative* (London, 1839), pp. 33–35.

43. *Jour. of Com.*, January 6, 1835, and July 18, 1837; *Niles*, XLIX, 37 (September 19, 1835); L, 73 (April 2, 1836).

44. November 12, 1835.   45. *Niles*, L, 100 (April 9, 1836).

to a spirit of revolt. A number of papers were quick to take up the inference drawn by the *New York Commercial Advertiser* when it said in a special article on Lower Canadian affairs that the answer to the speech from the throne "dwells repeatedly and at great length upon the 'welfare of the province'—the 'advantage of the people'—the 'privileges of the house'—and the 'rights of the provincial legislature,' but not a word of loyalty or devotion to his majesty's person or government."[46] It was suggested further that the reasonable concessions held out by the Royal Commissioners and by Lord Gosford's speech led only to further demands and to a more arrogant tone.[47]

Up to 1836 it appears that although Americans had begun to take a definite interest in Canadian affairs their sympathy on behalf of the Canadians had not been crystallized to the point where they would openly or actively take sides against Great Britain.[48] In the beginning of 1837 active sympathy was aroused, not because of the local scene in the Canadas but because of what seemed to be the emergence of a downright coercive policy by British ministers.

The occasion which prompted this solicitude was the introduction and passage of Lord John Russell's Ten Resolutions in Committee in the House of Commons by a majority of 144 to 16, March 6, 1837. Although these Resolutions were based upon the proposals of the Commission of Inquiry headed by the conciliatory Lord Gosford, the *National Intelligencer* on April 11, 1837, agreed with the strong language of the *London Times* of March 10, 1837, that the Resolutions proposed forcible measures to bring the culpable Canadians to terms. So great was the interest in the Resolutions that both the *New York Commercial Advertiser* and the *National Intelligencer* published a three-column synopsis of the Commons debate of April 14.[49] Especial emphasis was given to the speeches of the members of the opposition. Ministers received only a small share of the space.

The attitude of the *London Times* and of other conservative English papers went further toward arousing sympathy for Canada in

---

46. Quoted in *Nat. Int.*, November 21, 1835.

47. *Niles*, L, 100 (April 9, 1836).

48. This is the considered opinion of the *Montreal Courier,* quoted in the *Com. Adv.* and the *Nat. Int.*, November 21, 1835.

49. May 29, 1837.

the United States. The *Times* denounced French Canada.[50] It cared nothing for it except as a channel for communication with Upper Canada. The French meant to sever their connections with Great Britain, it said, and then averred that "for themselves alone, they are not worth the keeping." But so long as the French Canadians were the medium of intercourse with Upper Canada they must be prevented from committing further extravagances. An Act of Parliament would accomplish this desirable end. Therefore the *Times* favored coercive measures if necessary. Coupled with the ministerial position, the attitude taken by the *Times* was just what was necessary to excite American sympathies for the French Canadians. Having been aroused by the apparent harshness of the British government and by the plight of Lower Canada it needed only an incipient rebellion in Upper Canada to enlist the active sympathy of Americans for that province also.

During the years 1836 and 1837 signs of an approaching storm were evident. In Upper Canada Sir Francis Bond Head, the lieutenant governor, was at variance with the Assembly most of the time.[51] His unwise tactics in the election of 1836, in which he took the stump on behalf of the Family Compact,[52] thereby helping to oust the reform majority of the previous House and to elect a Tory majority, was in bad taste, to say the least. Head thereafter rapidly lost his hold upon the large body of the people. In addition, Head's opposition to aliens and his insistence upon giving them "nothing but their bare rights" not only wounded the feelings of American settlers at whom such a policy was aimed but limited their opportunities and injured their position in the communities in which they lived. Head's hatred of everything which savored of republicanism or democracy was of the most exaggerated sort.[53] His unwise procla-

50. The *Times*, March 10, 1837, quoted in the *Nat. Int.*, April 11, 1837.

51. Head, *op. cit.* This gives a good account of his differences with the Assembly and of his reliance on the Family Compact. See also *Niles*, L, 249 (June 11, 1836).

52. The governing clique in Upper Canada. The term, as used here, is a misnomer, because intermarriage was the exception rather than the rule.

53. *New York Courier and Enquirer,* quoted in *Nat. Int.*, July 25, 1836. Head's own defense in his *Narrative* was that he feared republicanism and that "it is impossible to put down republicanism by soft words," p. 100, in

mations and speeches during the Canadian Rebellion period frequently incensed thoughtful Americans who might in the absence of such provocation have been more friendly toward British government in the Canadas and less friendly toward the insurgents.

In Lower Canada excitement grew as the months of 1837 sped on with an accompanying food shortage and the beginning of a financial depression. Clashes occurred between civilians and the garrisons as early as July.[54] The active sympathy for the French Canadians which had already assumed considerable proportions in the United States now took the form of bold and violent denunciation of the British ministerial attitude toward the colonies. It appeared to Americans that Albion was pursuing the same "insolent invasion of [Canadian] rights" that "gave rise to the American Revolution." It also appeared that the Canadians were preparing to resist continued British control of colonial government. With a successful revolution behind them, Americans now began to look forward to the breaking of the storm with mingled feelings, even as their forefathers had on a previous occasion more than a half-century before.[55]

dispatch to Glenelg, May 28, 1836. He thought that "in a British colony, *British interests should be paramount* . . .," pp. 103–105, Head to Glenelg, June 1, 1836.

54. *Montreal Herald,* July 17, 1837.

55. *Boston Atlas,* quoted in *Jour. of Com.,* July 18, 1837; *Nat. Int.,* August 25, 1837; *New York American,* quoted in *Jour. of Com.,* September 1, 1837.

CHAPTER III

THE BORDER IN FERMENT

THE PRESS AND PUBLIC MEETINGS

A HUNDRED years ago vehicles for spreading news and opinion were limited to weekly or semiweekly newspapers, an occasional daily in New York and Washington, and a few quarterly magazines. There was, to be sure, the ubiquitous village store. And there were public meetings—called for almost every purpose—to express joy, sorrow, or indignation. Expression of opinion in writing was subjected to few limitations, for it was the custom to excoriate in no measured terms the persons, ideas, or societies which writers disliked. The public press was by no means averse to printing what today might commonly be regarded as slander or what might lead to diplomatic protests or perhaps to severance of normal diplomatic relations.

When, in November, 1837, news of the Lower Canadian Rebellion began to trickle into the United States, press opinions varied greatly but were not, on the whole, extreme in expression. As was to be expected, the causes of the Rebellion were likened to the causes of the American Revolution, and the independence of Lower Canada was hopefully anticipated. Not only that but the independence of Lower Canada, it was expected, must necessarily be followed shortly by the independence of Upper Canada and the Maritime Provinces, thereby securing for the United States a settlement of the troublesome northeastern boundary and the free navigation of the St. Lawrence. Canadian independence would have the added advantage of expelling Great Britain from North America and of making it possible to develop "an American policy in Canada [which] would augment incalculably the political strength and commercial resources of the United States."[1]

At that, no overt act of active intervention in behalf of Canada was recommended by the newspapers in the seaboard cities. They urged neutrality instead, in such characteristic comments as "the Canadians must fight their own battles," and "we shall not depart

1. Correspondence in *Nat. Int.*, December 2 and 7, 1837.

from our neutrality in this contest, or have our Government com-
promited by any act or measure which may sustain or aid this family
quarrel.''² The conservative Whig papers in Washington, New York,
and Albany, as well as the Democratic papers, anticipated that whatever the justification for the Rebellion might be, the Rebellion itself
would shortly be quelled by British arms. They expected that the
final result would be none other than the strengthening of government in Lower Canada. The *New York Albion*, a strongly Anglophile paper, together with others concluded that, far from being oppressed, Canadians enjoyed the most complete privileges that British
citizenship conferred; that, in consequence, loyal Canadians would
rise to the colors while many Englishmen in the United States could
be relied upon to enlist under the Queen's standard.³

That the attitude thus expressed in the leading newspapers was by
no means universal in the seaboard cities is attested by dispatches
from New York City to the *National Intelligencer* on December 2
and 5. In one of them we read that "99 out of 100 people here wished
success to the Canadians." It was expected also that the people living
in the counties lying immediately to the south of the Canadian border would exhibit an active and open sympathy for the Canadian
rebel cause. And this is exactly what they did, for it must be remembered that the Lower Canadian Rebellion and that of Upper Canada
which followed it affected the whole of the settled frontier of the
United States west of Maine.

Here was a region settled by small tradesmen and farmers, Jacksonian Democrats and religious fanatics, a region not yet linked up
by rail to the main centers of population to the south, a region where
production remained largely in the handicraft stage, and where un-
employment regularly accompanied the winter months.⁴ Into the
midst of this area stole a less than average crop along with the economic depression of 1837, so that where scores had hitherto been idle
during the winter, now many more neither toiled nor spun. Where

2. *Ibid.*, December 5 and 7.

3. *Nat. Int.; N.Y. Evening Star; New York American; Com. Adv.; Jour.
of Com.; Albany Argus.*

4. Cf. W. P. Shortridge, "The Canadian-American Frontier during the
Rebellion of 1837–1838," *Canadian Historical Review*, VII (March, 1926),
13–26.

therefore idleness, combined with a precarious existence, gave rein to radicalism, it was not difficult for men to be fired with a desire to aid those whom they believed to be oppressed. Moreover, in addition to giving aid to the Canadians, these sons of the northern border hoped to assist in the expulsion of the British from North America. The love of the unknown, of adventure, was a dominating motive. And finally they looked upon filibustering as a useful means of gaining a livelihood during the winter, of securing good land in Canada, and of winning glory and renown.

Spurred by these various motives, Americans, especially the borderers, expressed themselves in action in two ways—through public meetings and through the organization of filibustering expeditions, both of which showed clearly how strong, in the case of many Americans, were pent-up feelings against Great Britain. For these American people, the greater part of whom belonged to the inarticulate masses, there were no other ways of influencing public opinion or of forcing the government of the United States to assist in securing the freedom of the Canadas. The press was controlled for the most part, even in the border towns and cities, although there were important exceptions, by the more "respectable," that is, the small-propertied and professional classes. The consequence was that while the newspapers, regardless of their political affiliation, contained long and sometimes flaming accounts of happenings along the border, the most influential of them were likely to advise moderation and caution to the end of preventing such border conditions as would bring about an armed clash with the British. Would-be abettors of the Canadians' cause had perforce to turn to other means of influencing public opinion and securing assistance. And yet these other means, notably public meetings, often fell under the control of or were called together by the more conservative elements among the American people.

Public meetings held during the winter of 1837–38 by those who sympathized with the Canadians went through a number of stages. At first there were such meetings as the one held in Buffalo on December 5, the very day that armed rebellion broke out in Upper Canada. Like other early meetings elsewhere everything about this Buffalo meeting was dramatic. The Coffee House, the largest hall in the city, was hired for the occasion. When the doors were opened a band struck up the "Marseillaise," while 1,500 people poured into the building amid noise and confusion. When order and quiet were at length established certain influential citizens were elected officers. From William Lyon Mackenzie came a letter expressing regret that other circumstances prevented his attendance, and thanking the people of Buffalo for their vigorously sympathetic attitude toward the cause of reform in Upper Canada. Several fiery speeches were then delivered, a resolution "approbating" the Upper Canadian Rebellion was passed, and the crowd dispersed in orderly fashion. Similar meetings were held in Oswego, Ogdensburg, and Troy in New York, and in Montpelier in Vermont. They all passed innocuous resolutions in favor of the Canadian reformers and those in rebellion, but they did nothing more.[5]

Up to this time no active organization—for military purposes—of discontented Americans and refugee Canadians had been undertaken anywhere along the American border. But with the arrival of Mackenzie in Buffalo on December 11, after many hairbreadth escapes before arriving there, open recruiting began. This gave occasion for a series of public meetings, sponsored by some of Mackenzie's friends to arouse enthusiasm for recruiting and procuring financial assistance, and by others to curb excessive enthusiasm for the Canadian cause. On the evening of December 11, the first of three meetings, presided over by Dr. Cyrenius Chapin, Mackenzie's host, was held in the Coffee House. "Every foot of the house, from the orchestra to the roof, was literally crammed with people—the pit was full —the galleries were full—the lobbies were full—the street was full— and hundreds were obliged to go away without being able to gain admission."[6] Rumors began to spread of the aid that was already being made available for the Canadians. One man had subscribed $500 and another had left open a room containing forty muskets for recruits. The meeting was adjourned, however, until the following evening when it was expected that Mackenzie would address it.

With Mackenzie's presence assured, over two thousand persons crowded into the hall. But in the intervening twenty-four hours a momentous thing had happened. Less radical persons than Chapin had apparently banded together with the consequence that the eminently respectable Dyre Tillinghast, Supreme Court commissioner

5. *Nat. Int.*, December 15, and *Observer* (New York), December 16.
6. *Ibid.*, December 23, quoted from the *Commercial Advertiser* (Buffalo).

for Erie County, was elected chairman. Mackenzie was given a tremendous ovation and made a strong but florid speech. A number of men volunteered for service in the so-called "Patriot Army."[7] It was requested that arms and ammunition be left at the Eagle Tavern, Patriot headquarters. A "Committee of 13," which remained active throughout the Rebellion period, was appointed to confer with Mackenzie and his associates. Then the meeting was adjourned until the following evening.

By that time the mayor of Buffalo and General Potter of the New York militia, together with 150 others, had issued an open letter to the people of Erie County. In it they urged all who were aiding the Canadian cause to desist on pain of a threat to call upon the local magistrates to take measures to preserve peace and neutrality.[8] At any rate, the report of the Committee of 13 must have sorely disappointed the more adventurous who gathered on December 13. According to their own interpretation, the committee had been appointed for the sole purpose of receiving donations "for the struggling patriots of Upper Canada." They would not and could not countenance or aid illegal measures such as the current open arming and drilling of volunteers in Buffalo. These measures had been taken without their knowledge and against their advice. They were determined to fulfill the purpose for which they had been appointed, that is, receive donations, but they refused to aid an armed force in violation of their duties as American citizens and of obligations created by treaties with Great Britain. To aid the suffering Canadians was a charitable undertaking; to fit out armed expeditions was quite beyond the law. They would have nothing to do with it.

In similar vein, on December 20, a meeting in Middlebury, Vermont, "resolved" that it was the right of every American to think, feel, and speak in the cause of liberty, but not his right to violate the neutrality laws of the United States. In New York City, on December 27, an effort by E. B. O'Callaghan, the refugee editor of the *Montreal Vindicator*, to stir up enthusiasm for the Canadian cause

7. The "Patriot Army" was composed of all those who enlisted under the leadership of Mackenzie and numerous "generals." Their purpose was to invade the Canadas, particularly Upper Canada, and establish republics in those provinces.

8. *Nat. Int.*, December 27; *Observer* (New York), December 30.

in a crowded meeting in Vauxhall Gardens led merely to a vote to appoint a committee of three in each ward to raise money to alleviate the sufferings of Canadian exiles in the United States.

Meanwhile the recruiting of Americans and Canadian refugees for the Patriot army had been vigorously carried on from Vermont to Michigan. To make matters worse it seemed that neither civilian nor military authorities would take effective action to prevent recruiting and filibustering. Opposition to this situation crystallized first in Buffalo, as told above, and in Burlington, Vermont, when on December 12 twenty-three leading citizens requested Governor Jenison to issue a proclamation designed to check illegal recruiting, arming, and drilling. The letter is an illuminating example of the idealism and practical economic sense of the more substantial Americans resident near the border. It was quite absurd, they said, to arouse those harsh feelings which had "almost subsided" since the War of 1812. The commercial benefits of peace were much too great to be hazarded for the more dubious results of war. Since the Rebellion in Lower Canada was the consequence not of grinding oppression but of a family quarrel, Americans should not "dignify every case of resistance to an established government with the name of liberty . . . and we should remember, that though it may often be generous it is not always just, to adopt the quarrel of the weaker party." Interference of any sort was unjustifiable, and all right-principled men, as friends of peace and order, would remain aloof from the quarrels of Canadians with their government. The preservation of neutrality would secure the certainties and blessings of peace whereas interference in Canadian affairs might result in war with Great Britain with its attendant "lesser evils of restrictions of trade and of freedom of general intercourse with Canada."[9]

At the other end of the border, at Detroit, recruits for the Patriot army were gathering, drilling, and holding secret meetings in early January, 1838, in preparation for an attack on Bois Blanc Island and the Canadian shore. At the request of the governor of the newly created State of Michigan, a large number of influential Detroit citizens met in public meeting on January 6 and passed resolutions con-

9. *North Star* (Danville, Vt.), December 20, 1837; *Vermont Chronicle* (Burlington), December 20. For an attack on this letter see the *Burlington Free Press*, December 21.

demning surreptitious recruiting. They then organized a guard of one hundred men, called the Brady Guards in honor of Brigadier General Hugh Brady of the United States Army, to protect the town from the likelihood of looting by the Patriots and from possible attack by the "Royalists" from Upper Canada.[10]

Meetings were held for still another reason. The border between Lower Canada and Vermont was believed to be threatened by the Lower Canadian authorities who had issued a proclamation putting a price on the heads of the leaders of the rebellion in that province, most of whom, like Papineau and Nelson, had fled to the United States. In Vermont it was rumored that an attempt was to be made by irregular bands from Lower Canada to abduct the refugees by force. It was also rumored that the Lower Canadian militia would be marched into Vermont in pursuit of fugitives. Indignation meetings were accordingly held in St. Albans and Swanton on December 11, and again in St. Albans eight days later, as also in Vergennes and Montpelier, the capital. Dozens of resolutions were passed. On one matter there was universal agreement. Whereas the governor had hitherto taken no measures to provide the people with arms for their own defense, and whereas he had failed to call out the state militia, these Vermonters insisted that they must arm themselves, organize volunteer companies, and be prepared to defend themselves, their property, their honor, and the Canadian refugees in their midst. They were determined to resist the Canadians who were reported making ready to destroy border towns and isolated farmhouses.[11]

By the beginning of 1838 the whole border had been aroused to interest in the Canadian rebel cause. But large as had been the attendance at the public meetings, the majority of those present belonged to the inarticulate, if noisy, masses. Hence the meetings fell into the hands of the more conservative elements of society; and this very leadership gave the meetings, as a rule, an atmosphere of respectability which resulted in the passing of resolutions, the greater part of which were anything but assertive of radical and revolutionary principles. At most, the meetings confirmed the widespread sympathy for the Canadians, but overt acts to assist the Canadian rebels they discouraged.

10. *Nat. Int.*, January 23, 26, 27, 1838.
11. *North Star*, December 23 and 30, 1837.

Patriot Plans

Failure to secure active support from the press or by public meetings did not, as indicated, deter the friends of the Canadian reformers from organizing a Patriot army, whose avowed purpose was to assist Canadians to win their independence from Great Britain. Its organization began in Buffalo upon Mackenzie's arrival as a refugee on December 11, 1837. Recruiting at this stage was carried on openly, and volunteers wandered around armed with muskets that were stolen or given them. Within two days plans had been so matured that handbills were posted about the city. They read: "Patriot Volunteers will rendezvous this evening, at nine o'clock, in front of the Theatre, prepared to take up their line of march, By order of the Commanding Officer."[12]

The line of march led to Niagara Falls and thence, by boat, across the river to Navy Island. Here the diminutive force established itself and on December 15 ran up a flag of liberty. A provisional government of Upper Canada was organized and a proclamation was issued which announced that the objects of the government were " 'to secure perpetual peace, founded on a government of equal rights to all, secured by a written constitution,' civil and religious liberty, the abolition of hereditary honors, laws of entail and primogeniture, etc., a government republican in character,—a free trial by jury— the freedom of the press and a vote by ballot, free trade, and the opening of the St. Lawrence to the trade of the world."[13] A few days later a second proclamation offered three hundred acres of land in Canada and $100 in silver before May 1 to each volunteer who joined the Patriot forces.[14] To the incentive of adventure was now being added the promise of personal gain.

The Navy Island expedition was regarded as a considerable undertaking, both by Americans and Canadians. The island, situated on the Canadian side of the river and described by an overenthusiastic eyewitness "as about equal to the fortress of Gibraltar," was admirably suited for a base for filibustering, that is, if the Patriots aimed

12. *Commercial Advertiser* (Buffalo), December 14, 1837.

13. The proclamation is in Lindsey, *Mackenzie,* II, Appendix G, pp. 363–369. The quotation is from the *Vermont Chronicle,* December 23, taken from the *Commercial Advertiser* (Buffalo), December 16.

14. Lindsey, *op. cit.,* II, 131.

chiefly at being safe from attack from the Canadian mainland and secure from interference from the American shore. At first Mackenzie's followers numbered a mere handful, but so great was the excitement created by the expedition and so negligible were the attempts to prevent recruiting that the total enlisted force numbered 523 by December 26.[15] Within the next two weeks there were additional enlistments which probably brought the total up to between eight hundred and one thousand.[16]

Over this motley crew, ill clothed, ill housed, badly armed, but well fed during the first three weeks while enthusiasm was at its height, Mackenzie placed in command Rensselaer Van Rensselaer of Albany, a son of General Solomon Van Rensselaer of 1812 fame and a Whig political boss. It was an ill-considered choice for so important a command. .Young Van Rensselaer was, in the language of the day, "a gin-sling, sottish looking genius of twenty-seven, but apparently much older from disease and dissipation." He knew nothing of military strategy or tactics, and was incapable of taking advice. Despite these limitations, he appears to have been successful at first in maintaining discipline through the simple expedient of keeping his men busy throwing up breastworks and mounting a few cannon and a mortar. Thus securely entrenched against attack, he began with Mackenzie to lay plans for an advance against the British forces on the mainland.

The plan of campaign involved the direction and coördination of two other bodies of Patriots with the main force at Navy Island. Dr. Charles Duncombe, a former member of the Upper Canada Assembly, was already operating in the London district in the hope of entering Hamilton from the west. From Navy Island Mackenzie dispatched Thomas Jefferson Sutherland, erstwhile painter and lawyer, to take command in Detroit and the vicinity and raise additional recruits. Sutherland was to take Malden opposite Detroit, and proceed

15. *Commercial Advertiser* (Buffalo), December 27. This paper was strongly opposed to the Patriot activities and disparaged them as much as possible.

16. This is based on the estimate made by Nathaniel Garrow, United States district attorney for northern New York. Richardson, *Messages*, III, 399–400. One estimate was 600 (*Niagara Chronicle*, reported in the *Montreal Gazette*, February 8, 1838). Other estimates were as high as 1,500 to 2,000.

to Hamilton, where it was expected that he would join Duncombe and Van Rensselaer in a victorious march on Toronto. With the fall of that city, they anticipated that Upper Canada would be won without much fighting.

Success, in reality, depended upon the lack of military strength and determination in Upper Canada to keep the invaders out. To meet invasion Sir Francis Bond Head, the lieutenant governor, called out the militia and requested military assistance from Lower Canada. A battery was set up at Chippewa opposite Navy Island and military forces were concentrated at that point for defense against attack. Then Head began a waiting game. Neither he nor Colonel Allan MacNab, speaker of the Assembly and commander of the Upper Canadian militia, believed it necessary to attack Navy Island,[17] assuming correctly that the Patriots "must abandon their position before long in any event." Actually Head and MacNab relied on the civil and military authorities of the United States to take forceful measures to prevent bloodshed. But the American civil officers were either too far away, took too long to get to the border, or had insufficient authority to deal with the situation when they got there. Had the state militia been called out, it would have given no material assistance because it would have been recruited from among the sympathizers with the Patriot cause. Detachments of the national military forces were not readily available. Even if they had been available, they would not have been sent to the border because Washington had not yet awakened to the possible consequences of allowing armed bands to prepare to invade British North America. In any case, inaction led to a tragic occurrence which inflamed not only the border but all the United States and the Canadas, and to some extent Great Britain itself. This event was the destruction of the steamboat *Caroline*.

Within a few days after the occupation of Navy Island, the number of volunteers had increased so rapidly that there developed an acute shortage of transportation facilities to and from the American shore. To meet the needs of the Navy Islanders, the American-owned steamboat *Caroline*, of forty-six tons, was cut out of the ice at its dock on December 28 and put into immediate service by her owners.

17. Charles W. Robinson, *Life of Sir John Beverley Robinson, Bart.* (Edinburgh, 1914), pp. 228–229. Also *Com. Adv.*, January 17, 1838.

Transporting supplies for nearly a thousand men and carrying new recruits and large numbers of sightseers and visitors to Navy Island gave promise of a thriving ferrying business. But even before the ship was placed in service, Colonel MacNab had determined to prevent its use as a supply ship. On December 29, therefore, he commissioned Commander Andrew Drew, R.N., to command a nocturnal expedition to destroy the *Caroline*. Drew's force of seven boats and fifty men set out that evening for Navy Island where they expected to find the *Caroline* moored for the night. Not finding the ship there, they continued across the river to Schlosser in New York State where they discovered the *Caroline* made fast to a dock. In addition to the crew there were on board some twenty passengers who had been unable to secure accommodations at the single small tavern in the village. Nothing daunted, since his instructions authorized him to destroy the ship wherever he found it, Drew led his men aboard. In the general melee which followed, one man, Amos Durfee, was killed and several were wounded. The ship was set on fire and towed out into the current of the Niagara River where it sank before it reached the Falls.

No other incident during the entire period of border troubles from 1837 to 1842 produced a comparably electrifying effect upon Americans, Canadians, and Britishers. It remained to bedevil relations between all three peoples. Eventually, in 1841, it might even have led to war had Alexander McLeod, a Canadian, been convicted and executed in New York State for the part he was alleged to have taken in the destruction of the *Caroline*.

The first symptoms of excitement were the great fear which gripped the border from Buffalo to Rochester and the violent indignation which swept the entire border, as well as the whole of the United States. As soon as the first rumors of the burning of the *Caroline* reached Buffalo, the acting mayor issued a proclamation which promised that all possible legal measures would be taken against further invasion.[18] The Forty-seventh Brigade of militia from Erie County was ordered to assemble at once. Similar activity prevailed at Lockport and Rochester, eighty miles eastward.[19] Preparations for defense against further attack from Upper Canada provided a most

18. *Commercial Advertiser* (Buffalo), December 30, 1837.
19. *Democrat* (Rochester), December 30.

unusual bustle and excitement. But there was one significant note struck at Buffalo. The people were clearly warned in the proclamation that they should attempt no retaliation which might bring war between the United States and Great Britain. By contrast, in the Canadas, there was great rejoicing over the destruction of the *Caroline*. As a token of its appreciation, the Upper Canadian Assembly presented swords to MacNab and Drew.

Preparations to prevent invasion gave way within a few days to noisy demonstrations against the British and to demands that the United States government require satisfaction from Great Britain. Extremists like those at Richford, Vermont, resolved that it was the right of every American citizen *"who can,* to cross the line into Canada, and volunteer to help the *patriots* to obtain their liberties, and execute justice on their oppressors, and those who have shed innocent blood in the United States."[20] Elsewhere, as at Ogdensburg, New York, where tempers ran high, persons like Smith Stillwell, the respected collector of customs, were elected chairmen, and the resolutions passed by the meetings were less flamboyantly belligerent in tone.[21] The public meetings were, however, symptomatic of the increased interest in Canadian affairs which was aroused by the attack on the *Caroline*. There was increased Patriot activity in Vermont. From Cleveland, the collector of customs reported that the people had gone "mad" after hearing the news of the *Caroline*, that it was vain to attempt to enforce the laws until the excitement died down.[22] N. S. Benton, the district attorney from Little Falls who arrived in Buffalo two days after the destruction of the *Caroline*, declared that the Navy Islanders were increasing so rapidly that he was unable to cope with the situation.[23] Yet Navy Island was abandoned on the afternoon of January 14.

The reasons for this are not hard to find. Partly as a consequence of a one-day arrest on January 4, Mackenzie's influence and his followers' faith in him were seriously impaired. Within a few hours after news of the *Caroline* reached Washington, Major General

20. *Montreal Gazette,* February 27, 1838.
21. Department of State, *Miscellaneous Letters.* Smith Stillwell to Van Buren, January 8, 1838. Hereafter referred to as *D.S. Misc. Letters.*
22. *Ibid.,* Starkweather to Hon. J. W. Allen, January 8.
23. *Ibid.,* Benton to John Forsyth, Secretary of State, January 3.

Winfield Scott was on his way to the border to take command. His threat to seize all steamboats which were hired out to the insurgents put a stop to normal communication between Navy Island and the mainland. Hitherto the weather had remained amazingly moderate, but now on the twelfth it became bitterly cold for the first time. Provisions began to run low. On the thirteenth Scott had an interview with Van Rensselaer[24] and impressed upon him the utter absurdity of continuing the expedition. It was hardly any wonder that Navy Island was abandoned on January 14, and that all arms belonging to New York State were given up.[25] Van Rensselaer was himself arrested and bailed out like others before him. Hereafter, except for occasional sporadic outbursts like that of the succeeding February 24, the Buffalo area assumed an atmosphere of relative calm.

Even before Navy Island was abandoned the two "coöperating" forces under Duncombe and Sutherland had come to grief. After threatening the London district for a few weeks, Duncombe was forced to flee to the United States. Many of his men also fled and joined Sutherland's forces at Detroit. Sutherland, meanwhile, had organized at Cleveland an "Emigrating Committee" to enlist men and secure contributions, and had arrived at Detroit with some eighty or a hundred men.[26] Upon his arrival at Detroit he found perhaps an additional 700 men already enlisted and prepared for adventure.

Detroit was admirably situated as a base for attack against Upper Canada. It lies at the eastern end of the Detroit River, some thirty miles above Lake Erie. The terrain rendered military maneuvers relatively simple; the many islands in the river afforded admirable rendezvous; and ease of access to Canada was assured by an absence of swift currents in summer and a frozen surface in winter. A low, flat country on both sides afforded excellent opportunities for farming and grazing, so that the Patriots need never lack for food.

Sutherland's plan of campaign, not unlike that at Navy Island, involved establishing a base on Bois Blanc, a British island, nineteen miles from Detroit. From here he intended to attack Malden on the

24. *Poinsett Papers*, X, 24. Scott to J. R. Poinsett, Secretary of War, February 3, Private.

25. *Nat. Int.*, January 22, 23.

26. *D.S. Misc. Letters*, Samuel Starkweather, Collector of Customs at Cleveland, to J. W. Allen, January 8.

mainland, as the initial step in an advance against Toronto. But all of Sutherland's plans went awry. The expedition's principal ship ran aground on January 8 and was attacked by the Canadian militia. Governor Mason of Michigan and General Brown of the state militia visited the stranded vessel and, lacking authority or means to force them, persuaded the remaining Patriots to disband.[27] Sutherland himself was arrested shortly afterward but was soon released.

The Patriot failures at Navy Island and Bois Blanc came before their thirst for adventure was quenched and before they realized the difficulties inherent in organizing effective campaigns in the face of opposition at home and against regular and militia forces in the Canadas. Bois Blanc brought to an end the earliest attempts to succor the Canadians. Many of the volunteers returned to their homes. For the moment, now that Duncombe, Sutherland, Mackenzie, and Van Rensselaer had come to grief, quiet appeared to reign over the frontier.[28]

Peace and quiet proved to be more apparent than real. No sooner had Navy Island been abandoned than a more or less coördinated plan was hatched to attack the Canadas on Washington's birthday at three different points along the border from Michigan to Vermont. Of his total force on Navy Island Van Rensselaer was reported to have enlisted about five hundred to serve at Detroit. A majority had reached the vicinity of that town by February 1, although many stragglers were noticed by Lieutenant Homans of the navy as he traversed the Black Swamp near the western end of Lake Erie.[29] Shortly thereafter the Detroit area became a scene of confusion and disorder as a consequence of looting and requisitioning of food and other materials by the Patriot leaders. By February 24, three detachments, totaling from six to eight hundred, were ready to advance. On that day, 150 men under the command of Donald McLeod, adjutant general of the Patriot army, began a movement across the ice to what is now known as Fighting Island. Forty-eight

27. *Ibid.*, D. Goodwin, United States attorney for Michigan, to Forsyth, January 16.

28. See letters from Cleveland and Detroit, January 26 and February 1, in *Nat. Int.*, February 1 and 9.

29. *Nat. Int.*, February 17. A letter from Colonel Worth to Major General Scott, submitted in debate in the House of Representatives on February 16.

hours later they had been dispersed by a well-directed fire from the Canadian mainland. On February 28 another skirmish took place farther up the river. March 1 and 2 saw the final advance, against Pelée Island, fade into defeat. Once more it was reported that the western frontier was quiet.

Of the three proposed advances against the Canadas, that against Kingston was the only one which started on February 22. Throughout the previous week Mackenzie directed preparations from Watertown, New York, some twenty-five miles from the border. Food and arms were moved to the mouth of French Creek which flows into the St. Lawrence opposite Gananoque, sixteen miles east of Kingston.[30] Here the Patriots gathered, some three to five hundred in number, on the afternoon of the twenty-second, while people from miles around came to witness the invasion. Under the leadership of Van Rensselaer, the force occupied Hickory Island within Canadian jurisdiction. Van Rensselaer was eager to advance at once. He called for volunteers. Eighty-three offered to follow him. A second call brought only seventy-one; the third a mere handful of thirty-five. There was now no alternative but to retreat, for it was too bitterly cold to remain on the island overnight without shelter. Thereupon these disheartened invaders beat a precipitous retreat across the ice as darkness fell. In fact, so speedy was their return that their leaders found great difficulty in getting the arms and supplies transported back to the American shore.

Since November, when the Lower Canadian Rebellion had been quelled, the Patriots had been busy in northern Vermont collecting muskets, cannon, powder, ball, provisions, and money. Recruiting stations were opened—even in Montpelier, the capital. Yet with the exception of a minor skirmish on December 6, when forty Patriots were driven back by a handful of Canadian volunteers at St. Armands, no efforts were made to invade Lower Canada until the end of February. So quiet did the frontier appear that Brigadier General

30. "At Kingston the officer in command has been more alarmed during the last week than at any period of the troubles, and insists that there are not less than two thousand brigands assembling at Watertown and five hundred at French Creek, provided with pikes and artillery to cross and attack the steamboats." Sir John Colborne to J. B. Robinson, February 19. Quoted in Robinson, *op. cit.*, p. 230.

John E. Wool, the United States Army commander in Vermont, found it unnecessary to call out the militia. It was evident toward the end of February, however, that an attack upon Lower Canada was being planned. On February 25, the arsenal at Elizabethtown, New York, was looted of a thousand muskets. On the following day, while Wool was calling out the militia, the Patriots began to concentrate on the frontier. On February 28, effecting some degree of order in Alburg, Vermont, under the command of Dr. Robert Nelson and his associate Coté, they moved across the border. There they raised a flag and proclaimed the Independent Republic of Lower Canada, with Nelson as its first president and head of the provisional government. In a second proclamation, Canadians were urged to join the new republic and to aid the cause of revolution. In return for assistance, they were promised protection of person and property.[81] Unfortunately for the success of Nelson's venture, the British forces were advancing from the north and Wool was coming up from the south. Believing that he would receive less harsh treatment from the Americans, Nelson decided to retreat into Vermont. On the afternoon of March 1, the whole force of six hundred badly disillusioned protectors of Canadian freedom surrendered themselves and their arms to Wool, who took the leaders into custody.[32] And this ended for some time to come any serious effort in Vermont to succor the Lower Canadians.

While the expeditions against Upper Canada, intended to take place on Washington's birthday, were being organized, serious friction began to develop between Van Rensselaer and Mackenzie. To make matters worse they began to attack each other openly, Mackenzie going so far as to say that he had invariably urged his friends "to withdraw their confidence" from Van Rensselaer "in matters connected with Canada."[33] Two days after the fiasco at French Creek he

81. "The Declaration of Independence of the People of Lower Canada" is given in Nat. Int., March 12. The proclamation to the "People of Canada" is in an enclosure of Colborne to Glenelg, March 3, 1838. Q, CCXLIV, 448–449.

82. Wool's dispatch to the War Department is quoted in the Albany Argus, March 5, and Nat. Int., March 9.

83. Letter to the editor of the Jeffersonian (Watertown), February 22, quoted in Bonney, Legacy of Historical Gleanings, II, 99.

terminated by letter "all military and political connection" with Van Rensselaer.[34] The latter retaliated by attacking Mackenzie in a Syracuse paper, denouncing him as a "loafer" and questioning whether he had at any time possessed the confidence of Upper Canadians. With their confidence and their support, Van Rensselaer claimed that the British troops could have been driven out that winter. "But," he added, "the worst tyranny, [the Canadians] conclude rationally, would be better than [Mackenzie's] loafer Government."[35] To cap the climax, a tremendous reaction set in against the principal Patriot leaders all along the border. Verdicts of incompetence were pronounced against them. After Pelée Island McLeod and others were openly denounced as cowards. At French Creek it was said that "Mackenzie has showed himself equally selfish, heartless, unprincipled, and cowardly; and so great is the revulsion of feeling here [St. Lawrence County], that . . . if he should venture here again he would be handed over to the tender mercies of the Canadians, without ceremony or pity." And even a month before this he had already become "the most unpopular man in Buffalo."[36]

With the failure of every attempt to invade the Canadas, and with their leaders in disrepute, there was nothing for the Patriots to do but return to their homes, there to await more favorable opportunities to take up arms under new leaders who would use new methods of recruiting. They had not long to wait, for within two or three months secret societies began to be organized and to cause both American and Canadian authorities greater annoyance and anxiety than they had heretofore experienced. The first phase of filibustering, which came to an end in March, was but a prelude of what was to come.

34. *Ibid.*, II, 105. 35. *Nat. Int.*, March 5.
36. *Ibid.*, March 7.

CHAPTER IV

CURBING THE PATRIOTS

The Civil Authorities

Of the many factors which were responsible for the collapse of Patriot plans during the early months of 1838, the restrictive influence of the United States government was important but not primary. In his military capacity as commander-in-chief the President was expected to use the military forces of the United States only for the purposes of curbing rebellion or repelling invasion. By constitutional limitation he had no control over state militia forces. In his civil capacity under the neutrality laws he lacked authority adequately to deal with filibustering.

The Neutrality Act of 1818,[1] Section 2, provided for a fine not exceeding $1,000 and imprisonment not exceeding three years for any person who, within the territory of the United States, should enlist or cause others to enlist in the armed forces of a foreign power while an insurrection was going on in that country. Section 6 provided the same punishment for anyone who initiated or was the instigator of a military expedition against any foreign power. The act was therefore chiefly "penal, not preventive."[2] This statement really sums up the whole case for neutrality as it was understood in 1818 and as it continued to be understood until the Act of 1838 replaced the former measure.

The President's position was made no easier by the press, which insisted upon the strict enforcement of the laws of the United States, in order that a war with Great Britain might be averted. The case was well put on December 9, 1837, by the *Albany Argus*, which could by no means be called a pro-British paper, when it said,

We trust that whatever may be the partialities of our frontier citizens, they will take no step to compromise the neutrality of the United States, or tend in any degree to interrupt the amicable relations subsisting between the British and American governments. And such could scarcely

1. 3 *Statutes at Large*, 448, 449.
2. *Congressional Globe*, VI, 83, January 8, 1838.

fail to follow the recruiting of troops within our territory, or the assemblage of meetings in aid or approval of the Canadians.

This was the universal hope of the moderate press. It was willing to allow preventive and not merely penal measures to curb organized filibustering, providing Congress would but pass the required legislation.[3]

It is to be noticed that what the *Albany Argus* opposed was group or organized action; this alone in its opinion would be a violation of neutrality.[4] In fact, it held that "to preserve our *national* neutrality, it is not necessary that individuals should withhold their sympathy, or even their aid. No existing treaty between this government and England or any other government exacts so much as that." The important question hinged on whether individual aid should be suppressed, and for some time this seems to have been the issue at stake. There is little doubt that along the frontier the opportunity for individuals to take part in the Canadian quarrel was conceived of as a right,[5] which, it was held, did not involve an infringement of neutral relations or of international law by the United States.

Whatever the President might think of this view, his task and that of the civil officers of the several border states were made more difficult by the obvious loopholes in the neutrality laws and by the capacity of Americans and exiled Canadians for taking advantage of

3. One cannot help thinking, concerning the case of Texas which was discussed many times in making a comparison with Canada, that either Jackson allowed Washington's principles to be stretched out of all recognition or that he deemed that they did not apply to the Texas situation at all. It may properly be argued that in Texas the rising was a spontaneous one against Mexico and that after Texas had declared its independence the principles of Washington's proclamation and of the Act of 1818 could not be put into effect because Americans entered Texas before enlisting for service and were therefore outside of the jurisdiction of the United States.

4. December 19, 1837, quoted with approval from the *Democrat* (Rochester).

5. For a scathing denunciation of this attitude, see a quotation from the *New York Evening Star* in the *National Intelligencer*, January 8, 1838. On the other hand, certain sections of the press, such as the *Philadelphia Gazette*, December 14, 1837, and the *New York Journal of Commerce*, December 20 and 22, 1837, were genuinely puzzled as to whether the United States could legally prevent Americans from giving aid to the Canadians.

these lacunae. Van Buren had the unpleasant task of disapproving officially of all militant activity engineered by the Patriots while at the same time his hands were tied by lack of executive authority to prevent it. It is an open question, however, whether he or any of his advisers were acutely aware of the possible implications of the border troubles, or of the vast discontent there, or of the deep-lying sympathy of the border people for the Canadian rebel cause. To the President and official Washington, filibustering was an expression of a momentary mood; they expected it to cease as soon as its mercurial sponsors were called upon to desist.

With this in mind there was issued on November 21, 1837, a proclamation,[6] which unfortunately had no teeth in it. American citizens were called upon to obey the laws of the United States. They were warned that should they fall into the hands of the Canadian governments they would receive no aid from the United States. The proclamation was followed a few days later by Van Buren's message to Congress. "A state of feeling on both sides of the frontier," he wrote, "has thus been produced which calls for prompt and vigorous interference." Even if insurrection existed in the Canadas, the United States should remain neutral and should attempt to restrain its citizens. "This Government," he added, "recognizes a still higher obligation to repress all attempts on the part of its citizens to disturb the peace of a country where order prevails or has been restored." The high moral purpose expressed in this passage was vitiated, however, by what the President added in the succeeding paragraph. While he pointed out that the organized activities of filibusters might lead to the regrettable consequence of war, he admitted the propriety of an expression of sympathy by Americans for Canadians in their struggle for freedom. He ended by placing upon Congress the entire responsibility for determining whether the existing neutrality laws were "sufficient or not to meet the actual state of things on the Canadian frontier."

The state of affairs on the frontier did not yet appear alarming enough to require the calling out of the state militias or the sending of additional military units to the border. In fact, as late as December 27, 1837, John Forsyth, the Secretary of State, assured Gov-

6. Richardson, *Messages,* III, 485–487.

ernor Jenison of Vermont[7] that it was not thought necessary to send troops to the frontier "for the protection of our citizens along the line, or for quieting any reasonable apprehension; but if the course of events should . . . render it expedient, a sufficient detachment [would] be furnished for the purpose." Meanwhile, on December 7, Forsyth addressed identical letters to the governors of Vermont, New York, and Michigan, and to the United States district attorneys and marshals in those states.[8] In these letters he requested their assistance in observing insurgent activities and their prompt efforts to arrest anyone who made hostile preparations against Canada. The Secretary of the Treasury likewise sent a circular letter[9] to all collectors of customs requiring them to coöperate in every legal way with other federal officers to preserve the neutrality of the United States. More specific instructions were also sent as soon as the delays consequent upon the slowness of the mails permitted. In one case, on December 21, 1837—ten days after Mackenzie and Dr. John Rolph, another prominent leader in the Rebellion, had arrived in Buffalo—N. S. Benton, the United States attorney then most active in northern New York, was ordered to go to Buffalo at once, to ascertain facts, and to exercise due vigilance to prevent the recurrence of criminal acts.[10]

State and local officers likewise bestirred themselves. The governors of New York and Vermont issued proclamations[11] enjoining the citizens of those states to desist "from their unlawful proceedings . . ." and "to co-operate with the officers and magistrates of the United States in their efforts to suppress such violations of law and to bring the offenders to punishment." The "good people" were implored not to interfere "with the domestic concerns" of the Canadian provinces nor to aid political refugees in such a manner as to violate the principles of neutrality. Mayors, councilors, and others ferreted out the plans of the Patriots so far as they were able or were inclined to do so and sent information to state and federal authorities. They

---

7. Department of State, *Domestic Letters,* XXIX, 268. Hereafter quoted as *D.S. Dom. Letters.*

8. *Ibid.,* XXIX, 250–251, 260. Also *Jour. of Com.,* December 14 and 16, and *Vermont Chronicle,* December 20, 1837.

9. *Observer* (New York), December 30.

10. *D.S. Dom. Letters,* XXIX, 261.

11. *Vermont Chronicle,* December 20, and *Observer,* December 30.

cajoled the Patriots, they entreated them, and they threatened them. All to little avail.

The fact is that the efforts of the civil officers were largely ineffectual. To the majority of the American press this was not apparent until after the turn of the year, but not so with certain Britishers whose sympathy with American institutions was none too great. Both I. W. Cowell, agent for the Bank of England in Philadelphia, and James Buchanan, the British consul in New York, to say nothing of Henry Stephen Fox, the British minister in Washington, insisted that neither the President nor the governors had the power to enforce the laws or to restrain their people.[12] They believed that many officials who sympathized ardently with the Patriot cause were, for that reason, loath to use what power they possessed. Besides, politics entered into the matter. The Whigs were said to be strongly attracted to the Patriots in order to embarrass the administration. The Texas annexationists, who had by no means lost interest in annexationism, would gladly overthrow British dominion in North America. And finally the immediate and considerable interest of the border population in Canadian affairs rendered almost impotent an already feeble Executive.

Whatever pressures were brought to bear on Van Buren and his Cabinet, and there were many,[13] nothing could induce the President to send military detachments to the frontier until the destruction of the *Caroline*, on December 29, 1837, made such action imperative.[14] News of the attack on the *Caroline* reached Washington just before a presidential dinner party began. Van Buren arrived somewhat late. Before joining his guests, he remarked to Major General Winfield Scott, "Blood has been shed; you must go with all speed to the Niagara frontier. The Secretary of War is now writing your instruc-

12. *Q*, CCXLII, 371–372. I. W. Cowell to . . ., December 15; *idem*, p. 279. Buchanan to James Stephen, December 26; *G*, CCXXIV, 86–125. Fox to Gosford, December 18, Confidential.

13. *New York Morning Herald*, December 11, 1837; *Van Buren Papers*, XXXI, 7158–7159. C. J. Ingersoll to Van Buren, December 24, 1837.

14. *Poinsett Papers*, X, 159. Col. W. J. Worth to J. R. Poinsett, Secretary of War, Watervliet Arsenal, January 3, 1838; *ibid.*, X, 160. Poinsett to W. L. Marcy, governor of New York, January 5, 1838, Draft *"Private and Confidential"; D.S. Misc. Letters*, Poinsett to Forsyth, January 6, 1838.

tions."[15] The following day, January 5, a proclamation[16] was issued which went one step further than that of November 21. It gave warning that all those "who shall compromit the neutrality of this Government by interfering in an unlawful manner with the affairs of the neighboring British provinces will render themselves liable to arrest and punishment under the laws of the United States, which will be rigidly enforced. . . ."

Despite this show of the executive teeth, the President was actually not certain of his power to enforce the proclamation; and it seems reasonably clear that coercion by military force was one of the last things he desired. The evidence is contained in the instructions[17] Scott received from the Secretary of War. He was authorized to request the governors of New York and Vermont to call out the militia to defend the frontier. But it was impressed upon him that "the Executive possesses no legal authority to employ the military force to restrain persons within our jurisdiction . . . from violating the laws by making incursions into" the Canadas. Poinsett therefore gave Scott "no instructions on that subject, but request that you will use your influence to prevent . . . excesses." And finally Scott was told that "the President indulges a hope . . . that you will be able to maintain the peace of that frontier without being called upon to use the force which has been confided to you." But the die was cast. The day the news of the destruction of the *Caroline* reached Washington marks the end of a policy of attempting to curb illegal acts by the use of civil agents alone. It marks the beginning of a policy of using the military as a prop for the civil authorities.

THE NEUTRALITY ACT OF 1838

The likelihood of retaliatory acts as a consequence of the destruction of the *Caroline* made it necessary for the President to secure more adequate powers to prevent filibustering. Accordingly Van

15. *Memoirs of Lieut.-General Scott, LL.D.*, written by himself (New York, 1864), I, 306–307.

16. Richardson, *op. cit.*, III, 481.

17. *D.S. Misc. Letters,* Poinsett to Forsyth, January 6, 1838, enclosing Scott's instructions. Also *ibid.*, Forsyth to N. Garrow, January 5, 1838, in which Garrow was informed that the President "has no right to use the military force in execution of the laws, except when the civil authority has first been successfully resisted."

Buren sent to Congress on January 5, 1838, a special message in which he pointed out that the Neutrality Act of 1818 gave him power merely to punish offenders after offenses had been committed, "provided that the parties can be found." The attention of Congress was called "to this defect in our legislation," and it was told that "the Executive ought to be clothed with adequate power effectively to restrain all persons within our jurisdiction from the commission of acts of this character." Congress was requested to revise all laws relating to the subject of neutrality.[18] Three days later in a message concerning the *Caroline* Van Buren asked for a special appropriation to cover emergencies. The Congress granted this, to the extent of $625,000, without much delay; but the President had to wait more than two months before he got his neutrality law.

When Van Buren's message of January 5 reached Congress, that body was so absorbed in acutely recriminatory political debate that it was a triumph that any legislation was able to emerge at all. In the fight over neutrality the real object of proposed bills was frequently misunderstood, misrepresented, or forgotten, amidst a welter of party wrangling and mutual recrimination. Nor were asperities by any means confined to the walls of Congress. The opposition press damned the President in season and out, first, for not issuing proclamations of neutrality, and second, for not using all the powers conferred upon him by law.[19]

In the Senate, where the presidential message was first debated, there was a rather general agreement, even between Clay, Calhoun, and Thomas H. Benton of Missouri, that if existing legislation were found to be inadequate, it should be revised to give the Executive sufficient power to avert serious trouble. In the House, on the other hand, the debate became acrimonious at once. Members argued about the imminence of war, whether the Maine boundary question should first be considered, whether the army should be increased, and whether the President had or had not exercised all his powers to prevent illegal acts on the frontier.[20]

18. Richardson, *op. cit.*, III, 399.

19. For example, the following New York papers: the *Evening Star, Gazette,* and *Journal of Commerce;* and the *National Intelligencer.*

20. Debates on the President's message and the bill are in *Congressional Globe,* VI, *passim.*

Although abolitionism was being hotly debated at the moment, the Senate found time by January 18 to pass a neutrality bill designed to prevent Americans from giving assistance to revolutionary movements against neighboring governments. Whereas the Act of 1818 was applicable to maritime warfare and privateering, this Senate bill of 1838 was designed to prevent, in addition, trade in arms and munitions across inland frontiers. Its weakest point was that it provided no penalties for infractions of the law.

It was not until January 19 that Benjamin C. Howard of Maryland, chairman of the Committee on Foreign Affairs, was able to introduce a bill in the House. A week later it was reported again from the committee, not in its original form, but as the Senate bill with several amendments. Debate was, however, postponed from time to time until February 16 when Howard succeeded in getting a hearing by securing the consent of the House to suspend its rules. He presented correspondence which described the massing of the Patriots for an attack against Windsor. He reminded the House that the protection of the frontier and the preservation of neutrality "were entirely thrown upon the military arm instead of the civil, and it was so, because there was no existing law to meet the case." The real object of passing a new act was to increase the civil powers of the Executive and to reduce the influence of the military. It was one of the guns in a barrage directed against those who were then, in debate, espousing the cause of a larger standing army.

The bill provided that vessels, arms, and persons could be seized and detained if it appeared that they were about to be engaged in hostilities against any foreign state or colony whose territory was contiguous with that of the United States. Vessels and arms were to be detained until the owner or owners had deposited bonds to double their value against their reëmployment in illegal activities, or until the President ordered their restoration. Persons who were detained and later released on bail were to give such additional security as the judge might require. The extension of the civil authority was provided for by giving the President power to order judges, marshals, and district attorneys to the scene of action "for the purpose of the more speedy and convenient arrest and examination of persons charged with the violation" of the act. Finally, the President was authorized "to employ such part of the land and naval forces of the

United States, or of the militia, as shall be necessary to prevent the violation and enforce the due execution of this act. . . ."

In defense of the measure Howard laid emphasis upon four major objects of the bill. First, it would enable the United States to fulfill its obligations to other countries. Second, it would do so without in any way limiting "the legal and justifiable" right of Americans to trade abroad, even in time of war. Third, it would prevent Americans from stirring up insurrection or assisting rebels in a foreign country, and thus remove the probability of war. Fourth, the great object of the bill was to increase the civil powers of government so that the civil authorities could come to the assistance of the military who were acting under the terms of the Act of 1818.

Innocuous as the bill was and despite Howard's masterly explanation of it, the opposition swung into action at once. The four major issues, as well as a host of lesser ones, were hotly debated over a period of three weeks. It was contended that the bill fundamentally altered the principles upon which export trade rested because it sought to restrict trade with one of two parties in a neighboring state in which a rebellion was proceeding. The neutrality of the United States, it was said, could not possibly be jeopardized if trade were allowed to continue with both parties. The bill, it was claimed, lacked "the one great principle of all penal laws." It provided for a penalty for infraction of the law without first making infraction a penal offense. In the third place, the bill was denounced for containing unconstitutional provisions. It vested "dangerous and unusual powers in the officers of Government." It attempted to destroy the constitutional right of citizens to bear arms. And it violated the principles of "the fourth amendment" [sic] which provides for freedom from arrest without due process of law. Finally, there was the question of the relative roles which should be assumed by the civil authorities on the one hand and the military and naval on the other. To Francis W. Pickens of South Carolina and others it seemed clear that the constitution expressly provided for the use of military and naval forces for repelling invasion and attack, and for no other purpose. On the other hand, the militia could be used for quelling internal disturbances. Moreover, since the spirit of the constitution suggested that the people as a whole should assist the President in putting down domestic disturbances and since the militia were the people themselves organized into units under military regulations, it stood to reason that the militia and not the regular army should be put into action on the Canadian border. Howard of Maryland objected even to the use of militia because the duty of maintaining order "could be as well performed by the civil authority." He insisted that the civil power "ought first to be applied, and when it failed, there would be time enough to call in the aid of the military power."

During the days that followed both debates and amendments centered around certain questions such as trade in arms and munitions during a rebellion, private property's right to protection, the right of persons to bear arms and to be immune from arrest, provision of penalties for infractions of the law, curbing the extension of the powers of the President by limiting the duration of the act and refusing to grant him power to the extent provided for in the Senate bill.

Press opinion of the debates was hardly flattering. Even the anti-administration *National Intelligencer* agreed with certain members of Congress who stated that haste was imperative if war with Great Britain was to be averted, and who were willing to postpone all other business until a neutrality bill was passed. Two arguments for haste recurred. One was that disturbances on the frontier were becoming so serious that war could be averted only by granting the President authority to suppress the Patriots at once, a statement that was flatly denied by John Quincy Adams and others. The second was that the debates were largely futile and were merely impeding the discussion and passage of legislation of greater and more immediate importance. To annoy the friends of the administration the opponents of the bill kept up a constant attack by comparing the attempted vigor of Van Buren in the Canadian situation with Andrew Jackson's dilatoriness in the case of Texas.

At length, when members' nerves were well frayed and the patience of a majority of them had become exhausted, the previous question was put and carried by eighty-three to fifty-one. The main question, that is, the Senate bill with the amendments added to it by the House Committee on Foreign Affairs, was voted on and defeated by eighty-eight to seventy-six. The House was aghast. It was not prepared to refuse a neutrality bill altogether, regardless of Fox's statement to Palmerston that some voted against the bill because it was too cumbersome, others because they disliked restrictions placed upon personal liberty, but that the majority who voted against it were "actuated by no other motives, than by a secret hope and wish that by so doing they may in some way benefit the cause of rebellion in Canada."[21] That this most certainly does scant justice to the House is seen by the fact that debate was immediately resumed and the defeated bill was shortly referred back to the Committee on Foreign Affairs, whence it emerged in a new dress on March 1.

The new bill was definitely a compromise measure and as such passed the House on the following day, in the face of a spirited attempt of the opposition to prevent its passage. It provided for the seizure and detention of vessels and "other means or materials" by executive or court order, after which judicial procedure was to be resorted to. In any case, a delay of three months was provided for before the owner could regain possession. Nothing in the act was to be so construed as to interfere with any trade "to or with any parties engaged in war: which trade is now authorized either by treaty or the law of nations." The right to bail and to jury trial of persons who were arrested was guaranteed. The President was authorized to call out the military, naval, and militia forces to prevent violation of the act.

In the Senate there were added several amendments which were designed to reduce considerably the additional powers conferred upon the President by the newly passed House bill. In the first place, it was provided that only vessels, vehicles, arms, and ammunition, and not vessels and "other means and materials," could be subject to seizure. It was also provided that the seizure of these goods was to be limited to enterprises carried on against states or colonies *conterminous* with the United States and with which it was at peace. Nor was the Senate willing to allow the power of seizure to be exercised until an expedition had been prepared and was about to leave the United States.

21. Q, CCL, 42–45. February 26, 1838. Fox cannot be relied on all the time. That he had little sympathy with the nature of government in the United States may be seen in this very letter where his castigation of "licentious democracy" remains unexcelled.

The next amendment provided for the right to trade in arms and ammunition so far as the law of nations allowed. Here an elaborate distinction was made by James Buchanan, chairman of the Foreign Relations Committee, between trade in arms by sea and across interior boundaries. The latter alone would be prohibited by the present bill. Finally, the duration of the act was limited to two years.

Upon resubmission to the House, that body accepted (not without several attempted amendments) all but that clause which dealt with the trade in arms. Conference committees fortunately reached an agreement which provided for the legitimacy of the trade in arms and munitions and "any other trade" by sea which could therefore have been lawfully carried on. On March 9 both houses passed the amendment and on the tenth the President signed the bill.

Just what additional power did the President receive for the enforcement of order along the frontier? The penal provisions of the Act of 1818 remained intact but the President was no more able legally to prevent the organization of expeditions against Canada than heretofore. Moreover, Congress succeeded so well in cluttering up the act with provisions for legal and judicial procedure which had to be followed before vessels, arms, and munitions could be detained after seizure that the power of the civil authorities was quite as much restricted as it had been before. Trade of a questionable character could still be carried on under the guise of legitimacy. In whatever way one looks at it, it would seem that the labor of the mountain had brought forth little more than a mouse. The act did, however, have one effect which its sponsors had made conspicuous effort to circumvent. To grant to the President the power to call upon the military, naval, and militia forces, together with special appropriations to suppress disturbances, gave the Executive a striking force and a power which the civil officers with all due deference to their integrity could not be expected to exert unaided. What is of especial interest, then, is that despite the intentions of Congress to the contrary it was the military forces upon which the government eventually depended to keep order along the frontier.

On the other hand, any fair evaluation of the act must take account of the influence it exerted upon the minds of the American people. It is certain that they felt it would be effectively enforced. On

March 1 two petitions and remonstrances from Vermont were presented in the House of Representatives. They protested against the
passage of the bill and requested the recall of all orders for the seizure of arms and ammunition.[22] In commenting upon the passage of
the bill, the *Globe* expressed the prevailing opinion when it said on
March 12, "It is expected that our fellow-citizens in that part of the
country [the Canadian border] will, at once, submit to the law, and
return peacefully to their homes." In December, 1838, the enforcement of the act brought some six hundred persons together in Buffalo
to demand its repeal.[23] But by this time the more important papers
were completely out of sympathy with the activities of the insurgents
and were demanding an act with much "more energetic provisions."[24]
It may be said, in spite of the weakness of its provisions, that the act
did serve to restrain the border population, and that is the very best
evidence of its usefulness.

While Congress was engaged in debating the neutrality bill, the
Upper Canadian legislature acted more rapidly.[25] Of the three acts[26]
passed on January 12, the first two provided for the trial and punishment of all persons who were charged with treason or treasonable
practices for having taken part in the Rebellion in December, 1837,
or who might engage in treasonable practices thereafter. Restrictions
were placed upon trial by jury and the right of habeas corpus. The
penalty of "corruption of blood" was to be imposed upon those who
were found guilty. This involved forfeiture of the right of the convicted person and his heirs to hold property or public office in the
future. Both acts were limited in duration to the end of the following
session. The third act, "An Act to protect the Inhabitants of the
Province against Lawless Aggressions from Subjects of Foreign
Countries, at Peace with Her Majesty," provided that both aliens
and British subjects who invaded Canada should be tried before
courts-martial and, if convicted, were to be punished by death or by

22. The *Globe,* March 1, 1838.
23. *Nat. Int.,* December 18, 1838. The meeting was held on December 5.
24. *Ibid.*
25. In Lower Canada the governor and council were endowed with both
executive and legislative powers as a consequence of the suspension of the
Constitutional Act by the act of Parliament.
26. 1 Victoria, c. 1, 2, and 3. *Statutes of Upper Canada,* 1838.

such other punishment as the court might direct. The governor was given power to waive trial by military for trial by civil procedure.

The reason for this grant of discretion to the governor seems to have been "to excite less hostile feeling in the United States" by allowing less summary procedure in certain cases than would have been possible if martial law had been universally in force.[27] The legislature thus hoped through the threat of court-martial to deter invasion of Canada, and at the same time to maintain the civil-law system in full vigor. It was a wise precaution as subsequent events were to prove.

Although these acts were designed to strengthen the authority of the Executive in preventing lawlessness, they were, to repeat, primarily penal and not preventive. Fortunately the successive lieutenant governors of Upper Canada were not compelled to rely solely upon these laws to maintain order, for they were already well endowed with power, both civil and military, to exert control over would-be rebels and invaders.

INCREASING THE MILITARY FORCES

To provide the Executive in Upper Canada and in the United States with adequate authority to deal with border troubles was but a part of the demands made upon the provincial legislature and upon Congress. Congress found itself forced to consider the propriety of increasing the army and the militia while the Upper Canadian legislature was confronted with the need for reorganizing the local militia.

On November 30, 1837, the total paper strength of the United States military forces was 7,958,[28] but it is probable that the actual strength was not much over 5,000. Of this number the majority were stationed in the West and the South and were currently engaged in fighting Indians in those two areas.[29] In fact, when the *Caroline* was destroyed on December 29, 1837, nine out of the army's thirteen regiments, including all of the artillery, were in Florida. Of the remaining forces nearly all were stationed at considerable distances from Buffalo. For some years there was not a single American soldier

27. Robinson, *op. cit.*, p. 219.
28. *American State Papers, Military Affairs,* VI, 1022.
29. H. P. Beers, *The Western Military Frontier, 1815–1846* (Philadelphia, 1935).

stationed along the St. Lawrence or Great Lakes east of Fort Gratiot at Port Huron, Michigan, at which point there was a paper strength of 122 in 1836.[30]

The necessity of keeping troops in the Indian country rendered it unwise to shift military units from the South and West to the St. Lawrence. Yet the continuing dispute over the northeastern boundary, and now the Patriot war, required the presence of troops along the northern frontier. So it was, in the absence of sufficient reserves to meet current needs, that a bill for the increase of the army was reported in the Senate on January 9, 1838, eleven days after the *Caroline* affair. This bill was based upon the recommendations of Major General Winfield Scott in pursuance of a request from the Secretary of War concerning the additions necessary to defend adequately the northern and eastern boundaries of the United States.[31] Without knowing about the outbreak of rebellion in Lower Canada but with the northeastern boundary dispute and the Indian situation in mind, Scott recommended, on November 19, 1837, a minimum addition to the army of five regiments of artillery and three of infantry to provide against aggression and "to preserve the permanent posts from the gradual waste of time." The bill therefore provided for an increase of 6,650 noncommissioned officers and men and for a considerable reorganization of the army as well.

Since the bill was not eventually passed until July 5 it would be wearisome to take up the debates in detail. But there were some fundamental issues involved in its passage which split its defenders and its opponents into two hostile camps. Nor did the battle rage in Congress alone. The press took up the issues. Correspondents exchanged animated letters in the newspapers and journals. The increase of the army became a national question.

The two chief issues around which controversy raged in the country and in Congress[32] were related to the size of the projected increase and to the propriety of maintaining a large standing army. All other issues centered around these. As first introduced, the bill

30. *Register of Debates* (Senate), XIII, Appendix, p. 11. *Report of the Secretary of War,* December 3, 1836. There were a few companies of infantry and artillery in Maine.

31. 25 Cong. 2 Sess., Senate Doc., No. 88. January 9, 1838.

32. For the debates, see *Congressional Globe,* VI, *passim.*

provided for both the reorganization of the army and the increase of personnel, with the avowed purpose of making available a large force to combat the Indian menace on the western frontier and to safeguard the northern border. In both houses the western members took the lead in defending the bill, and in some cases, along with eastern members, in demanding an even larger increase than was provided for. How, they asked, could a standing army of 15,000 become a menace to the liberties of 14,000,000 Americans? Such an army was too small to protect the frontier against Indian attacks. It could by no means underwrite arbitrary government throughout the country at large. The opponents of the bill were, however, strong enough to limit the total strength of the army to 12,500 and to prevent reorganization. In the end the army bill also became a compromise measure.

At the end of three months of dreary and repetitious debate, with its bill torn to pieces by the House although twice passed by the Senate, the administration bethought itself of another line of approach. If it could not get a sufficiently large and satisfactorily reorganized army, it would attempt to have a bill passed for the reorganization of the militia. The Militia Act of 1792 had provided that all males between the ages of eighteen and forty-five should be liable for service, whereas the new bill changed the age limits to between twenty-one and forty. But it proposed to distinguish between the *active* militia, which was to form one tenth, and the *general* militia, which was to form nine tenths of the whole. The *active* militia was to be selected by the states and those who composed it were to remain under state control. They were to attend camp for six consecutive days each year, and their period of duty was fixed at nine months in case of hostilities. If the plan was carried out there would be about 250,000 *active* militia, which as *Niles' Register* remarked, "will not be inferior in drill to the regular army, and ready to take the field at a moment's warning,"[33] an opinion which was not, to say the least, very flattering to the army. To finance the plan an appropriation of $10,000,000 was asked for. At the same time it was urged that this arrangement would be the most effective argument against the increase of the regular army.

If the administration leaders had hoped to throw a sop to the anti-

33. *Niles*, LIV, 194 (May 26, 1838).

military group they must have received a rude shock by the opposition to the militia bill which immediately arose. Not even the *Globe* came to their rescue, for in an editorial on June 7 it denounced the measure both from regard to the "safety and honor" of the United States and "of enlightened economy." The militia would be far too expensive to maintain, and, besides, a militia would draw men from the soil. In the House, Isaac Bronson of New York estimated that the militia would cost from four to six times as much as the regulars. He claimed also that they were far less efficient. These were the classic arguments of all the opponents of the bill.

As the debate continued it looked as if no bill of any sort would pass. Between June 26 and July 2 no less than thirty-six members of the House took part in the debates, some of them a number of times. From June 14 to the end of the session on July 9 the House met in all-day-and-evening sessions every day except Sunday, and the army bill was discussed in every session until it was finally passed on July 5. It provided for an increase of about 4,650 instead of 6,650, enlistment for five years, and a new scale of pay for the ranks. No thoroughgoing reorganization was allowed.

In the Canadas the size and organization of the military forces were not subject to the control of the provincial legislatures but were determined by the War Office in London. Military expenses were met out of the military chest. In Lower Canada even the militia was in 1838 subject to the jurisdiction of the governor and council. This was not so in Upper Canada where a bill to reorganize the militia was introduced into the legislature on December 29, 1837.[34] Like the later militia bill in Congress, it met stiff opposition and its passage was held up for two months.

Insofar as a militia tradition rather than a military tradition existed in Upper Canada, the militia was regarded, as in the United States, as a force recruited for temporary emergencies and subject to the continued control of the legislature, and particularly of the Assembly. In this case, opposition seems to have come from those who objected to an extension of the control of the Executive over the lives of the people, for the bill aimed to amend and reduce into one act all the militia laws of the province in such a way as to give to the lieutenant governor unlimited power to call out the militia and to

34. *Journal of Assembly, Upper Canada, 1837–38*, p. 21.

control it. As finally passed on March 6, the act[35] made males between the ages of sixteen and sixty liable for duty for a period of nine months in time of rebellion or invasion. Penalties of a fine or imprisonment were to be imposed for refusal to serve. The militia could be marched into Lower Canada or anywhere in British North America when preparations were being made to invade Upper Canada. In case of emergency, the senior officer in any county or riding was authorized to call out such members of the militia as he considered necessary, after which he was to report his action to the lieutenant governor. The act applied to the militia who were actually serving at the time.

BRITISH AND AMERICAN JOINT EFFORTS

During the months that Congress and the Upper Canadian legislature were debating, the civil and military authorities in both countries were faced with difficult, and even critical, situations. Navy Island and later Patriot projects which endangered relations with Great Britain had to be prevented. But the most dangerous problems arose from the destruction of the *Caroline*. The attack upon this ship was chiefly responsible for the widespread spirit of retaliation in the United States and for the aid which was given to the Patriots. Moreover, the commendation of the attack by Sir Francis Bond Head, the defense of the action by Colonel Allan MacNab, and its justification by the Upper Canadian press drew the ire of all classes of society in the United States.[36]

Under the circumstances war between Great Britain and the United States was universally expected. Although the American press hoped that war would be averted, it was certain that war would become inevitable if filibustering continued.[37] In Lower Canada, Sir John Colborne, the governor, expected "serious consequences" to result from continued violations of neutrality, and in Washington, Henry Fox, the British minister, asserted that "war might occur at any time due to events on the frontier." Peace depended upon "the firm and successful assertion" of authority in Canada. Uneasiness was noticeable in ministerial ranks in London and in Washington. From London went instructions to Quebec that there were to be no

35. 1 Victoria, c. 8. *Statutes of Upper Canada,* 1838.
36. *Nat. Int.,* January 19, 1838.   37. *Ibid.,* January 27.

further violations of American territory.[38] In Washington the government was concerned over preventing invasions of the Canadas.

Happily for relations between the British and American governments there was being expressed in public dispatches an entire confidence by each government in the rectitude of the other.[39] Yet the Canadian authorities and Fox in Washington, as well as the Canadian press,[40] kept up a continual stream of complaints against the American government for its inability to restrain its citizens. To this government, paralyzed as was its military arm by lack of troops and its civil arm by lack of authority to prevent arming, drilling, and association, the problem of prevention was well-nigh appalling.

The appointment of Major General Scott as commander of the forces on the frontier was a most happy one. From all sides came plaudits of the man and of the soldier. Traveling first to one front and then to another, even in the bitterest winter weather, the indefatigable Scott became the hero of the hour. The *Buffalo Commercial Advertiser* was probably not exaggerating at all when it said on February 9 that "the names of Scott and Worth alone have contributed more to arrest the border difficulties than the combined civil authorities of the country. . . ."

Under Scott's command were three able officers: Brigadier General Hugh Brady and Colonel John E. Wool, already mentioned, and Colonel William J. Worth also mentioned above. Colonel Wool, a rigid disciplinarian, usually called "General" because he had at one time held the post of inspector general of the army, was placed in command on the Vermont front where, regardless of the sharp opposition of the press and the people, he brought Patriot efforts to an end much more quickly and successfully than was done elsewhere. Brigadier General Brady commanded the other end of the frontier, his headquarters being in Detroit. Now past sixty and universally beloved, he received glittering commendation as one who had "the

38. For Colborne's, Fox's, and Glenelg's statements see *Q*, CCXLIV, 161–163, 447; CCL, 90–91, 131–136; CCLVI, 57–60, 125–127; also *G*, XXXVIII, 128–137, 274–281.

39. *G*, XXXVIII, 128–137, 274–281, 351–356; *Q*, CCLVI, 187; *Stevenson Papers*, VII, 26843–26844. Palmerston to Stevenson, March 4, 1838.

40. *G*, CLXXXIV, 4–8; *Q*, CCLVI, 421–427; *Montreal Gazette*, January 13, February 24, 27, March 3, 1838.

honorable scars of a hundred well fought fields." In fact the *Detroit Free Press* said of him, "If there is a citizen of Michigan who wears the bright honors of an *American Patriot*, it is General Hugh Brady." Colonel Worth, a man in his middle forties and an exceptionally efficient officer, was in command of the northern district with headquarters at Buffalo. He was commonly regarded as one of the ablest officers in the army. Of all who were stationed on the Canadian frontier none was more esteemed than he. Almost always when Scott was mentioned in the border press from Buffalo eastward, Worth was mentioned also. In Scott's reports to the War Department it was Worth who was most frequently cited, not alone because he had the most difficult sector to command but because of the vigor and ability he displayed in carrying out his duties.[41]

On the Canadian side Lieutenant General Sir John Colborne[42] was not merely governor of Lower Canada. He was also commander-in-chief of the armies in the Canadas. He had had a long and honorable career and was to see twenty years of service after leaving North America. Portraits of Colborne represent him as a tenacious, wrinkled old bulldog of a soldier who never knew when he was beaten. Yet there was a kindliness about him, as revealed by his letters, which few outside his immediate associates suspected at the time. Under his command were a few regular officers, whose service had been long but whose ability was slight, and an occasional militia officer, like Colonel MacNab, of considerable ability but little service.

Scott was sent to the frontier on January 6. As he proceeded, he ordered several detachments of army recruits to join him; for, again, no regular troops were on the St. Lawrence border. In the course of time he had about four hundred regulars under his command. But, as he himself said, "rhetoric and diplomacy" were his chief weapons, his "countrymen and friends" his chief enemies, and "a little correspondence with the British authorities beyond the line" formed

41. For estimates of Wool, Worth, and Brady, see Fayette Robinson, *An Account of the Organization of the United States Army* (Philadelphia, 1848), II. These officers, together with Scott, were not without a meed of praise in the Canadas. See *G*, CLXXXIV, 12–13. Sir George Arthur to (Colonial Secretary), May 4.

42. For a biography, see C. G. Moore-Smith, *The Life of John Colborne, Field-Marshal Lord Seaton* (London, 1903).

"an episode of the whole." In his addresses to "immense gatherings of citizens, principally organized sympathizers, who had their arms at hand," he used all the rhetoric at his command to "inspire shame in misdoers, or excite pride in the friends of the Government and country." Often he ended his speeches in dramatic fashion, exclaiming, "I stand before you without troops and without arms, save for the blade by my side. I am, therefore, in your power. . . . All of you know that I am ready to do what my country and what duty demands. I tell you, then, except it be over my body, you shall *not* pass this line—you shall *not* embark."[43]

Words and speeches were not enough. He had to rely to a large extent on other weapons, such as the militia, the confiscation of arms and supplies, the commandeering of ships which the Patriots had engaged for service, and coöperation with the British officers. As he went through Albany on January 11, he requested Governor Marcy and Adjutant General of Militia McDonald to accompany him to Buffalo, so that in case the militia had to be called out no time would be lost in correspondence between the federal and state governments. Marcy's acceptance of the invitation is but one example of the willingness of state and local authorities in all three states to call out the militia when asked to do so. At the governor's behest the Michigan legislature passed an act which provided for the enlistment of two thousand militia to protect the frontier. In Vermont, Wool had two companies of volunteer cavalry at his command. At Buffalo and near-by points volunteer companies were formed, especially after the *Caroline* affair. The Steuben Guards were formed from among the German element in Buffalo, and a force of one thousand men was enrolled among the militia under the command of General David Burt. In February the New York militia was called out by order of the governor.

The American and British authorities were at the same time carrying on a friendly correspondence and entering into joint plans. Poinsett, the Secretary of War, proposed to Scott a joint conference of the governors and the American and British commanders in New York and Upper Canada. But the proposal came too late to be carried out.[44] No less than four regiments of infantry and a body of

43. Scott, *Autobiography,* p. 308.
44. *Poinsett Papers,* IX, 166; X, 18.

artillery crossed from the Atlantic to Quebec in the winter of 1837 and 1838 through the territory in dispute between Maine and New Brunswick, a movement which was facilitated by a communication from the Secretary of State to the governor of Maine.[45] Upon the refusal of Rensselaer Van Rensselaer to give up the New York State arms which his men had pilfered, General Arcularius of the New York militia requested permission from MacNab to retrieve the arms if they were captured by the Canadian forces. The request was "cheerfully complied with."[46]

The incident in which good understanding and good faith were most needed was that associated with the steamboat *Barcelona*. Word came to Scott that the Navy Islanders had hired the *Barcelona* to transport their arms and equipment to some other rendezvous. Scott outbid the Patriots at once and placed the ship in the United States service. Meanwhile the British and Canadian forces were lying in wait to destroy her as she passed down the river. Scott got the situation well in hand, however, by communicating with Colonel Hughes, commander of the Canadian militia, to the effect that the *Barcelona* was now in the service of the United States government and must be allowed to pass unmolested. He pointed out that if the ship were fired at he would be forced to take military action. To back up his message he placed a cannon on the bank of the Niagara River opposite Chippewa. Had the *Barcelona* been fired upon or destroyed, retaliation by Americans for a second *Caroline* incident and military action by the United States could not have been avoided. Scott's own feeling was that the border population could not have been restrained at all.[47] Much later he felt that his action and his assurances to Hughes that the *Barcelona* would not be used for Patriot purposes had averted the immediate possibility of war.[48]

The civil authorities also communicated with each other. Sir Francis Head informed Governor Marcy on December 13, 1837, of his intention to prevent the invasion of Canada and requested Marcy's coöperation. Although he found himself prevented from cooperating in the manner suggested by Head by virtue of the consti-

45. *D.S. Dom. Letters*, XXIX, 248.
46. *Journal of Assembly, Upper Canada, 1837–38*, pp. 93–95, 99–100.
47. *Poinsett Papers*, X, 51. Scott to Poinsett, February 22, 1838, Private.
48. Scott, *Autobiography*, I, 313–316.

tutional control exercised over foreign affairs by the federal government, Marcy issued a proclamation on December 19 requiring the people of New York to respect American laws.[49] Again, when the *Caroline* was destroyed Marcy forwarded a strong but not offensive message to the legislature at Albany,[50] and he entered into a surprisingly moderate correspondence with Head. Later in January, after Colborne had asked Marcy to prevent Coté, Gagnon, Bouchette, and others at Plattsburg from supplying arms to Lower Canadians,[51] and Marcy had replied that the state government had no power to act, he wrote to Wool, to the collector of customs at Champlain, and to the Secretary of War to enlist their assistance. In like manner, though to a lesser degree, the governors of Michigan and Vermont assisted the Canadian governors.

In the Canadas there was a certain assurance that, given time, British military power was sufficient to deal with all emergencies. The immediate problem, of course, was the effective use of available military forces and the militia to repel sporadic attacks by the Patriots. The regular army in British North America numbered some 4,500, and, of these, about 2,000 were stationed in the Canadas. Since they were obviously not numerous enough to cope with widespread rebellion, the governors of both provinces called the militia into service. But when it became certain that to the danger of renewed rebellion there was added the danger of invasion by armed bands from the United States, retaliation by loyal Canadians, and possible war with the United States, the governors became alarmed and urged upon the Colonial and War Offices the dispatch of a large number of troops to the Canadas. Their fears were aggravated by a feeling that however sincere the United States government might be, it lacked power to restrain its border population.[52]

In London interest centered chiefly in the political upheaval and the rebellions in the Canadas, until news of the burning of the *Caro-*

49. *Journal of Assembly, Upper Canada, 1837–38*, pp. 97–98.

50. *Messages from the Governors* (New York), III, 678–680.

51. For the correspondence, see *Q*, CCXLII, 89. Colborne to Glenelg, February 10; *D.S. Misc. Letters*, Marcy to Poinsett, February 4, 1838.

52. *Q*, CCXLIII, 31–34, 204–208. Gosford to Glenelg, January 5 and 30, Confidential; CCXLIV, 447, 449. Colborne to Fox, February 28, March 9, 1838.

line sharply awakened the ministry to the danger that lurked on the frontier. Already on December 28, 1837, Glenelg had written Colborne that a major general and twenty-five other officers were to be sent to Lower Canada at once.[53] On December 30, Colborne was assured of reinforcement by two regiments. The total military force in British North America was to be increased to 10,000, exclusive of artillery, as soon as navigation should open in the spring.[54] With the news of the *Caroline* incident in front of them, the ministry decided to increase the previously ordered reinforcements by two additional regiments. Of the total forces, 9,200 were to be stationed in the Canadas and 2,700 in Nova Scotia and New Brunswick.[55] The decision to increase the regular force in the Canadas appears to have been accompanied by a decision to place the defense of the provinces entirely in the hands of the regulars, on the assumption that the militia was far too expensive and under the present circumstances probably unnecessary. They were, to be sure, as late as April 20 thinking primarily of nipping further rebellion in the Canadas and of preventing attacks upon the United States as a consequence of ill-advised plans of militia officers.[56]

The ministry was interested not only in increasing the military forces in the Canadas but also in preventing the discontented elements there from receiving arms and ammunition. Information was received that arms were being shipped to New York with the Canadian provinces as their ultimate destination. An inquiry set on foot in the Customs Offices in London and Liverpool elicited the information that no unusual shipments, so far as ascertainable, had taken place. None had been shipped from London since December 5, 1837. Only 3,444 muskets and 432 pistols had been exported from Liverpool during October, November, and December, and their ultimate destination could not be determined. Since it was the custom to ship arms under the caption of hardware, it was obviously impossible to state how many had actually been exported. The only shipment direct to Montreal was sent in August, but the ship, the *Colborne*, was reported lost at sea.[57] It is therefore not possible to tell what propor-

53. *G*, XXXVII, 131–133.   54. *G*, XXXVII, 154–158.
55. *G*, XXXVIII, 151–155.
56. *Q*, CCLVI, 173–174. Glenelg to Durham.
57. This paragraph is based on dispatches and enclosures dated between

tion of arms exported from Great Britain to North America found its way to the Canadian insurgents.

In the Canadas Sir John Colborne took every possible opportunity to prevent American aid being given Canadians and to prevent further uprisings there. Colonel Charles Gore, the deputy quartermaster general, expended some £300 provincial currency to send secret agents into the United States to ferret out the movements of men, arms, and munitions. By paying *agents provocateurs* sufficiently well he hoped to secure adequate information.[58] Volunteers came forward, the militia was called out,[59] and eventually on March 6 a new militia law was passed which made it possible to reorganize that force. All available regulars were put into service, and correspondence with United States authorities was maintained. Whenever possible the justices of the peace attempted to persuade Americans that the majority of Canadians were not disloyal to the Crown and to warn them that the Canadian militia were ready to defend their country. The spirit of the magistrates was summed up in the remarks of Ogden Creighton of Niagara when he said that although the civil officers in Upper Canada "were unprepared for the sudden invasion of the whole American people, . . . we have sufficient spirit left to say in the language of our respected Governor, 'Let them come if they dare.' "[60] Martial law was proclaimed on February 27 when trouble threatened and was withdrawn on April 27 when danger was past.[61]

The control of shipping on the St. Lawrence and Lakes Ontario and Erie became a matter of importance. Scott, Worth, and Brady consistently commandeered vessels which the Patriots intended to use or whose services they had contracted for. This was especially exasperating to the Patriots whose general, Donald McLeod, excori-

January 3 and 13, 1838, in *G*, XXXVIII, 25–34, 40–45; and *Q*, CCLII, 131–139; CCLIV, 842–843.

58. *Q*, CCLII, 319–323, 341–342. Spearman to Stephen, July 11, 1838.

59. There were 1,500 volunteers and militia ready for service at Kingston at the time of the French Creek affair on February 22, 1838. *Q*, CCXLIX, 284–290. Lieutenant James Harper, R.N., to John Burrows, March 5.

60. *Q*, CCXLII, 280–282. Creighton to James Buchanan, British Consul at New York, December 19, 1837. Also *Democrat* (Rochester), December 13 and *Jour. of Com.*, December 20.

61. *Q*, CCXLIV, 446, 459.

ated the actions of the American commanders, contending that violation by the British of the naval agreement of 1817, in that they had three armed vessels on Lake Erie instead of one, gave Americans, Patriots, and others alike, the right to use vessels on the Great Lakes for any purpose they chose.[62]

McLeod's complaint on February 16 that the British had violated the Rush Bagot agreement had no better bases than a similar complaint against the United States would have had. And yet two days earlier Glenelg had dispatched a letter[63] to Colborne in which he explained that Her Majesty's government thought it expedient to provide for "a small flotilla" on the St. Lawrence and Great Lakes "consisting chiefly of a few armed Steamboats adapted to that navigation." Captain Sandom, R.N., had been ordered to proceed at once to Canada. Glenelg was careful to explain that "it is not the intention of H. M. Govt. that any extensive preparations should be made for a Naval Force in Canada in addition to that which will proceed" there in the spring, "but only that due precaution should be taken for securing the means of carrying on any necessary operations on those Waters with the aid of small Vessels to be procured in Canada, & which might to a certain extent be available for the transport of Troops." Sandom was, however, not to be in charge of transporting all the reinforcements to Canada, and he was not "to form his force upon a scale sufficient for that purpose."

The obvious intent of these instructions was that the naval force on the Lakes was to be increased sufficiently to cope with a situation which the agreement of 1817 did not envisage. It would provide for a more adequate defense of the Canadas, and more especially of Upper Canada. Here was no more calculated violation of the agreement than the increase of American forces by two unarmed vessels in the following June.[64] The question of the increase of naval forces and the possible abrogation of the Rush Bagot agreement was not to disturb Anglo-American relations for some months to come.

62. Callahan, "The Neutrality of the American Lakes and Anglo-American Relations," *loc. cit.*, p. 95.

63. *G*, XXXVIII, 155–160.

64. *Letters of the Department of State to the British Legation in Washington*, VI, 95. Forsyth to Fox, June 12, 1838. Hereafter referred to as *D.S. Br. Legation, Notes to.*

CHAPTER V

RISE OF THE SECRET SOCIETIES

ECONOMIC conditions in the United States and Canada during the winter of 1837 and 1838 give us the key to the discontent which resulted in increasing disorder along the frontier. The closing of the banks, the stoppage of specie payments—though not in Upper Canada—and the curtailment of credit in the summer and autumn of 1837 had the effect of dislocating business and commerce even in centers remote from the chief cities. Many a small business floundered and its employees were thrown out of work. Farmers could not move their less-than-average yield of crops of that panic year. Agricultural laborers were soon without jobs. The outlook for business and agriculture was abysmal.

In no area did those who were discontented with conditions at home have a finer opportunity to give direction to their energies than along the Canadian-American border where, during the winter, Americans who sympathized with the Canadians found themselves comparatively free to organize openly and to make preparations for the invasion of the Canadas. But as spring approached and the Patriots were successfully rebuffed and dispersed, they were forced to abandon methods of organization hitherto used and to become secretive. This lulled both Canadian and American authorities into a false sense of security from which they were rudely awakened in May, June, and July, 1838; and the Patriots were to have new names.

No less than five different secret societies were established in the United States, three in 1838 and two the following year. The first of these, the Canadian Refugee Relief Association, was formed at Lockport, New York, on March 19, 1838.[1] Its purpose was to discover the number and location of Canadian refugees,[2] to assist them to find a livelihood, and to aid them to redress their grievances against the

1. Lindsey, *Mackenzie*, II, 186–187.
2. *Marcy Papers*, III, 32974–32977. Marcy to Wetmore, June 7, 1837. Marcy estimated that there were 1,500 refugees in New York State.

government in Canada. Dr. Alexander Mackenzie of Hamilton, Upper Canada, was elected president. Donald McLeod, the Patriot general, as chief organizer was to send agents throughout the country to organize branch unions. Headquarters were located at Lockport. Since its membership was not confined to Canadians and since it either did not oppose or was favorable to sporadic attacks against the Canadas, it appealed to all those who craved action.

The Association's first action was to engineer the destruction of the British steamboat *Sir Robert Peel* in American waters. While on its way westward to Oswego with passengers and freight the *Peel* stopped on the evening of May 28 to take on wood for fuel at Wells Island near Clayton. At about two o'clock the following morning it was boarded by some twenty-two men dressed as Indians. Rousing the passengers and crew with shouts of "Remember the Caroline," they forced everyone to go ashore, unloaded most of the cargo, and set fire to the ship. The leader of the attack was a famous river pirate, Bill Johnson, who hoped to become a second Captain Kidd. Together with his regular band of followers, for months Johnson was responsible for preventing the pacification of the border because of his looting and burning of houses and barns. Of his followers in the attack on the *Peel* ten out of eleven who were captured were Canadians.[3]

An intention to embarrass Captain Armstrong of the *Sir Robert Peel* was one of the motives of those who destroyed it. During the previous winter he had lived in Watertown, New York, where he was accused by the Canadian refugees of being a spy in the pay of the Upper Canadian government. The destruction of the *Peel* was therefore undertaken as an act of retaliation against Armstrong personally. A second object was retaliation for the destruction of the *Caroline*. In the present case it appears that plans had been laid for simultaneous attacks on eight ships at as many different points on the St. Lawrence.[4] But above all, the Association was bent upon embroiling the United States and Great Britain in war. A succession of in-

3. *Van Buren Papers*, XXXII, 7573–7574. Marcy to Edwin Croswell, June 2, 1838.

4. *Albany Argus*, June 1. George C. Sherman, United States district attorney at Watertown, to Marcy.

cidents or even, it was currently said, "another *Caroline* affair" would bring about that desired objective.

Turning toward Buffalo the Association now made two attempts to attack Upper Canada along the Niagara front. On the night of June 6, some three hundred Patriots planned to cross over to Lewiston, but their courage failed them at the last moment when they heard that a party of American soldiers was on its way to take them into custody.[5] A few days later, under the leadership of Colonel James Moreau, an American, and Major Benjamin Wait, a Canadian, and others, some two hundred to four hundred men in small groups of twenty or thirty crossed over to Navy Island and Chippewa. Unable to advance further into Canadian territory because the Canadians failed to rise to assist them, they established a camp at Long Swamp between Grand Island and Chippewa Creek, whence a detachment marched over to Short Hills, twelve miles distant. On the night of the twentieth they either attacked a party of lancers in Overholt's Tavern or else became involved with them in a tavern broil. The consequence was that the invaders lost four of their number, burned down the tavern, and forced the lancers to surrender. They allowed them, however, to go free after they had confiscated their arms, ammunition, clothing, and horses, and although the British expected another attack the following night, none materialized. Unfortunately for the invaders they remained in the vicinity of Short Hills too long. As they were leaving in small groups for the United States on the twenty-third, they were overtaken by British and Canadian regulars and militia, and thirty-one of their number were taken prisoners. Among them were Moreau, Wait, Samuel Chandler, and Donald McLeod, the "general" who was chief organizer of the Canadian Refugee Relief Association.[6] With the dispersal of those who took part in the Short Hills affair, the efforts of the Association seem to have come to an end.

In the meantime, excitement over the attack on the *Peel* produced an incident at Brockville, Upper Canada, which further inflamed the frontier. On June 2 the American steamboat *Telegraph* called at

5. *Q*, CCXLIX, 431–432. Arthur to Colborne, June 8.
6. This account is based on correspondence in *Q*, CCXLVI and CCXLIX, and upon newspaper reports, e.g., *Buffalo Commercial Advertiser*, *New York Journal of Commerce*, *Niles' Register*, and *National Intelligencer*.

Brockville on one of its regular trips. While lying at a dock it was boarded by a number of unarmed men who ransacked the cabins, but without doing much damage. As soon as possible the captain began to move the ship to the upper wharf. Being ordered to heave to and thinking that additional passengers were about to come aboard, but apprehensive of trouble, he kept the ship some twenty feet from the dock and directed the passengers to be sent out in a boat. After an exchange of words with those on shore, the captain began to shove off. Thereupon some militiamen, who had been standing around, fired at the ship, but without doing it much material damage except to put some bullet holes through the walls of the ladies' cabin. That the attack on the *Telegraph* occurred in retaliation for the destruction of the *Peel* there is little doubt.[7]

While these disturbances were keeping the border people wrought up, another secret society, the Sons of Liberty, was being formed.[8] About the beginning of June, 1838, a large number of Canadians crossed over into Michigan in order to escape the surveillance of the Canadian authorities. Thereupon an association was formed "for revolutionizing Canada." It was composed mostly of Canadians, but with American leaders. Lodges were formed. Henry S. Handy, a former government clerk in Washington and now a Patriot general, was made commander-in-chief, and every member took the following oath to obey him or his aide, "General" Roberts:

You do solemnly swear, in the presence of Almighty God, that you will bear allegiance and fidelity to the SONS OF LIBERTY engaged in the PATRIOT service and in the cause of CANADIAN INDEPENDENCE—that you will obey the orders of your superior officers in whatever department you may serve—that you will never communicate or in any way divulge the existence or plans of said association. You also swear that you will devote your time, your person, your interest in promoting said cause, so far as may be consistent with your other duties—that you will never sell, barter, or in any way alter any badge that may be bestowed upon you for the purpose of designating your rank in said association. You

7. *D.S. Misc. Letters,* Bishop Perkins and Smith Stillwell, collector of customs, Ogdensburg to Sen. Silas Wright, Jr., June 3, 1838. Also *Nat. Int.,* June 11, and *St. Lawrence Republican* (Ogdensburg), June 12.

8. Lindsey, *op. cit.,* II, 192–195.

also swear that you will not disclose or in any way communicate to any person the contents or purports of this Oath, and that you will not converse with any person in reference to this Oath, except in Convention, or with the man who first presents it to you.

Confidential agents with commissions signed by Handy were sent into the Canadas to form revolutionary societies and enrol trusty persons. It was intended to place persons with authority to grant commissions in each square mile of settled country. Commissions were to be granted to captains; colonels were to be elected by the separate associations or lodges. One hundred special agents were to be kept constantly on the move, each doing a patrol of ten miles. They were to traverse this distance both ways each day, thus keeping in touch with their fellow agents, and keeping up a continual correspondence with Handy. To develop a fighting force there were to be formed in the Canadas two hundred companies, one hundred strong, a total of twenty thousand men, who could be called into action speedily by the one hundred special agents. In Michigan, where the disaffected were gathered together under Handy's command, a plan was made to attack Upper Canada on July 4.[9] The first objective of the Sons of Liberty was Windsor. Having captured it they intended to send out couriers to inform the Canadian people of the success of their venture, and to stimulate a general rising.

To launch an attack of such magnitude, arms and accoutrements had first to be secured, and to acquire them Handy relied on his ability to plunder the Michigan state arsenal. Some of the guards at the arsenal in whom Handy placed implicit confidence had served with him on a number of occasions, notably in the preceding February. These men were to leave the windows of the arsenal unlocked and were to give the keys to "General" Roberts, Handy's aide. Roberts acquired two scows of twenty tons each and towed them to within a few rods of the arsenal. By such means it was hoped to obtain some fifteen thousand stand of arms and sufficient ammunition with which to supply the majority of the twenty thousand men in Canada who were expected to be organized in the companies one hundred strong. Fifteen cannon were also to be taken over on the expedition.

At this point, a man named Baker upset Handy's plans. Falsely

9. This account is based largely on *ibid.*

stating that he was acting under Handy's orders he collected a body of forty freebooters and set out on June 26 on a plundering expedition along the Black River. After robbing some country stores the men found themselves pursued by the American steamboat *Gratiot*, but with the exception of one man they were able to escape after running their sloop aground. Five others were captured later. Of the six only one was an American.

At a Patriot meeting held the same evening in Detroit the thirty men who were to loot the arsenal at Dearborn were chosen. Both Baker's expedition and the meeting put Brigadier General Brady on the alert. He changed the guards at the arsenal and secured it against attack. So it was that a few days before the attack planned for the Fourth could be carried out, the conspiracy collapsed "from the want of arms." Handy and Roberts now appealed to Cleveland and to London, Upper Canada, for aid, only to be met with a rebuff, for Handy was replaced in command of the forces of the Sons of Liberty by "General" L. V. Bierce. Under the new leadership the society lay low until December, when, with a new group, the "Hunters," of the "Hunters Lodges" they tried and failed to capture Windsor and Sandwich. Thereafter, they seem to have disbanded as a society and to have merged with the Hunters.

Formed in May, this was the most important of all the Patriot associations.[10] It was the most widespread, it had the best and most effective organization, it absorbed all the other groups in the course of time, and it was the most feared. It originated in Vermont because it was thought that the Patriots should transfer their activities to Lower Canada as a consequence of the reverses which they had met in the west. Organization proceeded rapidly until a vast network of lodges spread over the northern part of the United States, as well as into some southern states and the Canadas.[11] In the north every village and every town was said to have had a lodge. Estimates of membership range as high as two hundred thousand but more conservative figures totaling forty thousand to fifty thousand during 1838 and

10. *Q*, CDIX, 46–146. Arthur to Glenelg, October 22, 1838. Also seven enclosures giving firsthand accounts. *D.S. Misc. Letters*, George H. McWhorter, collector at Oswego, to Levi Woodbury, Secretary of the Treasury, September 14.

11. Toward the end of 1841 the *London Morning Chronicle*, quoted in

1839, the years when the Hunters were most active, are likely to be nearer the truth.[12] Members were drawn from all walks of life. Neither office nor occupation was a deterrent to membership. Said a Jefferson County (N.Y.) paper: "Laborers left their employ; apprentices their masters; mechanics abandoned their shops; merchants their counters; magistrates their official duties; husbands their families; children their parents; Christians their churches; ministers of the gospel their charge, to attend [the] meetings" of the Hunters.

The militant nature of the society made secrecy imperative so that each member was required to take the following oath:

I swear to do my utmost to promote Republican Institutions and ideas throughout the world—to cherish them, to defend them; and especially to devote myself to the propagation, protection, and defense of these institutions in North America. I pledge my life, my property, and my sacred honor to the Association; I bind myself to its interests, and I promise, until death, that I will attack, combat, and help to destroy, by all means that my superior may think proper, every power, or authority, of Royal origin, upon this continent; and especially never to rest till all tyrants of Britain cease to have any dominion or footing whatever in North America. I further solemnly swear to obey the orders delivered to me by my superior, and never to disclose any such order, or orders, except to a brother "Hunter" of the same degree. So help me God.[13]

Jour. of Com., November 15, made startling allegations when it published the following list of lodges in the United States and British North America:

Maine	99	Virginia	21	Missouri	39
Vermont	107	Maryland	16	Iowa	2
New York	283	Delaware	2	Louisiana	11
Michigan	54	New Jersey	17	Upper Canada	81
New Hampshire	78				
Wisconsin	7	Lower Canada, nearly the whole population organized into lodges.			
Illinois	21				
Indiana	14	New Brunswick, a few.			
Ohio	86	British North America, elsewhere—scattered.			
Pennsylvania	49	United States, elsewhere—100.			
Kentucky	11				

12. *Q,* CDXVI, 101–107. "Report from the Select Committee of the House of Assembly of Upper Canada," April 30, 1839. Enclosure in Arthur to Normanby, May 11, 1839. This estimates the strength of the Hunters at not less than 40,000.

13. Lindsey, *op. cit.,* II, 199 n.

To insure still greater secrecy one had to be initiated through a number of degrees to become a full-fledged member. As in other secret societies there were special signs, words, grips, codes for correspondence, and methods of rapping to gain admittance to lodges.

Although the Hunters' movement began as early as May, 1838, centralized organization on a large scale was not effected until the Cleveland convention, in session from September 16 to 22. At that time a program of action was agreed upon. A republican government for Upper Canada was formed with a president, vice-president, secretary of state, secretary of the treasury, and secretary of war. There was also to be a commander-in-chief of the forces, with many other military and naval officers. To guarantee the fiscal needs of the new state a republican bank was formed with a capital of $7,500,000. Paper money was to be issued. The invasion of Upper Canada was determined upon.

As the movement spread, the most important lodges came to be situated at Lockport, Rochester, Buffalo, Cleveland, Cincinnati, and Detroit, with minor lodges in eastern New York and Vermont. Of all the lodges, that at Cleveland was regarded as the headquarters of the society, while the one at Rochester was looked upon as the chief center in the East.[14]

From July to November, 1838, a relative absence of incendiarism and the like rendered the frontier comparatively quiet. It was the quiet which precedes the storm, for the outward calm merely concealed the extensive organization of Hunters Lodges and the gradual ripening of rebellion in Lower Canada. It was not altogether an accident that the Hunters' attack on Prescott in Upper Canada and the November rebellion in Lower Canada nearly coincided. Lower Canadians were secretly supplied with arms from the United States. The

14. In 1839 two additional societies were formed (ibid., II, 238–242). The Agricultural Meeting at Auburn, N. Y., was stillborn. The Canadian Association organized in Rochester by Mackenzie, and an auxiliary, the Association of Canadian Refugees at Cincinnati, were designed to pursue Fabian tactics. To secure the independence of the Canadas was their ultimate objective but they proposed to refrain from direct action until the Canadians themselves should first strike out for independence. Neither association possessed directive vigor or competence. Their membership soon dissolved, to be absorbed to a considerable degree by the Hunters.

Patriot leaders were kept informed of the progress of discontent in the Canadas.[15]

The approximate date for the attack on Upper Canada was determined upon at the Hunters' Cleveland convention in September. Immediately after the convention they began to secure arms and provisions, enlist men, especially the unemployed, acquire ships, and organize the territory from Syracuse to Ogdensburg in preparation for the forthcoming assaults along the frontier. To divert attention from the central point of attack, they spread rumors that advances were to be made at several points. By early November their plans were complete and squads of men totaling a thousand or more began to converge on points between Watertown and Ogdensburg.

From a report[16] which gives the names of 140 of a total of 157 prisoners captured a few days later by the Canadians at Prescott, it appears that practically every man was a laborer, dependent for the most part upon seasonal employment. Twenty-three trades were represented and there were sixty-five who called themselves laborers. There was one teacher and one "gentleman." The majority of the men were very young. Twenty-seven were in the teens, seventy were in the twenties, eighteen were in the thirties, and the remaining seventeen whose ages are given were in the forties and fifties. Appeals were made to their hope of self-aggrandizement by promises of a wage of $8 a month, a bounty of $80, and 160 acres of land in Upper Canada. According to the available evidence one fourth were Hunters. Of these, eleven had been responsible for getting forty-six others to join the expedition. So far as can be determined, fifty-eight came from those counties of northern New York east of Oswego which border on Lake Ontario and the St. Lawrence River, five were from Canada, and two were Englishmen. Two thirds of the prisoners went across the river voluntarily while the remaining third were forced to go. A few Europeans who spoke a little English were taken along as menials without their understanding the nature of what they were being sent to do.

15. *Q*, CCXLIX, 566–567. Arthur to Colborne, October 24; and pp. 588–590. Colborne to Campbell, October 29.

16. *Q*, CDXIII, 247–270. Arthur to Glenelg, February 5, 1839. Enclosure No. 12, "Alphabetical List of Prisoners taken at or near Windmill Point, below Prescott . . . on the 12th November, 1838. . . ."

In so far as they could, the Hunters made the most careful preparations for the attack on Prescott. For example, Wingate Davis of Salina, New York, who had already distinguished himself, was sent to Toronto in the latter part of October where, for a week, he spent his time "dining with, wineing [sic], and playing checkers with ten or twelve English Army officers." Thence he went to Port Hope, Cobourg, and Kingston to learn all he could from the Canadian people. Everywhere on the trip he met Hunters who assured him that the majority of the Canadians were ready to rebel and that they would join forces with the Patriots as soon as they had gained a foothold in Canada. Back in Salina he found Canadians who insisted that the Upper Canadians would rebel again before the winter was over. Assurance was also given him that an army of from fifteen to forty thousand men "would be concentrated on the border to invade Canada at the first opportune moment."[17]

Their preparations completed, the Patriot army began to move toward Prescott. On the night of November 11, the steamboat *United States* took in tow at French Creek two schooners which were loaded with considerable quantities of arms and ammunition, and a few cannon. As the flotilla approached Prescott a council of war was held by Von Schoultz, a thirty-one-year-old Pole in command of one vessel, and Bill Johnson—erstwhile river pirate—the commodore. But no decision for a definite plan of action was arrived at. The *United States* then cast off and proceeded to Ogdensburg, while the two vessels attempted to make their way across the river below Prescott without being discovered. In this they were unsuccessful. A sentry spied them and gave the warning. As they sailed down the river, one vessel ran aground. The other with about two hundred men reached Windmill Point, a mile and a half below Prescott, where a landing was effected, the mill, built of stone, was occupied, and breastworks were thrown up under Von Schoultz' direction. The original plan of capturing Fort Wellington during the night had failed.

For the next five days the position of the Patriots was precarious. To be sure, on November 13, the militia and regulars were unable to dislodge them. Major Young, the officer commanding the military

17. Gardner B. Chapin, *Tales of the St. Lawrence* (Rouses Point, 1873), pp. 358–360. Davis' statement may be discounted in part because it was written so many years after the events occurred.

forces at Prescott, thereupon withdrew his men but posted a guard strong enough to prevent their escape. The following day another attack was delivered in which the British lost forty-five killed and wounded and took thirty-two prisoners and a few guns. Two days later a final sortie was made. This time eighty-six prisoners were taken and sixteen, wounded, were removed from the mill. All the Patriots' arms, twenty-six kegs of powder, and three cannon were captured. On November 17, the remainder of the adventurers surrendered with "a white silk flag, having an eagle and a star painted on it, with the words, '*Onondaga* Hunters,' '*Canada Liberated*,' fancifully worked upon it. . . ."[18]

From the first Von Schoultz had expected to receive aid from Ogdensburg and from the Canadians, but the latter did not rise in rebellion. When he discovered his plight he sent to Ogdensburg for boats to take his men back to the United States but the British kept a steamboat cruising back and forth on the river and Colonel Worth at Ogdensburg commandeered all the boats there. Worth, however, realized the plight of the men at Windmill Point and allowed the steamboat *Paul Fry* to go over to effect a rescue. It returned without any of the men for the reason that they were unable to leave the mill because of the strong British guard that surrounded it and because Captain Sandom, R.N., on the *Victoria*, was on guard to intercept attempts to aid the beleaguered men. Consequently all were forced to fight it out on the Canadian side. Of those who were not killed all but one or two were taken prisoners.

After the disaster at Prescott the Hunters and the Sons of Liberty made plans to invade Upper Canada once again. "General" Bierce was given instructions to proceed to Detroit and to attack Windsor. By November 29 he had a force of some four hundred men at a rendezvous near the mouth of the Detroit River.[19] On December 1 they

18. Good descriptions of the battle of Windmill Point are in Lindsey, *op. cit.*, II, 205–211 and E. C. Guillet, *The Lives and Times of the Patriots* (Toronto, 1938), chap. xiv. Contemporary reports are in Q, CCXLV and *D.S. Misc. Letters*. The quotation is from the *Kingston Chronicle*, repeated in *Nat. Int.*, November 29, 1838.

19. In Buffalo arms were seized in transit and some 150 to 200 men were prevented from sailing for Detroit because of inclement weather. *Nat. Int.*, November 30.

marched to within four miles of Detroit where they joined another party and were outfitted as if for a protracted winter campaign. Two days' delay took place. Men began to desert. Eventually, on the evening of the third, the force marched openly into Detroit, boarded the steamboat *Champlain*, and in the early morning of the fourth crossed over to Windsor. Some five thousand people followed their movements with much interest from the American shore.

The delay incident to getting the Patriots[20] under way gave both the British and American military authorities an opportunity to concentrate their forces. Nevertheless, the Patriots, to the number of about two hundred, landed near Windsor under the leadership of Bierce, whose courage was of such a vintage that he kept well to the rear surrounded by a special bodyguard. Upon landing he addressed his men and issued a proclamation which had been drawn up five days earlier. The party then swung into action, burned the militia barracks and the steamboat *Thames* near by. Meeting with a cross fire from the British, they then retreated into the woods. Shortly afterwards Bierce and many of his men attempted to recross the river. The *Champlain* had departed; so they hailed a steamboat, the *Erie*, with Brigadier General Brady on board, but she refused to come to their aid. They were thus reduced to the use of canoes and open boats. The upshot of the raid was that the invaders lost twenty-five killed and forty-four prisoners. Four of the prisoners were shot on the spot without any semblance of trial by order of Colonel John Prince of Sandwich, the commander of the Canadian militia.[21]

20. It will be noticed that the two terms, Patriots and Hunters, are used interchangeably. This usage is quite consistent with the usage at the time. To be sure, not all the Patriots belonged to the Hunters or other secret organizations, but all of the latter were commonly called Patriots. On the other hand, the term Patriots, as used in the United States where it was regularly applied to both Americans and Canadians, must not be confused with the term as it was used in the Canadas, particularly in Lower Canada. There it was applied to the followers of Mackenzie, Papineau, and other leaders of the Rebellions of 1837, as well as to those who rose again in rebellion in Lower Canada in 1838.

21. For Prince's report of the raid, see the *Montreal Gazette*, December 18, 1838. Also *Q*, CCLXIV and CDXIII.

CHAPTER VI

CROSSCURRENTS OF OPINION

DURING the second half of 1838, a sharp change of attitude toward Canada and the Canadian situation can be traced in the United States. In the first place, the recurring failure of all attempts to invade the Canadas gave the lie to the idea that those provinces could be invaded with impunity. In the second place, there was a pronounced desire to avert war with Great Britain. In the third, it began to be understood more clearly that Canadians had no desire for the assistance of Americans in their struggle to achieve responsible government or a redress of grievances. Furthermore, Americans were to a large degree won over by the personal charm of Lord and Lady Durham and by Durham's efforts to impress upon them how conciliatory British administration in British North America could be. Each of these sources of changed opinion we may now consider in turn.

FILIBUSTERING

After some months of quiet on the frontier, the destruction of the *Sir Robert Peel* on May 29 had an electrifying effect. Along the American side of the border there was at first a tendency to rejoice that the *Caroline* had been revenged. But the incident caused so much ill feeling in Upper Canada that it was generally expected that the Canadians would resort to reprisals at once—an expectation that was only too well founded in view of the *Telegraph* affair at Brockville on June 2.[1] The result was that intercourse between Upper Canada and the United States on the St. Lawrence and Lake Ontario was temporarily slowed up or halted altogether. The daily boats between Toronto and Oswego were reported to have stopped running, and the *United States* was advised at Rochester, Oswego, and Sackett's Harbor not to visit Kingston. There were rumors that many ships refused to sail for Canadian ports until they had been provided with armed guards. Resumption of normal sailings was not long delayed, however, because, as the *Rochester Daily Advertiser* remarked,

1. Richardson, *Messages*, III, 478–479; *Nat. Int.*, June 11.

"the proximity of these states and the Canadas renders intercourse essential, and no common obstacle can long suspend it."[2] In the same vein, the *New York Journal of Commerce* observed on June 13 that "nothing has yet happened which cannot easily be settled. . . ." It had already suggested that "if 1,000 picked men on each side of the line were tumbled into Niagara and sent down the Falls, there would be no further trouble."

In the nation at large, the destruction of the *Peel* was regarded as "disgraceful to our national character, and pregnant with consequences of the most serious import."[3] The government of the United States was censured for keeping ten thousand men in Florida "fighting for swamps" when it should have had a garrison on the Canadian border. The leading papers demanded that the President send a larger force to the frontier at once if the United States wished to avoid getting "into a *mess* with England. . . ." They were opposed to filibustering and reprisals of every kind.[4]

As the summer wore on toward autumn, reports began to circulate that discontent in the Canadas might ripen into rebellion, and that a vast movement was on foot in the United States to assist the Canadians. Not only did the leading American papers oppose such assistance, but when rebellion did break out in Lower Canada in November they insisted that upon the preservation of neutrality depended the good name of the United States. After the *Peel* affair they had demanded that a larger military force be sent to the border. Now they repeated that demand, and asked for a stronger neutrality law. They absolved the United States from all obligation to give diplomatic assistance to captured Americans. They praised Sir John Colborne for issuing a series of restrictive ordinances which, under different circumstances, would have been anathema. It was clear that American opinion as represented by the most influential newspapers and magazines had veered sharply away from opinions held only a year before.[5]

2. Quoted in *Jour. of Com.*, June 11.

3. *New York Courier and Enquirer*, quoted in *Nat. Int.*, June 5.

4. The Albany, New York, Washington, and Boston press were all of the same opinion.

5. This paragraph is based on comments between November 12 and 22, 1838, in the following papers: *National Intelligencer* and *Globe*, of Washington; *Journal of Commerce*, *Commercial Advertiser*, *Courier and Enquirer*, *Daily Express*, *Sunday News*, of New York; and the *Richmond Whig*.

While this sharp reaction in opinion was taking place, Mackenzie was busy in New York City attempting to stem the tide both through his newspaper, *Mackenzie's Gazette*, which he began to publish on May 12, 1838, and through the organization of an Executive Committee headed by himself.[6] When news of the outbreak of November, 1838, reached New York he called together some thirty persons with a view to making plans to hold a series of public meetings.

The first of these, at which an admission fee of four for twenty-five cents was charged, was held at the Richmond Hill theater on November 13.[7] Unfortunately for Mackenzie and his plans, he had allied himself with the Loco Focos and other political "radicals," and he made. the egregious blunder of inviting Fanny Wright, a militant campaigner for women's rights, to deliver an address. The meeting was attended by more than two thousand people who became very disorderly when Fanny Wright began to speak. The following evening another meeting was held at Vauxhall Gardens. This time E. A. Theller, a Patriot "general," and his associate, "Colonel" W. W. Dodge, who had recently escaped from the citadel at Quebec, were present and spoke at length. But it was all of no avail. It was impossible to do much more than amuse the crowd. Despite Mackenzie's expectation to the contrary, New Yorkers were not as willing to aid the Canadians as they had been a year before.

Like the meetings in New York, others in Philadelphia, Baltimore, and Washington achieved nothing. It was not for want of sympathy for the Canadians that opposition to the meetings arose but, as the *Alexandria Gazette* pointed out, because "our 'sympathy' is more likely to be appeased than increased by the harangues of 'foreign agitators,' who, driven or flying from the scene of war, come here to sow the seeds of dissension between friendly nations." In Baltimore where the rebuff administered to the Hunters at Prescott was known prior to the meeting, it was reported that "almost all respectable citizens disapproved of it, and would have been glad to see it prevented, if that could have been done with propriety."

More than any other incident, the battle of Windmill Point was responsible for changing public opinion in the United States. It

6. James Buchanan, the British consul at New York, kept Palmerston informed of the movements of Mackenzie, O'Callaghan, and others.

7. *Mackenzie's Gazette,* November 14; *Nat. Int.,* November 14.

"had a salutary influence upon the public mind, by disclosing" the ineptitude as leaders "of those who had been foremost in promoting the expedition."[8] The *Oswego Bulletin* spoke of it as "the melancholy close of the 'glorious three days' at Prescott" and expected it would "dampen the ardor of many who have been sanguine in the cause." It was reported to Colonel Worth that "a great and rapid change has come over the people."[9] It was expected that those of the frontier, like their fellows of the interior, would soon look upon the recent agitation with sorrow and indignation.

As Hough pointed out, however, it was the leaders who became the object of attacks. "Cowardly scoundrels," they were called, and their lives were even threatened "for sending innocent and brave men where they *dare not* go themselves!" Both indignation and change of attitude along the border were also due largely to the belief that Canadians in Canada had "proved themselves cowards and traitors to the cause" and deserved no further assistance.[10] In New York and Washington, the Patriots were attacked in the press in no uncertain terms. Americans, it was believed, should be convinced, once and always, "of the utter hopelessness . . . as well as the wickedness of such attempts, and of the lasting opprobrium which attaches to them."[11]

The attack on Windsor, on December 4, met with equally sharp criticism. In Detroit it was condemned as "the most foolhardy, mad, and criminal enterprise that has yet marked their [the Hunters'] infatuated career. There is no justification or palliation for so miserable an undertaking." It was hoped that this "mad-cap expedition" and its "disastrous results" would teach "the utter hopelessness and wickedness of so uncalled for an invasion," more especially since not a single Canadian joined the invaders after they had landed at Windsor.[12]

By the end of the year Hunters and Patriots alike were everywhere

8. Franklin B. Hough, *A History of Jefferson County in the State of New York* (Albany, 1854), pp. 524–525.

9. Letter to Worth, November 20, enclosed in Worth to Poinsett, November 24, in the *Globe,* December 3, 1838.

10. *Watertown Jeffersonian,* quoted in *Nat. Int.,* November 27.

11. *Globe,* November 23; *New York Courier and Enquirer,* quoted in *Nat. Int.,* November 26.

12. *Detroit Daily Advertiser,* December 6.

in disgrace, their expeditions defeated, their plans nullified, and their future anything but bright. This gives a clue to the prevailing opinion that no further invasions of the Canadas were to be expected during the winter.[13]

WAR

The condemnation of continued filibustering and of continued interference in Canadian affairs may be explained in part by reference to the belief that if the border did not quiet down, war with Great Britain would become inevitable. It is therefore of some interest to discover whether there was mutual hostility or friendliness between the United States and Great Britain if we are to determine whether there was actually any possibility of war. It is also of interest to discover what reasons might be adduced for concluding that there must be war and what the advantages and disadvantages of war were expected to be.

With the exception of the *Times* and the *Morning Herald* whose editors betrayed a marked anti-American bias, both private and official opinion in London seem, on the whole, to have been friendly toward the United States.[14] There were occasions, to be sure, when ministers and others used rather vigorous language in referring to the United States government, but irritation was shortly displaced by a recognition of the impediments which curtailed the efforts of the federal authorities.[15] They were willing to accept the assurances of the United States and to remain on friendly terms with that country. Toward the end of 1838, when Van Buren issued his proclamation against filibustering, it was reported that "the happy prospect of our being able to continue in peace with America has diffused the greatest satisfaction throughout Great Britain and Ireland."[16]

In the United States these expressions of good will and friendship met a friendly but critical reception. Ever since 1815, although they

13. *The Buffalonian, Jour. of Com.*, and *Observer*, December 29.

14. Editorial in *Jour. of Com.*, June 1, 1838.

15. Stanley's speech in the House of Commons, March 6, 1838, quoted in the *Globe*, June 21. Stanley spoke of "the candid, honorable, and handsome manner" in which the United States had maintained faith with Great Britain; G, XXXIX, 142–149. Glenelg to Durham, July 20, in which he expressed gratification at the coöperation of the United States authorities.

16. *Nat. Int.*, January 9, 1839.

were anxious to avert war as long as possible, Americans had been certain that another war with Great Britain must surely come. This anticipation arose out of the many conflicting interests between the two countries on the North American continent. A characteristic opinion, voicing belief in the inevitability of war and also weighing its advantages and disadvantages for the United States, is found in an open letter published in New Haven, December 26, 1838, by one who signed himself "Spirit of John Hay."[17]

For the past year, he said, the press had talked of advantages to be derived from a war with Great Britain, and the *New York Express* had published a list of these advantages which had been "extensively copied and circulated." After listing all of those advantages which were commonly expected to derive from the establishment of the independence of Canada, the writer listed several additional benefits to the United States which he had culled from various sources. These included a repudiation of more than $140,000,000 of loans from Great Britain which had been used to finance internal improvements; the exclusion of British manufactures to build up those of the United States which would, in turn, give employment to Americans and make them "a truly independent people"; and finally, the employment of many "hot heads" in the army. All these advantages would derive from a war with Great Britain. They would be only partially realized as a result of war with any other nation.

There were those, of course, who pointed to the bitter consequences of war. Summarizing their views and his own, the writer claimed that the first result of war, judging from the War of 1812, would be the destruction of American commerce within three months. All labor upon internal improvements would be suspended, dividends from industry would cease, the cotton trade would be cut off. To win the war the British could and would send thousands of free negroes into the Southern States and enlist the Indians in the West, whose removal thither by the United States government would prove to be their incentive to destroy all the western towns and settlements. British supremacy in steam navigation would result in sudden attacks on the poorly defended coasts of the United States. Financially, war

17. *Q*, CCLXV, 24–41. "War with England. The Case fairly Stated, with an Address to President Van Buren and the members of Congress with whom rests the power of preventing that Calamity. By an advocate of Peace."

would impose a crushing burden. It would cost at least from $300,-000,000 to $400,000,000, and Canada would, in addition, demand compensation for all losses. From every point of view war would be morally unjust, more especially if it should come as a result of aggression against Canada. Finally, victory for the United States would end in disaster. The acquisition of Canada would be followed by the dissolution of the Union into three countries, the North, the South, and the West.

That war was considered a possibility and that many feared it could not be avoided, was the opinion of James Buchanan, who from long residence as British consul in New York knew personally all the leading men in New York State. In a long letter to Palmerston, of January 3, 1839,[18] he outlined fifteen reasons which led him and others to anticipate war between the United States and Great Britain: The whole frontier remained hostile to Great Britain, and the ill feeling had been intensified by the execution of prisoners in Canada. Recently hostility had extended to the interior. Canadian refugees, especially the French Canadians, were urging war in the hope of freeing Canada. The more radical groups, like the Loco Focos, were insisting upon the removal of all European government in America for the purpose of following a more pointed policy of isolation with respect to commercial and financial relations with foreign countries. Impairment of the President's prestige because he had been unable to enforce the laws, and the necessity of taking positive measures to secure his reëlection would induce his party to urge war as a final resort to maintain itself in power. The manufacturing and mining interests in New England and Pennsylvania, the West whose object was to secure control of the St. Lawrence, the abolitionists who hoped to secure the emancipation of the American negro, the mercantile interests that believed Great Britain would rather give up the Canadas than go to the expense of a war—all these were in favor of war. Jealousy of Great Britain colored American feeling to such an extent that several senators who wanted peace were certain it could not long be maintained. Canadian opinion, especially the singularly vituperative language of the *Toronto Patriot*, in its denunciation of American officials who had attempted to do their duty also contributed to the feeling of hostility in the United States.

18. *Q*, CCLXV, 18–23.

That these opinions were prevalent in the United States is confirmed by the amount of space given to them in all types of publications. Throughout 1838, but particularly in the latter part of the year, the more important papers advocated a threefold program for the prevention of war with Great Britain. The army, they said, should be enlarged, presidential powers should be expanded, and the neutrality law should be made more inclusive to cover all aspects of Patriot activities.

The widespread interest evoked in the United States by the Canadian troubles led to a more careful examination of conditions in Canada in comparison with those of the colonies of other powers. To their surprise Americans discovered that "there was no liberty essential to the preservation of life and the pursuit of happiness, that the People of Canada did not enjoy from their Government."[19] The law protected Canadians' personal and religious rights, and their property; they were tried by their own judges and jurors; they passed their own laws; and they were "exempt from taxation and oppression." The *United States Gazette* believed that, on the whole, the government of Canada "appears to have been administered with as much prudence and as little oppression as has been seen in any Provincial Government." The *New York Journal of Commerce* discovered that there was "still some freedom in Canada" when a meeting was held in Quebec on July 4 to express sympathy and good wishes for political prisoners, for those deported to Bermuda, and for Canadian refugees in the United States. The *New York Gazette* believed that "the Canadians have already as much liberty, and a great many more exemptions than we have ourselves!" The result was that those who believed that Canadians were already relatively free to order their own lives argued against interfering in Canadian affairs.

This point of view was, of course, not universally accepted or understood. The majority of Americans most probably could not believe that liberty could exist or prosperity increase in North America under a monarchical form of government. Other reasons had therefore to be advanced for leaving the Canadas to their own devices. One of these is found in the assumption that the vast majority of Canadians neither understood nor appreciated the value of liberty, that they had shown they were unworthy of it and "do not now . . .

19. *New York Evening Star,* quoted in *Nat. Int.,* June 15.

desire free government."[20] By December, 1838, there was a growing demand that the Canadians should be "left to themselves" and that no more sympathy should be extended to them.[21] If they really were seeking a change in their form of government, they should be allowed to seek it their own way.

Certain other significant reasons were advanced against assisting the Canadians. That the Canadas might join the United States or be annexed if they secured their independence could not be overlooked, but the advantages of such a union would be dubious. There would be a larger territory to defend. Assimilation of French Canadians, who had a strong attachment for Great Britain, would be exceedingly difficult. More important still was a further consideration: union of the Canadas with the United States would involve war with Great Britain, for it was quite beyond doubt that the Canadas could, prior to union with the United States, become independent only with British consent. From whatever direction one viewed the subject it seemed but common sense to allow Canadians to seek their own salvation.[22]

American concern over relations with Great Britain gives the clue to American interest in the Canadas. Compared with them the United States was large and powerful, but compared with Great Britain in terms of its developed wealth and prestige in world affairs, the United States was still a pygmy. Had it not been for the shadow of the British lion to the north, the Canadas themselves would hardly have attracted much attention in the United States after 1815, as indeed they did not until the Canadian Rebellions broke out.

THE CANADIAN SCENE

Canadians, on the other hand, were always aware of the existence of the United States. Loyalists abhorred the Republic, French Canadians viewed it with apprehension, English settlers were either attracted to it or had misgivings about it; none could ignore it, and all were aware of the remarkable progress that was being made. Invidious comparisons raised Canadians' ire. By virtue of their memories of successful resistance to American invasion from 1812 to 1814 and

20. *St. Lawrence Republican,* November 20, 1838.
21. *Philadelphia Gazette,* quoted with approval in *Jour. of Com.,* December 19, 1838.
22. For sharp strictures, see *Jour. of Com.,* July 3 and 23, 1838.

their knowledge of American expansionist sentiment, there was at no time entire friendliness in Canada toward the United States.[23] Nor did the efforts of the American border population or the supposed laxity of the United States government during the Rebellion period encourage a friendlier feeling in the Canadas. Throughout the year 1838 there was an abundance of evidence of ill feeling, even of hatred, toward the United States, although this was tempered at times by a willingness to accept professions of good faith at their face value.

Distinct aversion to American interference in Canada was expressed in statements of loyalty to the Crown, castigations of the Patriots, and vainglorious demands for war. Said the *Kingston Chronicle* in July, 1838, in making plain the Canadian attitude:

We say to the Americans we have been in daily intercourse with you, we have had large commercial transactions with you, we have even entwined ourselves with you by numerous family connexions, even by the nearest and dearest ties of relationship; we have witnessed with pleasure your prosperity; we have sympathized with you in adversity; but we never asked your aid, we never wished your help, to detach us from the mother country, to take from us the British Constitution, and to institute for it a republic; we tell you, and we say it advisedly, that nine-tenths of our

23. James Silk Buckingham, *Canada, Nova Scotia, New Brunswick and the Other British Provinces in North America* (London, 1843), pp. 30–37, 138–139. Buckingham was a noted British traveler who had spent three years in the United States and who visited the Canadas for some two months in 1839. In Toronto he found that "every opportunity is seized of disparaging America and Americans, and speaking of them with unmeasured contempt." In Montreal, "there is one point on which nearly all the British Canadians appear to agree, and that is, in abuse of the Americans toward whom, the feeling of hatred and contempt seems to be universal, and to be expressed on all available occasions."

In explanation, Buckingham remarked that British travelers were constantly comparing the material progress of the United States and the Canadas to the disparagement of the latter. Canadians retorted that "in some instances, the superiority of America to Canada is imaginary and not real; and in others, where it may be regarded as real, it is not so much owing to American enterprize as it is to English liberality in lending a large amount of capital to carry forward their great public works, which capital, if it had been invested in Canada instead of the United States, would have produced results equally advantageous to this country."

population prefer the form of government we have to yours; we tell you that we are not an ill-governed or oppressed people, we are almost wholly free from taxation, we enjoy full, free and perfect liberty.

Americans who attempted to invade the Canadas were referred to with a good deal of asperity by the loyal press. The *Cobourg Star* called them the "godless American rabble"; the *Kingston Chronicle* hoped they "will come in sufficient numbers to be easily discovered and remain long enough in one place to give our troops an opportunity to find out their whereabouts." The Executive Council of Upper Canada recommended the use of Indians. "These brigands," they said, "whose object it is to rob and plunder and destroy cannot lay claim to any of the usages of civilized nations."[24] Sir George Arthur, the lieutenant governor, upon receiving reports from the chief superintendent of Indian affairs concerning the Hunters' efforts to alienate the Indians, assembled the various tribes under their own chiefs and near their own settlements, "subject to such orders as any sudden emergency"[25] might require him to issue. Both he and the Executive Council were prepared to use Indians to repel invaders.

Peace, war, and military preparedness were continually discussed in the Canadian newspapers. The advocates of peace were less vociferous than the noisy advocates of belligerent policies. Of such a vintage was the *Toronto Patriot*. In language that fairly reeked, it hoped "that ill-blood will continue to spread and increase till it infect every man, woman, and child, of British birth, at home and abroad, and that it will increase in heat and violence till it be soothed by concession, or quenched in vengeance."[26] Elsewhere it announced, as it had "from the beginning," that "war with the United States is inevitable—INEVITABLE, we say again, IT IS; and it will be no COMMON war, but a WAR OF EXTERMINATION." Detroit, Buffalo, Rochester, and Oswego could be burned "as easy as falling off a horse." It demanded the cessation of intercourse with the United States.[27]

24. *Q*, CDIX, 98–126. "Statement of the Executive Council." Enclosure in Arthur to Glenelg, October 22. This was a reply to Arthur's request for information about the propriety of using Indians.

25. *G*, CLXXXIV, 93–96. Arthur to Glenelg, December 14.

26. Quoted in *Jour. of Com.*, June 26.

27. Quoted in *ibid.*, June 28. In Lower Canada the *Montreal Herald* led the demand for war. In December it urged immediate war. (*Nat. Int.*, December 27.)

The animus which lay behind such extreme declarations was due to the belief that the American people "DO WANT THE CANADAS AND WILL GET THEM IF THEY CAN."[28] Nor was the idea that the belief was widespread a delusion of the Toronto paper. There had been sufficient discussion of the subject in the United States to warrant the conclusion. It is not surprising, therefore, that the Tory press, in particular, made constant demands for a stronger military force, not alone to throw back filibusters, but to defend Canada in case of war with the United States.

DURHAM AND VAN BUREN

It was a happy coincidence that the new governor general, the Earl of Durham, arrived in Quebec in May, 1838, just when filibustering was about to be renewed, for it was he who was largely responsible for awakening the government at Washington to the consequences of further attacks on the Canadas. If Durham had done nothing else during his residence in North America, his contribution toward the continuance of peace between the United States and Great Britain must mark him out for special attention.

Lord Durham's appointment as governor general and his arrival in Canada were hailed with *éclat* in the United States; and throughout his residence in Canada in 1838 the American press continued to publish glowing accounts of him and his administration. This was due, in part, to his studied avoidance of giving offense to Americans and, in part, to the legend from the other side of the Atlantic that he was the "PEOPLE'S PEER." As a speaker he was said to be "more than ordinarily lucid, possessing apparently a penetration which finds nothing dark to itself, and a tact and power in illustration which leave nothing unexplained to others." Furthermore, throughout his public life he had "adhered to his principles with uniform consistency, and has ever been ready to advocate with calmness and moderation, but without pusillanimity, the rights of his oppressed countrymen."[29] Thus was the Durham legend built up in the United States.

Before long he was making friendly gestures toward the United

28. *Patriot,* quoted in *Jour. of Com.,* July 11.

29. A letter by the Washington correspondent of the *Baltimore Patriot,* quoted in *Nat. Int.,* August 21. The magnificence of Durham's entourage had previously elicited some unfavorable comments.

States. Visitors were welcomed to Quebec with the hope that "sentiments of mutual respect and admiration" would result "in preserving the most friendly relations" between the two countries.[30] In July, Durham visited Upper Canada where, partly to show Americans the potential strength of the British forces and partly to suggest that they would be used for the defense of Canada, he held at Niagara Falls a military review to which he invited a number of United States Army officers. After the review Lord and Lady Durham presided at a dinner where Americans were "very politely entertained"; and in the evening they presided at a ball where still more Americans from Buffalo and the vicinity were present. So successful was Durham in bearing himself with that ease and dignity in the presence of which class distinctions appear to vanish that he won all who came in contact with him. A correspondent from Buffalo who met him at the dinner wrote: "The course which he is pursuing has disarmed all hostility on this side. . . . On the contrary, there is a strong feeling in favor of Lord Durham . . . for we feel that the misrule of the Tories of the Upper Province is at an end."[31] A few days later the *New York Daily Express* remarked that "our countrymen owe him a great deal for the hearty good-will he has manifested for us. . . . We have no apprehension of war, when men thus liberal and enlightened are at the helm of affairs." Back in Quebec again, Durham pursued the policy of befriending Americans. Said the *Baltimore Chronicle* in an article entitled "Lord Durham National Hospitalities":

During the past summer many gentlemen from Baltimore have visited the Canadas, and we are rejoiced to learn that the hospitable treatment which they uniformly experienced at the hands of Lord DURHAM and the British officers has inspired them with the most favorable sentiments toward the British authorities, and greatly strengthened the friendly feeling with which the government of our old mother is habitually regarded by well-informed and well-disposed Americans. Lord Durham seems to have taken particular pains to render Americans sensible of the kind feeling with which he regards our country, and not only extended his civilities to those who fell in his way, but was at the trouble of seeking out all respectable gentlemen from the United States, whom pleasure or

30. *Montreal Courier,* June 15, quoted in *Nat. Int.,* June 22.
31. *Nat. Int.,* August 2, quoted from *New York Daily Express.*

business called to Montreal or Quebec, and offering to them the elegant hospitalities of his house. Such conduct on his part is well calculated to strengthen the natural affection between the two countries, and to prevent the possible occurrence of unpleasant collisions whenever any cause for difference may be supposed to exist. Courtesy on the one side begets kindness on the other, and national prejudices disappear and lose their influence in the genial glow of social fellowship.[32]

The statement that Durham studiously attempted to cultivate the good will of Americans is no mere figment of the imagination. We have his own word for it. Writing to Lord Glenelg on August 9,[33] he said that while he was on his recent trip to Upper Canada, he had "courted the most unreserved communication with all respectable Americans, for the purpose of impressing them with a more sound and accurate conception of the real state of things."[34] He had done this because he had considered it essential to undo the irritation caused by the "false statements, much exaggerated descriptions, perversions of the truth, insulting reflexions, provoking sneers and low-lived abuse" of the English-Canadian press; to wean Americans away from the hypothetical discussion of war; to illustrate his abhorrence of border troubles, which had hitherto been responsible for burdening the federal and state governments with the necessity of increasing the army and militia, and which had also been responsible for increasing the powers of the Executive, much to the annoyance of many Americans. Durham must also have done this for another reason. The border troubles had been brought about, he believed, by the worst class of Americans—"squatters, refugees, and smugglers." All accounts showed, however, that ninety-nine out of a hundred of "the respectable and influential citizens condemn the conduct of the frontier population and deprecate a war with England." Being convinced that "the United States government is a perfect nullity,"[35] he decided to win over the better classes of Americans and through their influence to put an end to excitement on the border.

32. Quoted in *Nat. Int.,* September 7. For a strongly unfavorable view, see *Democratic Review,* V (January, 1839), 15, 23–26.
33. *Durham Papers,* Sec. 2, I, 271–296. Secret and Confidential. This is probably Durham's most famous dispatch to the Colonial Office. He reverted to the subject again in his *Report,* II, 59–64.
34. He felt he had been very successful.   35. *Q,* CCXLVI, 119.

Very soon after his arrival Durham had an opportunity to give effect to his ideas. Three days after the destruction of the *Sir Robert Peel*, on May 29, and as soon as he received the news, he issued a proclamation which promised £1,000 reward for the capture of the perpetrators of the crime. On June 5, he dispatched Colonel Charles Grey, a member of his staff, on a special mission to Washington. After the diplomatic courtesies had been extended and Durham's desire to cultivate friendly relations with the United States had been expressed, Grey was instructed to state that Durham relied on the President to bring the criminals to justice. The vigor of Grey's instructions can, however, be realized only by reference to the instructions themselves.[36] Durham said:

At the same time you will make him understand that something more is required from the United States' government; that the redress of this particular outrage must also be accompanied by measures for the prevention in future of similar crimes. . . . I have a right to call on the American government to fulfill the most sacred of all duties, the due observance of the faith of treaties, and the strict maintenance of the rights of friendly powers.

Since it is a matter of controversy whether Durham was responsible for awakening the government of the United States to a sense of its responsibilities, it is worth while to consider Grey's mission in some detail. Grey was the bearer of a dispatch to Henry Fox,[37] the British minister in Washington, who, whatever language he may have used when conferring with Forsyth and Van Buren (and at times it was vigorous), never minced words when writing to Durham, Colborne, Arthur, and Palmerston. In this dispatch Fox was informed that Grey was being sent to Washington to tell him of Durham's determination to protect the lives and property of British subjects, and that Durham was convinced that the United States would feel that it was "due to their national honor to prevent the repetition of offences, the longer continuance of which, and of the impunity with which they have been hitherto perpetrated, is a disgrace to all civilized governments."

36. *Q*, CCXLVI, 102. Enclosure No. 2 in Durham to Glenelg, June 16.
37. *Q*, CCXLVI, 101–102. Durham to Fox, June 2. Enclosure in Durham to Glenelg, June 16.

Grey arrived in Washington on June 12.[38] On the following day he had his first interview with Van Buren. Two days later he had interviews with both Poinsett, the Secretary of War, and the President.[39] On that occasion Van Buren assured Grey "in the strongest manner" of his desire to preserve order; but "in a little stronger manner" than the President, Poinsett assured Grey of his desire for peace on the border. He repeated "more than once, that 'he pledged himself' " to place an additional force on the frontier as soon as Congress passed the increase of the army bill.

It happened, however, that on the day before Grey's arrival in Washington Poinsett had decided to order Major General Alexander Macomb, commanding general of the United States Army, to take over the command of the frontier in person.[40] Macomb's instructions required him to collect all the available regulars and to distribute them at the most exposed points along the border.[41] In pursuance of these instructions Macomb at once issued a general order. The question, therefore, is: What effect did Grey's arrival or the previous knowledge of his mission have upon Van Buren and Poinsett? Grey's own opinion was that while the United States government had hitherto displayed a "culpable inactivity," its sudden action on June 12 had been due to the firmness of the tone of Durham's proclamation of June 2, to the expectation of a communication from Durham through Grey,[42] and to a knowledge of the efficiency of the British military and naval forces in the Canadas.[43] Fox likewise insisted that Grey's mission made the United States government "fully alive to the extreme danger" of war,[44] and that more than at any other period that government was "sincere in their desire to suppress the border disturbances. . . ."[45] Lieutenant Governor Sir George Arthur,

38. Q, CCXLVI, 176–177. Grey to Durham, June 22. Enclosure No. 3 in Durham to Glenelg, June 23.

39. Q, CCL, 141–144. Grey to Fox, June 15.

40. D.S. Misc. Letters, Poinsett to Forsyth, June 11.

41. Q, CCXLVI, 176. Poinsett to Macomb, June 12. Enclosure No. 4 in Durham to Glenelg, June 23.

42. Q, CCXLVI, 176–177. Grey to Durham, June 22.

43. Q, CCXLVI, 164–167. Durham to Glenelg, June 23.

44. Q, CCXLVI, 169–172. Fox to Durham, June 16.

45. Q, CCL, 148–153. Fox to Palmerston, June 24. Fox thought, nevertheless, that the federal government's means of enforcing order were "lam-

for the first time since his arrival in Upper Canada, became convinced that the United States government was "sincerely engaged in discouraging" lawless attacks on Canada, but that it had not been so before Grey's mission to Washington.[46] Durham himself felt that the assurances of coöperation as a result of Grey's mission were good.[47] Lord Glenelg, the Colonial Secretary, commended Durham on the success of Grey's mission and approved of Durham's instructions to Grey.[48] Sometime later the *New York Journal of Commerce*, in a spirited defense of Durham, claimed that "in all probability he had been the means of saving the two nations from war."[49] The evidence, therefore, points to the conclusion that it was Durham's directness of approach that awakened the federal government to sharp and positive action.[50]

Durham was not one of those who let well enough alone. In this case, he intended to make doubly sure that the United States would coöperate. Upon Grey's return to Quebec on June 22, Durham immediately had instructions sent to Colonel Dundas and Captain San-

entably insufficient," and that the progress of American neutrality had "kept exact pace" with the increase of the military forces of Canada.

46. *G*, CLXXXIV, 27–33. Arthur to the Colonial Secretary, July 10; CLXXXIV, 33–42. Same to same, August 6.

47. *Q*, CCXLVI, 164–167. Durham to Glenelg, June 23.

48. *G*, XXXIX, 104–107, and *Q*, CCXLVI, 103. Glenelg to Durham, July 12.

49. September 7.

50. Pressure was brought from other directions. A number of New York and Washington newspapers, including the *Globe*, demanded the dispatch of additional military forces to the frontier. On June 5 Forsyth forwarded to Poinsett a report from N. S. Benton, dated May 31, which said that there were too many Canadian refugees and Americans in the United States bent on reprisals. "Past experience has fully demonstrated that the civil arm of the Government is not adequate to prevent these outrages from our territory . . . I am taking and shall pursue every measure in my power to have the offenders brought to punishment if the act of burning the 'Peel' within the territory and jurisdiction of this State be cognizable in the United States Courts of which I now entertain strong doubts." *D.S. Dom. Letters*, XXIX, 447. Certain that trouble was brewing, Wool left his post in Vermont on June 3 and proceeded to Washington to ask for a larger force. *Q*, CCXLIX, 428–430. J. McCord to Major General Clitheroe, June 7. In Washington, Isaac Bronson, member of Congress from Jefferson County, N.Y., wrote Poinsett on June 4, calling for the transfer of a regiment from Florida to the

dom, R.N., at Kingston to get in touch with General Macomb without delay. Reporting his action to Glenelg, he said: "It seemed to me of the highest importance to bring the fair intentions of the American Government to a practical test, as soon as possible after receiving such hearty assurances of coöperation." He believed that a good effect would be produced by the "sight of the two flags united in one common effort to put an end to this unnatural excitement on the frontiers." He intended, therefore, to direct the disposition of the military forces in such a manner that "no legitimate grounds of international jealousy need be apprehended on the part of the United States."[51]

By contrast, to all outward appearances, Martin Van Buren, President of the United States, was forced to play a less vigorous role. Durham's commission had conferred upon him almost unlimited powers in British North America where self-government was still far from being achieved. He was dependent for his position upon the Crown alone. No political party had jockeyed for position to secure his appointment. His most important decisions could be repudiated and countermanded without necessarily involving a major political catastrophe in England or in the Canadas. What he did, or did not do, did not materially lengthen or shorten the life of the political party to which he belonged. Van Buren's position, on the contrary, was precisely the opposite of this. Reared politically in the Jacksonian tradition he had been elected to office as Jackson's successor. The Democratic party which he headed represented a vigorous and boisterous expansionism which demanded a rapid extension of internal improvements, assistance to Texans in their struggle for freedom from Mexico, and larger opportunities for trade abroad. It was a militant democracy too, demanding payment of the French spoliation claims at the risk of war with France, and refusing settlement of the northeastern boundary with Great Britain except on its own

northern frontier. Poinsett replied on June 5 that troops could not be moved from Florida or the West. While convinced of the need of "a competent force" in the north, he would have to wait until Congress passed the act providing for the increase of the army (passed July 5) before he could "place a respectable force on the frontiers of Canada." *Albany Argus,* June 9, and *Jour. of Com.,* June 11.

51. *Q,* CCXLVI, 164–167. Durham to Glenelg, June 23.

terms. Under Jackson's leadership it had fought against granting special privileges, and the entrenchment of financial and political power in the hands of Nicholas Biddle and his friends. Democrats loudly demanded the extension of freedom everywhere, at home and abroad.

The difficulties which Van Buren met in his efforts to prevent filibustering were made no simpler by the political situation in New York State where Democrats were joined by Loco Focos and other radical groups in opposition to the efforts of the governments at Albany and Washington to enforce the neutrality laws.[52] Elsewhere along the border in Vermont, Ohio, and Michigan the President's adherents condemned him for pursuing too repressive a policy. The Whigs, for political and other reasons, spurred on in part by statements in the American press which were copied from English and Canadian papers, condemned Van Buren for not taking measures vigorous enough to prevent raids on the Canadas. The Whigs also accused him of not pressing American demands for redress upon the British, notably in the case of the *Caroline*.[53] Van Buren was accordingly confronted with a dilemma. If he took as strong measures as he could, he weakened his own and his party's position politically; if he did not take strong measures he laid himself open to attack by the Whigs on the ground that he was needlessly exposing the United States to the danger of war with Great Britain.

Van Buren's position administratively was weakened, as has been already recounted, by the limited increase in authority which was grudgingly allowed him by the Neutrality Act of 1838, and by the relatively small increase of the army provided for by the act of the following July. Besides, his orders had to be carried into effect along the border more largely by civil than by military officers. The latter came from some distance south of the border, and performed their duties efficiently in spite of having forces that were too small under their command. The civil officers, such as collectors of customs, deputy collectors, and deputy marshals, were in most cases natives of the localities where they served. Born and reared near the border, most of them were in sympathy with the Canadian rebel cause and with the Patriots, some of them were Hunters, and many of them

52. *Nat. Int.*, September 5.   53. *Ibid.*, September 7, 10, 21, 27.

neglected to comply with the instructions which they received to secure and forward information to Washington. Even in New York and other places distant from the border, there was some evidence of this.

What positive action could Van Buren take? Fortunately he dominated his Cabinet, and his Cabinet was in entire accord with his cautious policy of going just as fast and as far as public opinion required[54] and presidential powers allowed. Emphatically he did not hedge in his proclamations or messages to Congress, nor in his correspondence with governors. The United States, he said, had an obligation to prevent raids and other attacks on the Canadas. As President he proposed to fulfill that obligation to the letter in so far as he was authorized to do so by the constitution and the statute law. Although in his correspondence he more than once questioned the power of the government to keep order on the frontier and deplored its inability to do so,[55] to the public he never gave the slightest hint that political or any other considerations would keep him from executing the law. This much can be said of him, that however much he might engage in politics in private, as when he received a visit from Papineau and Robert Nelson in the company of Senator Silas Wright of New York,[56] all his public statements and acts concerning Canadian problems were said and done in complete disregard of their effects upon his own or his party's future.

54. On December 8, 1838, the antiadministration *National Intelligencer* said editorially of the President's annual message to Congress that it concurred heartily with all that was said concerning the duty of the government and the people, and was "satisfied that he will be sustained by public opinion."

55. Writing to Andrew Jackson on November 16, 1838, Van Buren said: "The Canadian affairs give us much trouble, but will I hope work off without serious difficulty." *Van Buren Papers*, XXXI, 7790–7793.

56. *Q*, CCLXV, 105–110. Fox to Palmerston, January 12, 1839, Confidential. Political affairs in the Canadas were not mentioned, according to a prior understanding.

CHAPTER VII

MILITARY AND NAVAL PROBLEMS: POLICY AND PRACTICE

MILITARY

DURING the early months of 1838 the military situation along the border had been anything but satisfactory. In the United States, where this had been particularly obvious, the President had been authorized by the Neutrality Act of March 10 to employ military and naval forces (which he did not have) to stop marauding expeditions against a foreign state, and a demand had grown up for an increase of the regular army on the Canadian frontier. During these same months, the British government took more positive action. It dispatched five thousand regulars to the Canadas and increased its naval strength in North American waters by sending out additional steam vessels. In the United States, it was currently rumored that the British were fortifying posts around the Great Lakes, and arming vessels upon them.

In the United States all this conspired to bring on a campaign for preparedness for war. Said the *New York Journal of Commerce* on June 8, 1838:

Jonathan is sitting quietly in his elbow chair, as careless as if nothing had happened out of the common course of things, or was likely to happen. . . . Meanwhile John Bull bellows and paws the ground, confident of his own strength, and wonders that we should heed his movements so little. . . . We do not much fear war. . . . What we ask is, to what extent are we to suffer the warlike preparations of our powerful neighbor to proceed, on our very borders, before we begin to guard against contingencies?[1]

This from the friendliest of American papers!

The United States government, apparently, paid little heed to

1. In answer to Palmerston's request for information concerning the "movements and preparations" of the American navy, Fox wrote that the United States was less prepared for war than at any time since 1814 and that British preparedness was a matter of awe to the United States. *Q*, CCL, 119–123. Fox to Palmerston, May 17.

widespread opinion of this character, for it regarded it as evidence of a temporary excitement, occasioned in part by fear of the consequences of the destruction of the *Sir Robert Peel.* Indeed, spurred on by Grey's mission from Durham to Washington, the government concentrated its efforts upon strengthening the military forces on the border, not as a measure of defense against the British, but to prevent secret societies and the like from interfering with Canadian affairs. To this end General Macomb was ordered to the frontier where, within three months, he had some two thousand troops under his command.[2] The government also attempted, without evident enthusiasm and without appreciable success, to speed through Congress the passage of the bill for the increase of the army.

In spite of these measures, the Canadian governors continued to distrust the capacity of the United States government to keep order on the frontier. Their distrust can be seen, in part, in the numerous requests they made for reinforcements of regulars from England, and in the action they took to get together large numbers of the volunteers and militia. Occasionally, in 1838, they called for reinforcements on the ground that the Canadas and the rest of British North America needed larger military forces, as a measure of adequate protection in case of war between Great Britain and the United States. Yet, so far as the governors took measures to strengthen the military forces, they took them chiefly with an eye to preventing rebellion from being successful should it break out again, and to keep Hunters and their kind from invading the provinces. It was not until later that they pressed for the defense of the Canadas upon what may be called imperial rather than provincial or local grounds.

To safeguard the provinces against rebellion from within and attacks of Hunters from without, the governors effected considerable reorganization and redistribution of the military forces, and strengthened defensive posts along the frontier. According to a plan drawn up on June 2, 1838,[3] in Upper Canada some three thousand regu-

2. *Q,* CDIX, 353. Macomb to I. R. T. Jones (lieutenant in the 43d regiment and British secret agent), October 30. Some time earlier Fox was informed by the United States government that there were 3,000 troops on the frontier. *Ibid.,* CCXLV, 158–163. Colborne to Lieut. Gen. Lord Fitzroy Somerset, October 20, Private and Confidential.

3. *Q,* CCXLVI, 88–89. "Proposed Distribution of the Troops of the

lars were distributed among the posts at London, Chatham, Toronto, and Kingston. The Montreal district was guarded by three thousand men, and the Quebec district by sixteen hundred. According to the plan, cavalry companies were also located at Chambly and La Prairie, not far from Montreal, to guard the approach from Lake Champlain. Artillery battalions were stationed at Toronto, Kingston, Montreal, and Quebec. The plan also provided for the use of militia and volunteers, the former to keep communications open along the St. Lawrence from Kingston to Coteau du Lac near Montreal, and the latter to guard the frontier at Niagara, and at Amherstburg on the Detroit River. In October, another distribution of forces was consummated with a view to guarding the Canadas against the extensive invasion which the Hunters were reported to be planning. In addition, believing that there were not enough regulars available to ward off invasion, Colborne called for some five thousand volunteers in Lower Canada,[4] and directed Sir George Arthur to raise an equal number in Upper Canada.[5] Instead, Arthur chose to heed the advice of the Executive Council and the Military Board of Upper Canada. He therefore called out thirteen thousand of the militia to serve for eighteen months.[6]

These measures were matched by an unremitting effort to secure arms to replace some thirteen thousand muskets that had been lost track of in Upper Canada during the winter of 1837–38. So badly off were the Canadian military authorities that in July they had in the Quebec arsenal only nine thousand stand of arms, three thousand of which were, in the same month, shipped to Upper Canada.[7] To

Line in Upper Canada," June 27. This differed slightly from the proposal of June 2, in that three companies were to be divided up between Niagara, Niagara Falls, and Brockville.

4. *Q*, CCXLVIII, 330. About 2,000 were to be used for local service only.

5. *Q*, CCXLIX, 568–574, 583–587. Colborne to Arthur, October 22 and 29.

6. For a sharp criticism of the militia system, see Thomas Rolph, *A Descriptive and Statistical Account of Canada* (2d ed. London, 1841), p. 261. Rolph remarked that the militia "is a hardship on the great body of laborers, and is but an incentive to drunkenness and disorder." Were they properly organized they would be "a respectable and available body for any purpose they may be required."

7. *Q*, CCXLIX, 487–491. Colborne to Arthur, July 6.

these were added a few muskets secured by buying what was available in stores in Detroit, Buffalo, Rochester, and other towns.[8] They were eventually supplemented at the end of the year by thirty thousand stand of arms, twenty thousand sets of accoutrements, and a goodly quantity of smaller arms which were shipped from England in September.[9]

To be certain that the Canadas would be adequately defended against the Patriots, Colborne ordered the engineers in June to establish a line of posts and barracks along the frontier, all the way from Lancaster (a few miles west of Montreal) to Sandwich on the Detroit River.[10] This was in keeping with Arthur's observation that the time was now ripe for action which at some later time might arouse the suspicions of the government of the United States.[11]

In comparison with the Canadian governors who took all these precautions against attacks by organized bands from the United States, the British government assumed that its immediate obligation was fulfilled once it had dispatched troops to the Canadas for the purpose of preventing further rebellion from developing. Orders were accordingly sent, first to Colborne and then to Durham, to disband the militia in the interests of economy.[12] It was only after Britain had learned of the *Sir Robert Peel* and the *Telegraph* incidents that the government showed any signs of recognizing the Canadas' need of defense against attacks from without. Even then, in the absence of requests from Durham for additional troops, Glenelg hoped that the regulars already in British North America would afford ample protection.[13] As late as October, after receipt of news of the

8. *Q*, CDXIII, 62–67. Arthur to Glenelg, January 2, 1839.

9. *G*, XL, 170–171. Glenelg to Durham, September 10. *Q*, CCLII, 119, gives a statement of quantities shipped in 1838. They had not arrived at Quebec by October 29. *Ibid.*, CCXLIX, 583–587. Colborne to Arthur. Arthur complained bitterly to Glenelg on November 14 that there were no supplies available for the militia and that none could be purchased. *Ibid.*, CDIX, 405–410. Confidential.

10. *Q*, CCXLIX, 464–467. Colborne to Arthur, June 25; also pp. 470–472, "Posts directed to be established in Upper Canada."

11. *G*, CLXXXIV, 13–19. Arthur to the Colonial Secretary, May 30.

12. *G*, XXXVIII, 211–218. Glenelg to Colborne, February 26; *Q*, CCLVI A, 173–174, 261. Glenelg to Durham, April 20 and June 12.

13. *Q*, CCLVI B, 15–16, 36–37. Glenelg to Durham, July 13 and 20.

plans and preparations made by the Hunters in September, the government declined to send more troops to the St. Lawrence area. It still assumed that there was sufficient military strength in the Canadas "to repel hostile aggression." Such an attitude, to be sure, was adopted largely because the British government did not wish to send unneeded troops to North America for fear of alarming the United States and straining the friendly relations which existed between that country and Great Britain.[14]

To the danger of invasion there was added in October the possibility of rebellion in Lower Canada. The communication of this information to London still left the government cold to pleas for additional reinforcements. The imperturbable Glenelg still hoped, as late as November 24, that military expenditures had been reduced.[15] But knowing that conditions in the Canadas rarely remained static for long, Glenelg gave Colborne a free hand to meet new dangers. He also authorized Colborne to raise as few volunteers as were positively necessary to defend the province against insurrection. Economy was to be the watchword.

Ministerial complacency and financial caution were shortly to be blown to the winds. On October 4, Fox sent Durham detailed reports of widespread secret organizations on the frontier which had been transmitted to him by the United States government.[16] Convinced by this information that it was imperative to place the condition of the Canadas without delay before the government at home, Durham altered his plan of returning to England by way of New York, and decided to sail directly from Quebec. He then wrote Glenelg, urgently requesting immediate reinforcements.[17] This dispatch and Colborne's two of October 31 and November 5 to the War Office finally brought the British government to a realization of the seriousness of conditions along the border, as well as the likelihood of renewed rebellion. Sensing this the government promised to send out three or four regiments at once, and additional arms and equipment for the militia when requisitioned.[18]

14. Q, CCLVI B, 151–156. Glenelg to Durham, October 26, Confidential.
15. Q, CCLVI B, 199–200, 204.
16. Q, CCXLVIII, 132–137. Confidential.
17. *Durham Papers*, Sec. 2, II, 409–412. October 22.
18. Q, CCLVI B, 223–226. Glenelg to Colborne, December 11. For addi-

Nor did the British government stop at these measures. In October, the United States government had communicated to Fox a statement of its inability to prevent by military action the rumored Hunters' invasion of the Canadas.[19] At Arthur's suggestion Fox proposed to Forsyth that the United States should sanction, in advance, any invasion of its territory which might result from reprisals or "hot pursuit" of filibusters.[20] Forsyth promptly and unequivocally rejected the proposal.[21] The United States, he said, would not permit British reprisals or invasions in hot pursuit, and the Canadas in turn were expected to take a similar view of reprisals and hot pursuit from the United States. To allow such violation of each other's territory would have "a most injurious effect on the friendly relations" between the two countries.

When Fox's dispatch, proposing hot pursuit, reached the Foreign Office, Palmerston dealt with that suggestion with his characteristic zeal and vigor. Within a week, instructions which had Glenelg's approval[22] were on their way to Fox. These instructions required Fox to state to Forsyth that the British government would deprecate retaliation for violations in spite of attempts to prevent them, but that if they should unavoidably occur

the United States government will see in the circumstances of the moment a sufficient excuse for the irregularity, and will not take it ill, if acts of positive War against Great Britain committed by Individual

tional correspondence, see CCXLIX, 591–609. By December 12, 1838, there were 11,703 effectives in British North America, and 1,923 were on their way from the West Indies.

19. Q, CCXLV, 158–163. Colborne to Fitzroy Somerset, October 20, Private and Confidential. The United States had 3,000 regulars on the frontier, of a total force of 8,653, as of September 30. See *Report of the Secretary of War,* November 28. That Fox had received from Forsyth a statement concerning the Hunters' activities was reported in the *Kingston* (Upper Canada) *Chronicle,* a report which was copied in the New York *Observer,* November 3.

20. Q, CCL, 257–270. Fox to Palmerston, November 19.

21. Fox merely referred to the probability of reprisals. *Notes from the British Legation to the Department of State,* XIX, Fox to Vail, November 3. (Hereafter referred to as *D.S. Br. Legation, Notes from.*) Also *D.S. Br. Legation, Notes to,* VI, 96–99. Forsyth to Fox, November 15, in answer to Fox to Vail, above.

22. Q, CCL, 255–256. (Writer unknown) to Backhouse, December 13.

citizens of the Union, should lead, not to retaliation for the sake of vengeance, but to some little overstepping of the Boundary of the Union, for the purpose of more effectually abating a danger which the authorities of the United States would in such a position, have been unable to control.[23]

The instructions were never carried out. Forsyth's adamantine reply of November 15 had put an end to the proposal before Fox's letter had even reached Palmerston. But the whole episode shows how acute was the problem of keeping peace on the border, and how alive, by the end of 1838, the British government had become to the need of the Canadas for military protection.

NAVAL

British and American military policy during 1838 was closely matched by naval policy. The scant attention paid to naval affairs prior to the burning of the *Sir Robert Peel* and the attack on the *Telegraph* in June was superseded by increased attention during the latter part of the year. Moreover, complications began to arise between the two countries over the interpretation placed upon the Rush Bagot agreement[24] by the British, who, faced with what appeared to be a desperate situation, began to increase their forces quite beyond the terms of the agreement.

United States action can be disposed of quickly. On June 12, Forsyth informed Fox that the government expected to employ on Lakes Erie and Ontario, in addition to the ships already in service, two unarmed steamers, commanded by naval officers and carrying fifty soldiers each.[25] No additional ships were commissioned for naval service during 1838.

The immediate consequence in the Canadas of the *Sir Robert Peel* and *Telegraph* incidents was a rush to secure shipping against attack on the Lakes and the St. Lawrence River. With this purpose in

23. *Q*, CCL, 311–316. Palmerston to Fox, December 15. Glenelg also sent a copy of the instructions to Colborne. *Ibid.*, CCLVI, 242–244, December 14.

24. The agreement restricted the naval force to be maintained on the Lakes on each side to the following vessels: on Lake Ontario one vessel of 100 tons and one 18-pound cannon, on the Upper Lakes two such vessels, and on Lake Champlain one similar vessel.

25. *D.S. Br. Legation, Notes to,* VI, 95.

view Colborne made two recommendations to Durham; first, that Captain Sandom, commander of the naval forces, should be authorized to fit out a small armed vessel to cruise among the Thousand Islands, and to hire additional steamboats if he should need them for service on the river or on Lake Ontario; second, that Sandom should be authorized immediately to hire a steamer for service on Lake Erie, and to fit out two gunboats to be stationed near Long Point.[26] Durham gave his approval. Next, he requested Vice Admiral Sir Charles Paget, commander of the fleet at Quebec, to allow officers and men of the *Hastings* and the *Hercules* to volunteer for service under Sandom, to whom orders had been given to act strictly on the defensive, and in Canadian waters only.[27] To be certain that the United States government would not misconstrue these actions, Durham sent all the correspondence referred to above to Fox so that he might prove to the President that "any preparations or equipments" that the British might make were "solely for the defence of our frontiers," and did not contravene the agreement of 1817. Durham promised that he would allow no act to be committed which could be construed as showing hostility to the United States.[28]

Turning next to the British government Durham questioned the advisability of retaining that article of the Rush Bagot agreement which provided for the specific armaments which each government might employ on the Lakes. Durham argued that since neither the United States nor Great Britain adhered strictly to the terms of the agreement prior to June, 1838, and since there was an increasing amount of disorder on the frontier, the agreement could not be adhered to without detriment to the Canadas.[29] Before long, Glenelg replied stating that the government was giving thought to the expediency of terminating or modifying the agreement in such a manner as to make possible the employment of armed vessels for the protection of the frontier during periods of filibustering and similar dis-

26. *Durham Papers*, Sec. 4, p. 230. June 8.

27. *Ibid.*, Sec. 2, I, 49–52. Durham to Glenelg, June 16. Paget's orders to the captains of the *Hastings* and *Hercules* are in *Q*, CCXLVI, 186.

28. *Durham Papers*, Sec. 3, I, 865–870. Durham to Fox, June 25.

29. *Q*, CCL, 306–309. (Writer unknown) to Backhouse, July 14, Immediate. Durham thought that a "small naval flotilla" would protect the frontier better than large military forces.

turbances. Durham was warned not to allow any violation of the agreement to occur.[30]

By the end of October, Colborne, who had taken over command in the Canadas at Durham's request, was confronted with the necessity of securing the border against the impending invasion of the Hunters. He accordingly ordered Arthur to hire as many steamers as possible on Lake Erie.[31] Arthur had, however, acted upon his own initiative and had acquired no less than four ships and had arranged for Sandom to charter a fifth. He recognized that this substantial increase of the naval forces violated the agreement with the United States, but he defended his action by pointing to the assurance given him by Durham of amicable arrangements with Washington.[32]

Arthur's naval policy received commendation from an unexpected quarter. He had kept in touch with Fox at Washington in order to be sure that he would not offend the authorities there. But Fox was a man after Arthur's own heart. He had no confidence in Americans or in their government. Consequently he recommended to Arthur that he continue to equip ships "without scruple and without reference to the Convention of 1817." He thought it was "beyond the possibility of things, that any American authority can be so monstrously unreasonable and perverse, as to raise a complaint or objection" when Americans themselves made the increase of the naval forces necessary.[33] Later he wrote to Forsyth in a more conciliatory tone. He did not apprehend the raising of any objection by the United States because the "armament is equipped for the sole purpose" of guarding the Canadas. It would be "discontinued at the earliest period, after which the causes which now create that danger shall have ceased to exist."[34] Fox's own explanation of this letter is decidedly interesting. He intended to forestall a request from Forsyth for an explanation of the reasons why additions were being made to the naval forces on

30. *Q*, CCLVI B, 34–37. Glenelg to Durham, July 20.

31. *Q*, CXLIX, 583–587. October 29.

32. *Q*, CDIX, 252–257. October 31, Confidential. In December, 1838, Arthur started to recruit a provincial marine. In the same month, Sandom recommended the purchase of two steamships for use on Lake Ontario and the upper St. Lawrence. In February, 1839, he was commissioned by the Admiralty to buy two steamships for Lake Erie. *Q*, CCLXIV, 28–38, 39–41, 42.

33. *G*, CCXXIV, 253–267. Fox to Colborne, November 16, Confidential.

34. *D.S. Br. Legation, Notes from*, XIX, Fox to Forsyth, November 25.

the Great Lakes. Forsyth had already indicated that he might have to ask for an explanation in order to answer questions in Congress. Fox had therefore decided not to ask for consent to equip additional ships. He "confined" himself "to stating the fact of the increased Armament and declaring the motives."[35]

Fox had, of course, communicated all this to Palmerston who, during the summer, had been seriously considering terminating or modifying the Rush Bagot agreement. The news of developments along the St. Lawrence, together with Fox's recommendations, had a telling effect upon Palmerston. Sounding out Glenelg, he said that since the British armaments had been "carried to a considerable extent without remonstrance or a representation from the government of the United States, it might perhaps be as well to let the matter rest as it does" and to refrain from suggesting any modification or termination until Washington should first bring up the question.[36] Upon Glenelg's concurrence, Palmerston immediately instructed Fox, should any representations be made to him by the United States government, to say that he would refer the matter to Great Britain. At the same time, he was to state that he believed the United States was animated by an equal desire to keep within the agreement of 1817, "as far as is consistent with the paramount consideration and imperative duty of Self Defence." The agreement was for the purpose of maintaining police protection in time of peace. If in recent months the United States had been able "to prevent open War from being carried on" against British North America, Great Britain would have had no occasion for increasing naval armaments. Hence "in this strange and anomalous state of things," that is, the invasion of British territory, the British government "must consider themselves released from all restrictions" concerning the means they should use to defeat attacks.[37]

In view of the conversations that were held and the dispatches that were sent, it is quite clear that the British government decided to consider the Rush Bagot agreement as a peace-time measure which

---

35. *G*, CCXXIV, 310–313. Fox to Colborne, November 29.

36. *Q*, CCL, 251–254. Backhouse to Stephen, December 10.

37. *Q*, CCL, 301–304. Backhouse to Stephen, December 14, Immediate; CCL, 311–316. Palmerston to Fox, December 15; CCLVI B, 240–242. Glenelg to Colborne, December 14, Confidential.

was inoperative during a period of border raids. This was an *ex parte* decision, arrived at without the consent of the United States. In that country, on the other hand, no questions had actually been asked officially and the government was lying low until it was forced by Congress or by public opinion to make official inquiries.

CHAPTER VIII

THE HUNTERS TRY AGAIN

PLANS

THE mobilization of public opinion, of government agencies, and of the military and naval forces, the suppression of a second rebellion in Lower Canada, and the failure of the Hunters to invade Upper Canada had in 1838 reduced to a nullity all attempts to secure the independence of the Canadas. But the Hunters remained undaunted. In spite of their rebuffs at Prescott in November and at Windsor in December, they persisted still. In the early months of 1839, they turned to the West where they expected to find a supply of men and materials. By April, it was reported that 1,500 Indians and 1,750 Americans, Canadians, Irish, and Dutch were ready for service in the area which stretched from Coldwater in Missouri to the Illinois and Fox rivers. To these were to be added several unspecified Indian tribes, as well as 4,000 men in Upper Canada. For cannon they turned to a Detroit foundry which apparently was willing to supply them, while 30,000 muskets, it was anticipated, would be available for purchase in the open market.[1]

The dissolution of these plans for lack of funds and because of the sharp opposition encountered on both sides of the border led the Hunters to give up, for the time being, their project of invading the Canadas. In its place they turned to plans for sending over "small marauding parties to burn, and destroy property, in the hope of producing retaliation,"[2] thus to maintain the ferment and eventually to force the United States and Great Britain into war. That there was little apprehension of this at the time in government circles in Upper Canada is attested by Arthur's report to Lord Normanby on June 8 that "the impending mischief is purposely magnified by a wicked class of people, on both sides of the Boundary."[3]

Incendiarism and other lawlessness could however lead to retaliation, and this all the governments concerned took action to circum-

1. These statements are based chiefly on Lindsey, *Mackenzie,* II, 235–238.

2. *C,* DCXIV, 136a–136b, 139–147. Colonel Airey to Captain Halkett, military secretary, May 6, 1839.

3. *Q,* CDXVII, 125.

vent. In January, 1839, a regulation required that all who left or entered the Canadas must be provided with passports. In March, Governor William H. Seward, of New York, issued a proclamation which promised a hundred-dollar reward for information leading to convictions for arson.[4] In Upper Canada, after the attack on the *G. S. Weeks*, in May, Sir George Arthur proceeded at once to Brockville and roundly denounced both innocent and guilty.[5] To allay the excitement caused by such border incidents and by a rumor that on July 4 the Hunters would make an attack on Lower Canada, President Van Buren, Henry Clay, and Major General Winfield Scott visited the border in June. The presidential visit, coupled with the failure of the projected Hunters' invasion to materialize, had a distinctly quieting effect. With some glee Colborne noted "improved feeling" along the border, and reported that enthusiasm for assisting Canadian refugees was on the wane.[6]

What had made matters more difficult to handle on the Canadian border was the sharp dispute between Great Britain and the United States over the New Brunswick–Maine boundary and the belligerent spirit which the dispute aroused in both countries. To the British with their need for a military road[7] from New Brunswick to Quebec, and to both New Brunswick and Maine with their conflicting interests over lumber and navigation of the St. John River, there seemed to be no satisfactory method of settling their differences. Relations grew worse until lumbermen and local authorities clashed in the disputed area in February, 1839. This came to be known as the "Aroostook War." Such clashes were in themselves not serious. But already, in 1838, the Maine legislature had appropriated $800,000 for defense and Governor Fairfield now dispatched the state militia into the area in dispute. Moreover, Congress passed a special appropriation of $10,000,000 for the protection of Maine. New Brunswick

4. This was published in full in the border press, albeit somewhat tardily. *St. Lawrence Republican* (Ogdensburg, N.Y.), April 9.

5. For press reports: *Montreal Courier*, June 10; *Nat. Int.*, June 17.

6. *Q*, CCLIX, 352–353, 401. Colborne to Normanby, July 2 and 28, Confidential; CDXVIII, 12. Arthur to Normanby, July 1.

7, *Stevenson Papers*, XIV, 28452–28454. Benjamin C. Howard to Andrew Stevenson, American minister in London, May 30, 1839: "Indeed, Mr. Fox once said to me very significantly that they could not do without that road."

prepared to call out both her militia and her regulars while Nova
Scotia appropriated $100,000 for military aid for her sister province.

The situation created by the Aroostook War required an immediate, if temporary, settlement. Major General Scott was sent to Maine
to preserve peace. With a show of asperity which was compatible
with his temperament but with a haste which was not, Fox signed an
agreement with Forsyth on February 27,[8] in which provision was
made for a temporary settlement. At the same time, he attacked the
government of the United States for being "as usual, weak, per-
plexed, and disconcerted; really desirous . . . to maintain peace,
but not daring to offend any State in the Union, however evidently
in the wrong."[9] Fox's mind was really on the Canadian frontier, for,
writing to Colborne he expressed the hope that the Aroostook War
would not excite the people along the St. Lawrence.[10] He secured an
understanding with Forsyth that until the acceptance or rejection
by the British government of the *modus vivendi* was received, the
United States would move no part of its regulars from the Canadian
border where he considered them to be "so usefully employed."[11]

With the removal of the immediacy of the northeastern boundary
dispute, with the British government insisting upon the necessity for
peace[12] and sending instructions to governors and to naval and military commanders to prevent the commission of any acts which might
arouse the American border people again, and with the governments
of the Canadas and those in the United States attempting to prevent
disorders, one would expect that the Hunters would cease making further plans to invade the Canadas. But the Hunters were not through
yet. Taking heart from a circular[13] entitled "Glorious News for the
Patriots," which was distributed on August 18, 1839, by the Committee of Safety, they met in convention at Lockport, New York, on

8. *G*, CCXXV, 147–153. Fox to Colborne, February 28, Confidential.

9. *G*, CCXXV, 124–131. Fox to Colborne, February 23, Confidential.

10. *G*, CCXXV, 147–153. *Supra*. On February 23, Fox had written: "Considering the present state of things in Canada, I am sensible of the more
than usual importance of maintaining peace if possible on the New Brunswick frontier."

11. *G*, CCXXV, 147–153. *Supra*.

12. *G*, XCII, 174–176. Normanby to Arthur, May 7.

13. *Q*, CDXX, 92–105. Enclosure in Arthur to Normanby, October 15,
Confidential.

September 28.[14] Assurances having been received of material assistance in Upper Canada, should an invasion be undertaken, plans were developed for an attack via Windsor. But like other better-laid schemes of the Hunters this one also went awry. Neither Americans nor Canadians had any stomach for large-scale invasions which, from experience, they knew could meet with nothing but failure. Colborne's considered statement that the "American brigands" were not organized in sufficient numbers to renew attacks, and that the disaffected in the Canadas were not prepared to encourage the Patriots,[15] sums up the situation in September, 1839. For that matter, evidences of returning prosperity had begun to chill the ardor of the disaffected in Canada and of their friends in the United States.

To meet the Windsor and other threats of the Hunters certain military precautions were taken in the United States. Scott, who had been sent to the frontier once more, ordered his officers to report promptly to the nearest British officer every fact "in the least important."[16] A number of independent militia companies were organized under the direction of state authorities at Oswego, Rochester, Buffalo, and Detroit.[17] The United States government dispatched additional regulars to the frontier, began to repair a number of old military posts, and decided to build a new fort at Ogdensburg.[18]

Military activity in the United States was more than balanced by military activity in the Canadas, where, throughout 1839, the governors felt that the United States could not curb filibustering and that the best way to afford protection to Canadians was to establish

14. Report of a spy to Arthur. *Q, CDXX*, 81–87. The straits to which the Hunters were reduced are apparent from reports circulated in the press. See *Oswego Commercial Herald*, quoted in *Jour. of Com.*, September 2.

15. *Q, CCLX*, 318. Colborne to Normanby, September 27.

16. *Q, CDXX*, 279–281. Scott to Arthur, November 9. Scott had given standing orders to this effect a long time before.

17. *Q, CDXIX*, 369. Arthur to Normanby, September 27, Confidential.

18. *Q, CDXX*, 33. Arthur to Normanby, October 15, Confidential. Posts were to be strengthened at Sackett's Harbor, Oswego, and Niagara. See also *Stevenson Letter Book, May 19, 1836—July 28, 1841*, pp. 186–192. Vail to Fox, October 31, enclosure in Forsyth to Stevenson, November 7. By April 12, 1839, there had been stationed along the Canadian border 1,674 of the army's 8,497 effectives. *Van Buren Papers*, XXXV, 8484–8489. Poinsett to Van Buren, April 12.

a large military force and build permanent military posts. The British authorities in Canada also anticipated that the act which provided for a temporary increase of the army and navy in the United States, whether the increase was made permanent or not, would necessitate additional military and naval forces in the Canadas.[19] As a consequence, all the measures that were proposed or that were adopted were directed toward the twin ends of preventing invasion by the Patriots and of protecting the Canadas against the United States in the event of war.[20]

To secure the first of these ends the Canadian governors were fortunately able to strengthen the military in three directions. They petitioned London for additional regulars and redistributed the regulars already in British North America to meet emergencies. In Upper Canada a Militia Act and later a Report on the Militia by a Special Committee of the Assembly encouraged the establishment of a large body of militia and volunteers for two years.[21] With the approval of the Colonial Office there were established in Upper Canada, in particular, special stipendiary police magistrates and police units at points along the border where incendiarism was to be expected or individuals might be subject to molestation.[22]

REBUKE

Apart from the incapacity of the Hunters and the preventive measures that were taken against them, the failure of the Hunters to secure active assistance from large numbers of Americans and Canadians may be attributed in large measure to the marked opposition of the press and public opinion to interference in the Canadas. By the beginning of 1839 even Fox had begun to discover a change of attitude among the American people. The "superior class of citi-

19. *Q*, CCLVIII, 23–31. Colborne to Glenelg, March 18, Confidential; CCLVIII, 183–192. Colborne to Normanby, April 16; CDXIII, 453–461. Arthur to Glenelg, February 19.

20. For a discussion of the problem of providing for the permanent defense of the Canadas, see chap. x.

21. *Appendix to Journal of the Assembly, Upper Canada (1839–40)*, II, 255–260. In Lower Canada the existing militia and volunteer forces were retained by special permission of the Colonial Office. *Q*, CCLXV, 445. G. J. Pennington to Stephen, December 3, 1839.

22. *Q*, CDXIX, 349. The Colonial Secretary to Arthur, October 28, 1839.

zens," he reported, "are trying to restore order."[23] The January number of the very partisan and influential *Democratic Review* remarked that the "duty . . . of *non-interference,* which no one calls in question on the part of the Government, is plainly equally imperative on the individual; and its violation is a crime of very grave complexion, for which no degree of generous ardor in a cause deemed worthy of such enterprise, can be recognized as affording a sufficient excuse."[24] In the same month the *New York Journal of Commerce* and the *Washington National Intelligencer* were led to publish sharper editorials than before. The *Journal of Commerce*[25] believed that

the game of pirating upon our neighbors has been carried far enough; and a little too far. Neither Canada nor Great Britain can stand it much longer. The American people would not have borne it so long. . . . Let it be understood that any individuals who . . . shall commit crimes [in Canada] will be ferreted out if they return, and given up to the British authorities for punishment,—and we ween the "patriot" operations will henceforth be very much curtailed in their proportions.

The sooner the Americans held in custody in the Canadas were sent to Botany Bay the better. A few months later when incendiarism was at its height, the government was urged from all directions to take a strong hand.[26]

The publication of Lord Durham's *Report on the Affairs of British North America,* news of which arrived early in April, also had a marked influence upon American public opinion. As pointed out by the *Democratic Review*[27] in June, 1839, and by the *North American Review*[28] in October, 1839, the nature of political developments in the Canadas had been seriously misunderstood in the United States. The *North American Review* believed that

23. *Q,* CCLXV, 173–191. Fox to Arthur, January 31, 1839, Confidential; CCLXV, 171–172. Fox to Palmerston, February 21. Fox thought that the change was due not to a change of heart in the American people, but because of Sir George Arthur's judicious treatment of the American prisoners in Upper Canada.

24. *Democratic Review,* V, 13.   25. January 9, 1839.

26. See reports in the *Nat. Int.,* April 8.

27. *Democratic Review,* V, 542–579.

28. *N. Am. Rev.,* XLIX, 373–431. "British American Politics," John Gorham Palfrey.

the colonial system . . . as it has been in operation in the adjacent provinces, and more especially of late years, has not been, either in design or effect, what the party lately in revolt has called it. There is no evidence whatever of intentional or even of active oppression of any kind, on the part of the mother country or its government, towards the colonies. The cases of 1776 and 1839 are, in this respect, as little analogous as they well can be.

Concession "has long been the order of the day. Nor has there been, on the part of the mother country, so far as British America is the case, any apparently intentional or interested misgovernment of her dependencies."

In so far as there had been inadequate development of internal improvements and resources, mismanagement of public lands, or excessive patronage, the Canadians were themselves responsible. Rebellion grew rather from defects in the form and procedure of government and from English ignorance and weariness of having to give thought to colonial welfare. In comparison with English and American political agitators, whose violence was tempered by the anticipation that they might some day come into power, the agitator in the Canadas "cannot go too far or too fast. . . . He may profess, promise, assert, deny, assail, or defend, at pleasure. He is a chartered fault-finder, fearless of ever being subject to the same fault-finding ordeal in turn." In the first stage, he demanded money for local improvements. In the second stage, he attacked by irregular methods those whom he could overcome in no other way. In the final stage, agitation became "a trade, and the agitator sees the loss of his capital in the redress of grievances. . . . Demand is now heaped upon demand; not to obtain justice . . . but to force from the ruling power a refusal of what is asked, that the work of agitation may go on, and its workmen prosper." The *North American Review* concluded therefore that in relation to the causes from which they sprang, the Rebellions had received far too much attention in the United States.[29]

Another significant change in outlook became apparent by 1839. Americans began to think of the Canadas as not merely a congeries

29. *Idem.* In similar vein the *Democratic Review* commented upon Durham's *Report.* It said: "In addition to the beneficial influence it is calculated to produce at home, we hope, too, that it will not be without its useful effect, on this side of the water, in putting to shame the flippant ignorance, and the

of colonial possessions, as not merely Canadian or British, but as North American, an area which for good or ill was emerging as a North American country in its own right, depending for protection upon British arms. With this country the United States must learn to live at peace. In the Canadas there was slowly developing, during the 1830's and 1840's, self-reliance and self-assurance; and likewise they were discovering that for better or for worse they were part and parcel of North America, that consequently they must compose their differences with the United States if they were not to remain the objects of expansionist interest. These concurrent discoveries and the resulting demarcation of national interest were to be of the utmost importance in the future relations between Canada and the United States.

PUNISHMENT

Intimately connected with the progressive decline of Patriot activity was the manner in which offenders were punished on both sides of the border. In the United States, two periods can easily be distinguished: the first lasting through 1838 when, owing to the continuance of Patriot influence, it was next to impossible to secure convictions; and the second in 1839 when in New York (but not in Michigan where Patriot influence was still comparatively strong) the leaders were not only convicted but imprisoned and fined. During the earlier period it was frequently impossible to secure credible witnesses; the accused, if taken into custody, had no difficulty in securing sureties for bail; and juries were hard to impanel. A few examples will show how next to impossible it was to secure legal action against any of the Patriots.

Prior to June, 1838, all the chief leaders—Mackenzie, Gagnon, Coté, Nelson, Van Rensselaer, Sutherland—had been arrested but immediately released on substantial bail. N. S. Benton, as district attorney for northern New York, reported to Forsyth on January 5, 1838, that the state of feeling along the frontier was such "as will render it very difficult to procure proof sufficient to warrant arrests

selfish illiberality, which have been so disgracefully exhibited, by a large portion of the American press, in their discourses upon the 'pretended grievances' of the Canadians, under the 'free and paternal government' of the English ascendancy." *Democratic Review*, V, 543.

and commitments."[30] In June he was forced to report that of the thirteen against whom indictments had been brought at the circuit court at Albany only one minor character had been convicted.[31] The circuit court at Buffalo had even less success.

The nonchalance of the indicted persons, many of whose cases were carried over until the October terms of the courts, and the outcome of their further trials was also significant. Of seven important cases to be tried at Little Falls, New York, only one actually came up. Nelson, Bryant, and Bill Johnson jumped their bail and did not appear. In three other cases, including Mackenzie's, it was decided to change the venue to the court at Canandaigua. In each case it meant postponement of trial until June, 1839, or later. It was very evident that the courts must bide their time. The wheels of justice were badly clogged.

The inability of the United States courts to convict had reverberations in the Canadas where at first there was a tendency to poke fun at "the amusing farce of judicial examination." But as 1838 came to a close and not a single important leader of the Patriots had been punished, derision gave way to anger. Said the *Montreal Gazette* on December 11, 1838: "Where is the individual . . . that has been prosecuted to conviction, and punished for his delinquencies? He has never been heard of in these Provinces, and we believe he is not to be found in the United States." Such incapacity suggested only one remedy—action of such a nature as should compel the United States to prevent "piratical aggressions" abroad.

During the early months of 1839, as has been seen, the Patriots became largely discredited. By June it was possible to proceed with

30. *D.S. Misc. Letters.*

31. *Ibid.,* Benton to Forsyth, June 21. Evidence of the strength of border opposition to these trials is shown by what took place in Watertown in June. Of the ten prisoners in jail awaiting trial for complicity in the burning of the *Sir Robert Peel* on May 29, only one was actually brought to trial, on June 22. The N.Y. *Whig* reported: "One thing is certain, that a disposition prevails to no inconsiderable extent, in our community, to favor the patriot cause; so much so, indeed, that it is exceedingly doubtful whether any of the individuals who are now awaiting their trial for the burning of the *Sir Robert Peel,* can be convicted, though the evidence against them is overwhelming." (Quoted in *Nat. Int.,* July 2.) The trial dragged on for days until Anderson was acquitted. The others being held in custody were perforce released.

the trial of Mackenzie and others who were by now no longer in good standing anywhere east of Michigan. Mackenzie himself was nevertheless confident that he would be acquitted by any New York jury. What was his surprise to find that after three hours' deliberation the jury which heard his case brought in a verdict of guilty. He was thereupon sentenced to pay a fine of $10 and to imprisonment for eighteen months.

It is hardly possible to overestimate the effect that Mackenzie's conviction and punishment had upon opinion on both sides of the border, in discouraging the Patriots, and in the renewal of confidence in the capacity of the United States government to bring to justice offenders against the statute law. The *New York Evening Star's* comment was typical.

The trial, conviction and sentence of Wm. Lyon Mackenzie may be justly considered a triumph of the laws and civil government and will atone in a measure for that unjustifiable outbreak, that recklessness of law and public opinion, that illegal attack upon a neighboring and friendly power, which nearly drove us into a war with England, and caused a wanton sacrifice of human life and treasure. . . . It should be . . . understood that the laws and treaties of this country with other powers must not be violated with impunity, no matter how strong the sympathy that may be got up in behalf of our neighbors.[32]

The *New York American* hoped that "others, both native and foreign, who think lightly of hazarding the peace of two nations . . . will take warning from this conviction."[33] This attitude made it possible to convict and punish other offenders against the neutrality laws. Among them were Van Rensselaer and Bill Johnson who were sentenced to imprisonment in October.

Yet Mackenzie was not without friends. The reported statement of Judge Thompson, who sentenced him, that "the case involved no moral turpitude, and that the defendant had acted with a zeal which actuates men who, however mistaken, think they are right," represented a fairly widespread attitude. Almost immediately some of the Whig papers began a campaign for his release. Six weeks after his trial, somewhat more than a thousand signatures were secured at a

32. Quoted in *Nat. Int.*, June 28, 1839.
33. Quoted in *ibid.*, June 28.

public meeting in Utica for a petition praying for pardons for Mackenzie and for one Case who was sentenced at the same session of the court.[34]

Successful prosecutions in New York and the East were not matched by similar success in Michigan and the West. In this area it was impossible in 1839 even to secure indictments against anyone who had taken part in attacks on Upper Canada. Nor did the federal courts in the West ever succeed in punishing any of the Patriots. Grand juries approved of the predatory expeditions of filibusters, sometimes vocally as a body, saying that they were openly sympathetic toward "any nation earnestly engaged in the assertion of its liberty and independence."[35] It was an attitude which was considerably strengthened by large numbers of immigrants from Upper Canada who settled in the American West during 1838 and 1839.[36] Some of these had left Upper Canada as refugees, some because of unsettled political conditions, others because of dissatisfaction with their economic status. Some had recently gone to Upper Canada from the United States, others were comparatively newcomers from the British Isles, while many were native-born Canadians. But whatever their origin or their complaint, they were dissatisfied. Once in the United States they discredited British government and enterprise in the Canadas.

The Canadian authorities had likewise to meet the difficult and pressing problem of the disposition of prisoners, some of whom were British subjects charged with treason, and others, American citizens, charged with felony. To mete out even-handed justice was a difficult task, for the continuance or quieting of excitement on both sides of the border depended to a large degree upon the severity or the leniency with which the prisoners were treated. It speaks well for the level-headedness of the governors and the military authorities that they

34. The *Globe*, August 8 and 26.

35. *Van Buren Papers*, XXXVI, 8598a. Statement handed out for publication by a Detroit grand jury, June 29, 1839. *Detroit Free Press*, July 1.

36. R. S. Longley, "Emigration and the Crisis of 1837 in Upper Canada," *Canadian Historical Review*, XVII (March, 1936), 29–40. The United States papers referred frequently to heavy immigration, particularly from Upper Canada. For examples see *Nat. Int.*, July 18, 1838, and the *Globe*, July 9, 1839.

recognized the difficulties under which they were forced to act, and that they acted in such a manner as to impress upon Canadians and Americans alike that, while justice would be swift, mercy was not far off.

As might be expected, the first persons to be taken into custody in the Canadas were many of those who had risen in rebellion in November and December, 1837. Toward these political prisoners the British government took an amazingly lenient attitude,[37] partly, no doubt, because most of them were followers of leaders who had fled to the United States and had found sanctuary there.[38] Although this policy of leniency was dictated by considerations other than the appeasement of American opinion, the release of prisoners was met by an immediate congratulatory response in the United States.[39] This was accompanied, to be sure, by accounts in the border press of the miseries suffered by prisoners in provincial jails[40] and by accounts of occasional visits to jails by American officers who reported that the prisoners, both Americans and Canadians, were "treated with humanity and with all the attention their circumstances require."[41] In similar vein, the *National Intelligencer* observed, "Unsuccessful rebellion, you know, makes 'vagabonds' and wretches of what successful rebellion would convert into demi-gods and heroes."[42]

The recommendations to mercy were particularly noticeable after Durham had proclaimed amnesty for all but those who had fled to the United States and the eight whom he had banished to Bermuda. Said the *New York Journal of Commerce*, after surmising that such clemency would prevent further rebellion from coming to a head, "We wish that the conduct of the British Government . . . may be duly appreciated. . . . History affords but few, if any, examples, in which a nation so confident in its own strength as Great Britain is

37. Two were executed in Upper Canada, but none in Lower Canada. For Glenelg's instructions to Colborne, G, XXXVIII, 1–12, 296–304. January 6, 1838, Separate, and March 19.

38. For efforts to extradite Mackenzie and others, see pp. 171–172.

39. *Globe,* December 26, 1837. "This is a just and merciful policy, and will do more to keep down popular rising than the severest measures could possibly effect."

40. *Buffalo Star; North Star* (Vt.), March 3, 1838.

41. *Burlington Free Press,* March 9; *Nat. Int.,* March 16.

42. April 21.

and has a right to be, ever displayed so large a measure of mercy."[43] Similarly the *Rochester Democrat* said that "the consequences of this most pacific Amnesty, cannot fail to be highly salutary and soothing."[44] In the face of this attitude it is hardly surprising to discover that when news arrived of the disallowance of Durham's ordinance banishing prisoners to Bermuda, the American press vehemently condemned Lord Brougham and the British government for undoing their own and Durham's work of pacification. With gloomy foreboding and almost in unison they predicted renewed rebellion in Lower Canada after Lord Durham's departure for England.

As a consequence of the various attempts to invade the Canadas during 1837 and 1838, there were in Canadian jails many American citizens who were being held on charges of felony. In the early months of 1838 there were such loud complaints from some of the prisoners themselves and so vociferous a demand among certain elements in the United States for an investigation that President Van Buren decided to make an inquiry, not because he attached "much credit to the complaints" but in order to quiet them. Forsyth thereupon arranged confidentially with Fox for the appointment of a special agent to investigate the many reports so widely believed in the United States. Aaron Vail, recently chargé d'affaires in London and later to be Under Secretary of State, was accordingly sent to Canada where he found that arrangements for prisoners were adequate according to the standards of the day and no worse than they were south of the border. Fox's opinion seemed to be vindicated when he stated that the United States government "appeared . . . to be marked by a strong and sincere desire of promoting national good-will."[45]

Vail had a further purpose, namely, to aid American citizens subject to penalty in Canada even to the extent of securing their release. His inability to make any headway with Arthur and Colborne in the spring of 1838 brought a cessation of intervention by the govern-

43. July 10.
44. Quoted in *Jour. of Com.*, July 18.
45. *D.S. Br. Legation, Notes to,* VI, 93–94. Forsyth to Fox, April 3; *G,* CCXXIV, 167–171. Fox to Arthur, April 3; CCXXIV, 172–186. Fox to Colborne, April 4, Confidential; *Q,* CCL, 94–98. Fox to Palmerston, April 10; *G,* XXVIII, 628–630. Glenelg to Durham, May 29, in which Glenelg expressed approval of Vail's appointment.

ment of the United States, but by no means brought to an end efforts of Americans to secure the release of their deluded compatriots. Petitions were forwarded to Arthur and Durham from New York City, Albany, Utica, and a number of smaller places. Toward the end of the year, particularly after the failure of the invasion of Prescott in November, many public meetings were held. Designed as they were to assist the prisoners, they condemned capital punishment, scored filibustering, raised funds to supply the wants of those in custody, acknowledged the right of the Canadian authorities to try offenders according to local judicial practice and under provincial statutes, admitted that the prisoners were receiving reasonable treatment, and attempted to correct opinion in the United States concerning the nature of Canadian affairs.[46] Sir George Arthur remained skeptical and critical. He thought that "the real motive" was not the prevention of the invasion of Canada but was "only to serve their guilty fellow-citizens now in the custody of this Government." But he added, "Still, it affords an expression of opinion most desirable to encourage, and is a valuable testimony as an admission of the injury which has been done."[47]

Arthur had a particularly difficult role to play, for under his jurisdiction came the great majority of the American prisoners. Had he been excessively harsh he would have encouraged retaliation by the Patriots; had he been too lenient he would have encouraged filibustering. How to steer a middle course which would at once satisfy Canadian public opinion, the requirements of the Colonial Office, and provide a deterrent to Americans called for balanced judgment and a firm policy.

At first, Arthur believed that severity would have a good effect.[48] As the months wore on and it appeared that the United States government was actually making a serious effort to curb the Patriots, and that some of the "more violent" American newspapers were picturing him and President Van Buren as "pulling in the same boat,"

46. *Q*, CDXIII, 50–53, 54–57; *Nat. Int.*, August 24 and December 7; *Globe*, November 28 and December 3; *Com. Adv.*; *Watertown Jeffersonian*; Hough, *History of Jefferson County*, pp. 525–528.

47. *G*, CLXXXIV, 97–100; *Q*, CDXIII, 6–9. Arthur to Glenelg, January 1, 1839.

48. *G*, CLXXXIV, 27–33. Arthur to Glenelg, July 10, 1838.

Arthur concluded that leniency would be the most profitable policy.[49] In a dispatch to Glenelg on February 5, 1839,[50] he argued that neither the banishment nor the imprisonment of all the Prescott and Windsor prisoners would be satisfactory. To put the men to work on the roads or other public works would be dangerous. Transportation to Van Diemen's Land (Tasmania) was the only alternative punishment, but was far too costly. The Kingston jails were overcrowded. He had, therefore, consulted the Executive Council of Upper Canada and had concurred with their opinion that most of the prisoners should be unconditionally pardoned. This policy he intended to pursue, without waiting for instructions from England, in order to produce a good effect in the United States and Canada.

The release of the prisoners, some in March, 1839, and others in May, July, and August[51] had the desired effect. The *Globe* represented public opinion when it said on May 6: "These instances of generosity on the part of the British authorities, will do much to allay the bad feeling which for many months past has existed along our northern frontier." This was precisely the attitude which Arthur had hoped to see develop. Speaking at Cornwall in June, he said: "I frankly avow to you that it has been with me an object of great anxiety to call forth a generous feeling from those who have acted toward this country with cruel treachery and wanton violence. If the endeavor be successful (and I still shall leave no honorable effort un-

49. *G*, CLXXXIV, 96–100. Arthur to Glenelg, January 1, 1839.

50. *Q*, CDXIII, 190–198. Fox was opposed to a policy of leniency. See his letter to Arthur, January 31, 1839, Confidential in *ibid.*, CDXIII, 464–481. For Arthur's reply, *G*, CCXLI, 2–5, 11–12. March 12 and April 24, Confidential.

51. In March, Van Buren contemplated sending his own son and Senator Silas Wright to Arthur and Colborne to intercede on behalf of the prisoners. This he was deterred from doing by the advice he received from Fox. *Stevenson Papers*, XIV, 28357–28360. Van Buren to Stevenson, received May 10. Van Buren asked Stevenson to approach Palmerston informally to request him to encourage Colborne and Arthur to extend clemency "as far as they can do so with safety to themselves, & without doing violence to public opinion in Canada." Stevenson did as he was requested. Both Palmerston and Russell thought that if they intervened as Van Buren had suggested, "it might produce the state of things all wish to avoid, e.g. more bloodshed, & excitement in Canada." *Stevenson Letter Book, Apr. 5, 1839—Nov. 9, 1839*, pp. 225–239. Stevenson to Van Buren, May 16, Private.

attempted to accomplish it) it will be to me a source of unbounded satisfaction."[52] In this he was not to be disappointed. Writing to Lord Normanby on July 1, he informed him with evident pleasure that both Van Buren and Scott had written him to the effect that the liberation of the prisoners had "worked most beneficially in allaying excitement."[53]

Pardons, acquittals, and discharges for lack of evidence were counterbalanced by seventeen executions and seventy-eight sentences of transportation for life.[54] The executions were not to Arthur's liking. He had a "strong natural repugnance" to capital punishment and disapproved of it in strong terms. Yet he was the executive head of a province and had to admit that "a case of extreme and obvious necessity" might "compel recourse to it." The seventeen executions seemed to him "to be absolutely necessary as awful examples to deter . . . a repetition of aggressions."[55]

Arthur was similarly reluctant to transport so many men for life. Had he been able to follow his impulses, he would have pardoned a number of them. This was made impossible by recent events along the border and by opposition in the province to further clemency. The security of the Canadas required the transportation of a considerable number of the convicted prisoners. Nevertheless, he hoped to

52. *Montreal Courier,* June 10, quoted in *Nat. Int.,* June 17.

53. *Q,* CDXVIII, 12.

54. *Q,* CDXX, 10–14. Enclosure in Arthur to Normanby, October 14, 1839. The following is a summary of a memorandum showing the disposal of Americans in custody in Upper Canada.

Acquitted by the several courts	6
Pardoned on various grounds	90
Discharged through want of evidence	11
Discharged as witnesses	10
Died in hospital	2
Executed	17
Transported for life	78
In custody and awaiting trial for felony	6
	220

55. The Executive Council had already placed itself on record in October, 1838, as opposed to capital punishment "in any case which can be safely avoided." *Q,* CDIX, 98–126. For Arthur's opinions, see his confidential correspondence with Normanby in *ibid.,* CDXV, 211–213, and CDXVI, 8.

ameliorate the lot of many of them and ordered the provincial secretary to send the colonial secretary of Van Diemen's Land favorable reports in the case of a number of the prisoners, together with the request that those so recommended might be singled out for favorable treatment.[56]

Meanwhile in the United States Mackenzie's friends had started a movement to secure an unconditional pardon for him. Petitions, bearing perhaps 300,000 signatures, were sent to the President and to Congress. At length the Senate prevailed upon Van Buren by petition[57] and Mackenzie was released on May 10, 1840. Nine years later both he and Papineau were allowed to return to their homes in Canada where they were able to enjoy in their declining years some of those political amenities which they had striven so hard to secure for their fellow countrymen.

Time has dealt kindly with these two leaders, and rightly so. Theirs was an effort born of no puny self-interest but rather one of determination to lift from Canada the blighting control of the Family Compact and the Chateau Clique. Quite naturally officialdom fought back and branded them as traitors and rebels. Quite the opposite was the attitude of many of their contemporaries who continued to believe them to be men of heroic proportions. Nor has time dulled this judgment. Indeed, as time has passed their stature has increased until today they appear as symbols of the aspiration to secure for all Canadians the greater freedoms which, under responsible government, have come to fruition in the Dominion of Canada.

56. *Q*, CDXX, 3–6. Arthur to Normanby, October 14, 1839. The prisoners were all granted free pardons by the British government in 1844. With one or two exceptions they returned to their homes in Canada and the United States.

57. *Congr. Globe*, VIII, 307, 385.

CHAPTER IX

THE McLEOD CASE

It used frequently to be said during the years following 1837 that had the *Caroline* not been attacked and destroyed in American waters by a British force acting under orders, many of the incidents along the border would not have occurred. It also used to be said in those years that if the British government would only have accepted responsibility for the act and apologized or granted redress for it the cause of the Patriots and Hunters would have been weakened very much. Whether or not such results would have followed, the consequences of the burning of the *Caroline* on the night of December 29, 1837, and the failure of the British government to accept responsibility or to grant redress were far-reaching indeed. As the most spectacular incident of the rebellion period it proved also to be the most important in its consequences, that is, in spurring on a spirit of retaliation and bedeviling relations both between Canada and the United States, and between the United States and Great Britain.

Since the night when the *Caroline* was burned, sheriffs, deputy sheriffs, and others in New York State had been on the watch to arrest everyone who was reported to have been a member of the raiding party. In the period between 1838 and 1840 several men were apprehended, but all were released for lack of evidence or other sufficient cause. Among them was Alexander McLeod, a deputy sheriff from Niagara, Upper Canada, who was twice arrested and twice released. At length on November 12, 1840, he was arrested a third time, at Lewiston, New York, and confined to jail in Lockport. He might have been released on bail offered by the Canadian authorities in the beginning had the local population not prevented it by barricading the jail and threatening his life, for they were incensed against McLeod whose duties caused him frequently to cross into the United States to secure evidence against the Patriot invaders of Upper Canada.

McLeod's detention for almost a year, pending judicial settlement of his case in the New York courts, might never have occurred if the British government had complied with the demand for an apology and redress for the *Caroline* incident which Andrew Stevenson, the United States minister in London, formally presented to Palmerston on May 22, 1838.[1] Palmerston merely acknowledged the minister's extraordinarily vigorous letter although the two men had already had several informal conversations which led Stevenson to anticipate that while Great Britain was unwilling to discuss redress, it would publicly justify the necessity of the act and assume responsibility for it.[2] Six months later, on November 6, 1838, Palmerston instructed Fox to admit, on behalf of Great Britain, the destruction of the *Caroline* as a public act.[3] But Fox, for some unexplained reason, did not carry out these instructions. From that time until Alexander McLeod was arrested in November, 1840, Stevenson met with no success in his attempts to secure any admission from the British government.[4]

Once McLeod was arrested and it became apparent that he was being held for trial in a New York court on charges of arson and of murdering Amos Durfee, it became a matter of British policy, if not of honor, to secure his release without a trial. In a letter to Forsyth on December 13, 1840,[5] Fox claimed—although admitting that his statement would have to be confirmed by the British government— that the destruction of the *Caroline* was "the publick act of persons obeying the constituted authorities of Her Majesty's Province." He hoped that the United States would see the necessity of releasing McLeod at once especially since "the case [was] naturally occasioning a great degree of excitement and indignation within the British frontier." He continued, "I earnestly hope that it may be in your power to give me an early and satisfactory answer." Forsyth's reply on December 26 expressed both a desire to prevent ill feeling and a deter-

1. *Despatches to the Secretary of State from United States Ministers at the Court of St. James*, XLV, Stevenson to Forsyth, May 24, 1838. Hereafter cited as *G.B. Despatches from*.

2. *Ibid.*, XLV, Stevenson to Forsyth, March 6.

3. *Q*, CCLI, 227. Palmerston to Glenelg, November 8.

4. For an excellent account of the McLeod case which disposes of the questions relating to the acceptance of responsibility by Great Britain for the destruction of the *Caroline*, the efforts of the United States government to obtain McLeod's release from judicial process in New York, and the innocence of McLeod, see Alastair Watt, "The Case of Alexander McLeod," *Canadian Historical Review*, XII (June, 1931), 145–167.

5. *D.S. Br. Legation, Notes from*, XX.

mination not to interfere with the jurisdiction of the New York courts. Neither he nor the President was "aware of any principle of international law, or indeed of reason or justice" which entitled offenders to immunity before legal tribunals even though they "acted in obedience to their superior authorities, or because their acts have become the subject of diplomatic discussion between the two Governments."[6] Fox was surprised and chagrined and in reply remarked upon the "very grave and serious consequences" which would result from adhering rigidly to Forsyth's position.[7] Forsyth retorted with asperity on December 31 that no further discussion would be "useful or proper" since Great Britain had made no reply to the demand for redress of May 22, 1838.[8]

Meanwhile Congress became interested in the issue. A few weeks after the arrest of McLeod, it took action. On December 21, 1840, Millard Fillmore of New York submitted a resolution in the House of Representatives calling upon the President to transmit to that body all the correspondence with Great Britain concerning the *Caroline* affair and McLeod.[9] On December 31 another resolution requiring the printing of the correspondence precipitated a long and acrimonious debate in which both parties aired all the political dirty linen they could gather. States rights, war and peace, the status of treaties with Great Britain all received attention. A few days later, in a more moderate debate, it was proposed to refer the whole subject to the Committee on Foreign Relations. Congressmen seemed to desire a continuance of peace with Great Britain, although many were still indignant over the hauteur of Fox's letters to Forsyth.

The political battle royal came in the following February, 1841, when Francis W. Pickens of South Carolina, chairman of the Committee on Foreign Relations, introduced the report which he had written himself, and the battle continued until the end of the special session of the new Congress in September, 1841. The report gave the facts of the case, stated the principles involved, and then proceeded to a violent attack on Great Britain, whose objects and ambitions

6. *D.S. Br. Legation, Notes to,* VI, 186–189.

7. *D.S. Br. Legation, Notes from,* XX, December 29, 1840.

8. *D.S. Br. Legation, Notes to,* VI, 190, December 31, 1840.

9. Resolutions and debates in Congress are in *Congressional Globe,* IX, *passim.*

knew "no bounds." It ended with the hope for a peaceful and honorable adjustment of the *Caroline* and McLeod cases. A fierce debate took place immediately. Fillmore and John Quincy Adams attacked the report on the ground that it was too bellicose. Pickens replied that it was a plain and fearless statement of fact, that it was not intended to ruffle feelings, that its real object was to prepare the people of the United States for the problems they must face, the chief of which was that of national defense. Fillmore and others took the opposite view—that it was unwise to stir up feeling against Great Britain until the United States was sufficiently protected on its frontiers to withstand attack. In the country at large the New York *Observer* expressed current opinion when it said on February 20 that the report was meant for home consumption only, in order to accustom people to speak above their breath when speaking of the British. In the Senate, except for a few innocuous speeches on March 1, there was no excitement.

At this point, that is, on March 4, 1841, Daniel Webster became Secretary of State. In an exchange of letters with Fox he completely reversed the position taken by Forsyth; he acknowledged that there was no justification in international law for punishing as criminals those who acted under military orders, but he averred that the federal government was helpless to interfere with the jurisdiction of the courts of New York. He held out hope that the case might eventually be transferred to the Supreme Court of the United States.[10] Fox, on his part, was able on March 21 to accept on behalf of his government full responsibility for the destruction of the *Caroline*.

In order to understand the ebb and flow of opinion on both sides of the Atlantic it is well here to give a summary of the progress of McLeod's trial. While Congress was debating *Caroline* matters in January, 1841, Canadian authorities in their turn, as said above, sought to secure McLeod's release from detention at Lockport, New York, by providing bail, but failed because of the opposition of the local mob. In February, Governor Seward sent a request to the chief justice of the Supreme Court of New York to preside at the forthcoming trial at Lockport and requested the attorney general of the state to de-

10. For a complete statement of the United States' official position, see *D.S. Br. Legation, Notes to,* VI, 196–210. Webster to Fox, April 24, 1841; also *British and Foreign State Papers,* 1840–1841, XXIX, 1129–1139.

fend McLeod in order to insure a fair trial.[11] On March 15 Webster ordered the United States Attorney General John J. Crittenden to Lockport to protect McLeod's interests.[12] Owing to a technicality, the trial was postponed until June, at which time it was decided to refer it to the Supreme Court of the state. In spite of the fact that the attack on the *Caroline* was carried out by a military force acting under orders and in spite of the acceptance by the British government of responsibility for the act, the New York Supreme Court upheld the jurisdiction of the state courts to try McLeod for murder and remanded the case for trial by the lower court. McLeod now had a choice of carrying his suit directly to the Supreme Court of the United States or of standing trial before a local jury. He chose the latter in order to avoid spending another winter in jail and because a verdict of not guilty in a local court would satisfy the border population of his innocence. The venue of the trial was now changed to Utica, and there McLeod was tried and acquitted on October 12, 1841.

Meanwhile, on June 10 and for three days thereafter, the United States Senate had been engaged in a vigorous debate, during the course of which party politics had been confused with the principles of international law.[13] The main questions debated were whether Webster in his letter of April 24 to Fox had abjectly accepted the demand for the release of McLeod and whether he had gone beyond his rightful powers in ordering Crittenden to defend McLeod's interests. Associated with attacks on Webster there was an outburst of glorification of American nationalism along with an almost fanatical hostility to all things British. Said Thomas H. Benton of Missouri in a ringing attack, "To strike—to crush—to plunder—to terrify—and to make peace—this is their policy. . . ." In advocating the maintenance of American national interests he declared that it would be "better far to throw away the books, and go by the heart. Then, at least, they [the Americans] would always have the consolation of being on their country's side." As for Webster, his letter of April 24 to Fox, "besides its fatal concessions," had been "deficient in manly tone—in force—in resentment to injurious imputations—and in enforcement

11. *D.S. Misc. Letters,* Seward to Forsyth, February 27, 1841.
12. *D.S. Dom. Letters,* XXXI, 360–363.
13. For the debates, see *Congressional Globe,* X, and Appendix.

of our just claims. . . . The letter demands nothing—literally nothing; and in that respect degrades us as much as the surrender upon a threat had degraded us." Webster's political friends, especially Rufus Choate of Massachusetts, defended him by asserting with substantial truth that Benton and others were attempting "to excite just [in the sense of "mere"] sensibilities" and were not trying to enlighten the country on the facts or the merits of the case.

In the House, where the debates began on June 24 and lasted until September, an attempt was made to embarrass the administration by assertions that Webster's capitulation could bring about only one result—war. As the debates continued, the tempers of the members rose. Redress for the destruction of the *Caroline* was insisted upon. In florid language Aaron V. Brown of Tennessee proclaimed:

Sir—the waves of Niagara have extinguished the fires of that vessel— they have silenced forever the agonizing shrieks of her remaining crew— but the cry for vengeance still comes up from her deep and agitated bosom, in tones louder than the thunder of her own mighty cataract.

The debates are particularly interesting because of the intensity of party spirit and because each side insisted that the other's policy would lead to war. Fittingly did the reporter remark at the end of the debate on July 13: "When the hour expired [that is, the time set apart for debate on McLeod and the *Caroline*], the subject was dropped, and the bill, making temporary provision for lunatics in the District of Columbia, was taken up and passed."[14]

In Albany too there were stiff debates in which party spirit was evident. But the tone of the debates there was set by Governor Seward, who insisted upon the preservation of the rights of the state in his message to the Assembly in May.[15] He would continue to do all in his power to secure a fair trial for McLeod, but he would allow nothing to be done which would compromise "in the least degree, the rights, dignity, or honor of this state." In his correspondence with Lord Sydenham, governor of the United Province of Canada, he was equally definite, and at no time did he relinquish his position in the slightest degree.

14. Quoted in the *Observer* (New York), July 17.
15. Charles Z. Lincoln, ed., *Messages from the Governors* . . . (1823– 42) (Albany, 1909), III, 932–933.

What was fair bait for legislators was, of course, fair bait for people in the country at large. In the press one finds six separate aspects of the McLeod case made a matter of attack or defense. The first was whether Great Britain, by admission of culpability in attacking the *Caroline*, had the right to demand McLeod's release; the second, whether Great Britain ought not first to grant redress to the United States; the third, whether the balance in weighing transborder offenses was not heavily weighted against the United States; the fourth, whether the State of New York had jurisdiction in the McLeod case; the fifth, whether Webster, in his defense of the British, had not sold out his American birthright; and the sixth, whether war was likely to result with Great Britain if McLeod was condemned and executed. The leading papers took sides and attacked each other with unusual vigor and heat. When Thurlow Weed's *Albany Evening Journal* praised the decision of the state Supreme Court for having upheld "the honor and dignity of the State," the *New York Journal of Commerce* commented: "This, in the estimation of the *Journal*, appears to have been the essential point at issue." Whether the United States and Great Britain should become involved in war with all its attendant evils was a matter of little importance in comparison with the vindication of Seward's position.[16] It and other papers pointed out that the leading members of the New York bar refused to accept the decision as valid.[17]

As the summer wore on and the time for the trial at Utica approached, a general apprehension appears to have arisen that McLeod would not receive a fair trial and that war with Great Britain would result. But as the day came nearer it was evident that excitement was dying down, largely because many who had formerly thought that McLeod ought to be punished now believed that American dignity and honor had been sufficiently sustained, and "that having carried the point, the punishment of McLeod could answer no end or object," that therefore the government of New York "would

16. *Jour. of Com.*, July 15. The *National Intelligencer* (Washington) and the *Daily Advertiser* agreed with the *Journal*. The *Globe* (Washington), on the other hand, stood staunchly by the official position.

17. *Jour. of Com.*, July 19; *Nat. Int.*, July 22; *Poughkeepsie* (N.Y.) *Eagle,* quoted in the *Nat. Int.*, July 22.

not be justified in putting him to death."[18] So little interest was exhibited in the trial itself that the courtroom was but one-third filled.

English opinion went through a number of phases in 1841. The first news of McLeod's arrest excited only moderate attention, although in certain quarters notable apprehension was felt. Lord John Russell in a personal note to Stevenson expressed the fear that "the Senate & public in the United States are acting in ignorance of the very strong feeling which will be excited here if McLeod is condemned."[19] When news of the January debate in Congress and of the Lockport grand jury's true bill reached England, the daily press printed it at length, and excitement went to fever heat. In anticipation of probable war, funds depreciated and the Bank suspended specie payments. Melbourne's guarded but incisive and threatening language and O'Connell's insistence upon the protection of British subjects abroad did nothing to allay the public frenzy. Palmerston became so disturbed that he urged Stevenson to write privately to Van Buren urging him to do all in his power to release McLeod, whereupon Stevenson reported to the President: "The excitement is indeed violent among all Parties & the case is treated as one of the most monstrous character. Some . . . talk of seizing and retaliating upon Americans here. One thing is certain, if McLeod is executed, there will be *immediate war!* Of this you may rest assured."[20] Speed was essential if trouble was to be averted.

During the following three weeks excitement subsided when it became known that McLeod would probably be bailed and discharged.[21] Besides, the soft words of ministers in the debate over the naval and military estimates had a soothing effect upon public opinion. But just at this point, March 7, news of McLeod's further detention and of Pickens' report reached England. London and the country were immediately thrown into an uproar. Stevenson reported that many thought war inevitable, although he himself did not expect it immediately, and he even hoped to avoid it. Nevertheless he went so far as

18. *Observer* (New York), October 9, quoted also from the *Jour. of Com.*
19. *Stevenson Papers*, XXIV, 30599–30600, February 2.
20. *Van Buren Papers*, XLII, 9904–9907, February 9.
21. *G.B. Despatches from*, XLVIII, Stevenson to Secretary of State, March 3. Stevenson still thought that McLeod's condemnation and execution "would inevitably have led to a rupture between the two countries."

to advise Commodore Hull, who was with an American flotilla at Marseilles, "to get nearer home and within reach of orders from the [Navy] Department."[22] Even Joseph Hume found feelings running so high against the United States that he refrained from questioning ministers in the House as he had previously intended.[23]

Most of the papers, according to Stevenson, were "filled with articles of the most revolting extravagance & violence, & well calculated to agitate and influence the public mind, already too much predisposed for violent & rash measures."[24] The *Times* headed its account, "Menacing and Insulting Report of the Committee of Foreign Relations of the House of Representatives." The *Morning Chronicle*, a government sheet, worded it: "Threatened War with England." The London correspondent of the *New York Journal of Commerce* reported that such declarations brought about

one universal feeling of anger and indignation upon every lip and feature . . . and I do assure you that I have never beheld, or read of, anything at all equal to the manner in which the whole community from the highest to the lowest, in the lobbies to the Senate, or in the thoroughfares of the streets, at the clubs of the aristocrats, or the parlors of a pot-house, were so completely convulsed. From several conversations which I have had this morning, with persons of various grades of life, from every enquiry that I can make, and from all the close observation of which I am capable, I do find that the excitement was, and is, most excessive; that England has felt herself insulted, outraged, and menaced, and that, in the language of the *Times*, "without the especial interference of the ALMIGHTY, any human means of averting war" does not seem to be entertained for a moment.[25]

22. *Stevenson Letter Book, July 10, 1836—September 27, 1841*, pp. 200–201. Stevenson to Hull, March 8.

23. *Stevenson Papers*, XXV, 30756–30757. Hume to Stevenson, March 10. E. V. Harcourt wrote Webster a friendly letter on March 12 in which he assured Webster that "there is in this country but *one* feeling on the subject among all parties and all ranks, that if he [McLeod] should be condemned, it would be such an outrage on *international* justice that we must throw away the Scabbard at once." He hoped for peace. Cf. *Daniel Webster Papers*, V, 16476–16477.

24. *G.B. Despatches from*, XLVIII, Stevenson to Secretary of State, March 9.

25. This is part of a long letter from J.W.G., the London correspondent, March 9, in the *Jour. of Com.*, April 7.

British honor had been outraged. Said the *Morning Herald* on March 17: "The release of Mr. McLeod is as indispensable to British honor as it would be creditable to American justice." Matters still appeared critical in the middle of March, but thereafter excitement tended to grow less. The Tories, generally referred to as the war party, were unwilling to undertake a war upon their own responsibility, although both the Tories and the Tory press remained adamant in their belief in the ultimate necessity of settling difficulties with the United States by force of arms. Melbourne's tottering government was not disposed to take measures which might lead to an immediate collision with the Republic unless measures looking toward military preparedness could be so interpreted. Hume, who again would have introduced the subject in Parliament, was induced by ministers themselves to keep silent. Moreover, the arrival of the news that Webster had been appointed Secretary of State and was giving the McLeod case his closest attention aroused an expectation among press and people alike that the United States would accede to the British demand for the release of McLeod. Consols went up half a point.[26] For the next three months little comment appeared in the London press.

The essential issues between the two governments and the two peoples are now quite clear. In the first place, the matter of primary interest to the British was the release of McLeod while to Americans McLeod's release was merely an incident associated with the far more important question of securing redress for the destruction of the *Caroline*. But McLeod's predicament involved another issue which Englishmen were either unable or unwilling to understand. They could not accept the explanation that under a federal form of government separate powers and responsibilities exist. They made it a point of honor to demand McLeod's release, whereas the United States government was unable to secure it by any fiat of its own. The complicating factor was, of course, that both the government and the states-rights citizens of New York made it a point of honor to insist that justice take its course, regardless of the international consequences of such a procedure.

It is not difficult thus to see that the intensity of English feeling

26. *G.B. Despatches from*, XLVIII, Stevenson to Secretary of State, April 7. Also correspondence of J.W.G. in *Jour. of Com.*, April 22; and re-

and expectation of war in March were matched again in August when it became known that the New York Supreme Court had refused to discharge McLeod. In both London and the provinces the press of all shades of opinion carried statements of the government's preparations for war or advocated such measures. In a particularly outspoken article on August 11, the *Times* asked if it were consonant with the dignity of Great Britain to wait until McLeod should be out of reach of help. Since his chance of a fair trial was minute, preparations for war should be expedited at once. According to the correspondent of the *New York Journal of Commerce*, this article "created quite an effect, and received eulogies of men high in authority with both Whigs and Tories." On the eighteenth the *Times* again trumpeted warnings of danger: "The time for diplomatic expostulation and legal argument, is . . . already past." It ill became the United States, so weak in naval armaments, to assume its present attitude toward McLeod and Great Britain.[27]

At this juncture the new Parliament met for the first time, on August 24. To quiet the country no mention was made in the speech from the throne of McLeod or of relations with the United States. Friendly assurances, it said, continued to be received from foreign powers. Palmerston's studied defense of his policies and his proof that good relations with the United States did exist were so successful that several Whig papers congratulated the country on its escape from war. The Tories were by no means satisfied, for at a meeting at the Colonial Club on August 30, presided over by Lord Mountcashel, a number of bellicose resolutions were passed, and these, together with speeches delivered by several influential peers, were printed in the *Morning Herald* the following day.[28]

Although the subject was still considered by Peel and Russell to be "one of deep importance,"[29] Aberdeen's "friendly and conciliatory" attitude toward the United States and the government's abstention

ports in the *Journal* from the *Times* (London), April 2; *Sun* (London), April 1; *Spectator* (London).

27. This paragraph is based on many quotations from the English press in the *Jour. of Com.* from August 24 to September 7, and on correspondence of J.W.G.

28. Quoted in *ibid.*, September 17.

29. *Stevenson Letter Book, March 21, 1839—October 22, 1841*, pp. 208–215. Stevenson to Webster, September 18.

from committing itself to a definite policy prior to the trial in Utica had a calming effect upon public opinion. The press became less active in denunciation of the United States.

But just as hostility toward the United States seemed to have calmed down, news arrived in England of an incident which occurred on the border between Vermont and Canada East (formerly Lower Canada) on September 19. On that day a band of volunteer dragoons crossed over into Vermont and abducted one Grogan, who, for the past two years, had gained notoriety for burning houses and barns in Canada East. The border peoples became extremely excited and the press on both sides of the frontier took up the issue. Fortunately Grogan was released by Sir Richard Jackson on October 4. While the incident showed that the greatest caution had to be pursued in handling the case of McLeod in order to avoid retribution from Canadians, and perhaps consequences of a more serious nature as well, the incident itself soon passed into the limbo of the ordinary in both Canada and the United States.

Not so in England. So much was it felt in London that Grogan's abduction would aggravate relations with the United States that, upon the arrival of the news, "the funds went down, speculators became paralysed, 'change was crowded,' the newspapers were sought for with extraordinary avidity, and rumors the most absurd, ridiculous, and terrific, were to be heard in all societies." Sunday papers added fuel to the excitement by announcing that "reprisals had commenced and war was inevitable." It was also reported that the British government was busy preparing the navy and army for emergencies. The *Times* aroused anxieties still more by printing a long letter in which the strategy for waging war with the United States was fully outlined.[30] English resentment and expectation of war had been awakened again. In this state of mind Englishmen awaited news of McLeod's trial. When the news of his acquittal arrived, they admitted that the proceedings were creditable to American justice, but they refused to grant that the question had been settled as to whether any court in the United States had a right to try him.[31]

Canadian exasperation with the United States exhibited a tone

30. Correspondence of J.W.G., October 20, in the *Jour. of Com.*, November 10.

31. *Morning Chronicle* (London), quoted in *ibid.*, November 22.

more even, but nevertheless sharp enough. In view of the intermittent but continuous trouble along the border, the British government was especially anxious to prevent retaliation against the United States. To this end Sydenham was ordered to restrain the Canadians. At the same time he was ordered to assure them of the Queen's "determination to protect them with all the weight of Her power."[32] In Canada West (formerly Upper Canada), Sir George Arthur was a tower of strength, ever on the watch to prevent border outrages. That there were no incidents of importance until September, 1841, speaks well for the good sense of Canadians and Americans alike.

A perusal of Canadian newspapers shows a great divergence of opinion and of editorial practice. Some Tory papers began shortly after McLeod's arrest "to speak with much warmth" and waxed hotter and hotter as the months went by.[33] A number of Reform papers advocated caution and refused to admit the likelihood of armed hostilities.[34] In general, it may be said that all disliked the thought of war with the United States, but while the Reform papers remained moderate, the Tory papers often assumed a bellicose tone. When the trial was over, all were relieved, but the Tories felt indignant still. Some day, they felt, there must be a final reckoning for all outstanding disputes.

It is evident that, coming as it did in the midst of a long-drawn-out dispute over the Maine boundary and of tension which resulted in filibustering along the St. Lawrence frontier, the immense amount of bad feeling stirred up in 1841 by the trial of McLeod gave the several governments concerned a great deal of uneasiness. Among the causes of their uneasiness were the many reports they received of the revival of the Hunters and other Patriots in 1841. For a year the Hunters had remained comparatively inactive, though they had sponsored attacks on ships, had blown up Sir Isaac Brock's monument at Queenston, and attempted to burn Kingston. Now in 1841 again there were rumors that they were organizing for another expedition against Upper Canada, that one of their objects was to cap-

32. G, CVIII, 170–172. Russell to Sydenham, March 8.
33. For example, the *Herald* (Montreal), *Montreal Gazette*, *Gazette* (Quebec), and *Patriot* (Toronto).
34. For example, the *Canada Times* (Montreal), *Chronicle* (Kingston), *Journal* (Hamilton), *Times* (Toronto).

ture McLeod, kill him, and thus precipitate war. There were rumors also of an expedition from Canada to rescue him. Under these circumstances we find Webster writing a personal note on March 11 to J. A. Spencer, now United States district attorney for the northern district of New York and counsel for McLeod, in which he said:

The President is exceedingly anxious for McLeod's personal safety and security. . . . The utmost care, we think ought to be used to prevent any attempt either to rescue him by persons from Canada, or to use violence towards him, by persons on our side. . . . The main object of this is, to press the high importance of guarding McLeod from all possible danger—consequences of the most serious nature might follow if he should become the subject of popular violence, either by his friends or his foes.[35]

Webster also assured Fox of the government's intention to protect McLeod by a military force under the command of Major General Scott.[36] From March until October reports of Patriot activities were constantly sent to the War and State Departments, and efforts, not always successful, were made to prevent the American border population from committing acts of violence against Canada.

In these various safeguarding measures Governor Seward took a leading hand. He refused to interfere with the jurisdiction of the courts, but he was determined to protect McLeod from violence. By September 1, 1841, he had visited Utica, the scene of the final trial; he had ordered an extra guard placed around the jail at Whitesboro; he had given orders that the militia officers of Oneida County be ready for duty, that a special volunteer artillery force of one hundred men be formed and armed at once; and he had also employed secret agents to "traverse the line of canals" to get information of any designs on foot.[37] During September, information was received of the accumulation at Utica of a large quantity of Patriot gunpowder, and Seward then redoubled his efforts. In a long letter to David Moulton, sheriff of Oneida County, he gave the most minute instructions for insuring McLeod's safety, both before and after the trial. "There is much reason," he said, "to apprehend that the coun-

35. *D.S. Dom. Letters,* XXXI, 357–358.
36. *G,* CCXXVII, 311–318. Fox to Palmerston, April 28.
37. *D.S. Misc. Letters,* Seward to Webster, September 3.

try would be involved in war if any injury should befall Alexander McLeod while he remains in the custody of the law. . . . The honor of New York and of the United States is more deeply concerned in protecting him against danger until [his] vindication be accomplished."[38] In fact, Winfield Scott even believed that Seward would give McLeod a safe passage out of the country, regardless of whether he were acquitted or convicted.[39]

Nor did Seward act alone. Webster's anxiety caused him to order both the district attorney and the district marshal of the northern district of New York to aid or to act concurrently with the state authorities, and he had a special company of artillery sent to Rome, a few miles distant from Utica. President Tyler issued a forceful proclamation on September 25 against filibustering. In the course of a long conversation with Fox on September 30, he informed the British minister that he hoped to avert trouble with Great Britain should McLeod be executed. To this end he would refuse Fox a passport and, if necessary, force him to remain in Washington, or at least in the country, until Great Britain had had time to reflect more fully on the various aspects of the case. This Tyler said in "a friendly manner, but firmly and resolutely."[40]

The McLeod case is an example of the enormous amount of ill feeling which can be generated by a misunderstanding which cannot be ended because of the absence of satisfactory machinery for the settlement of disputes between nations. So serious did it become that the Czar directed his ministers in London and Washington to state to the British and United States governments his deep interest in preserving peace.[41] He felt, in this instance, that since neither vital interests nor national honor was at stake, a settlement could be arranged. If it could, it would prevent a war which, if it began, would in all likelihood spread to Europe.

To speculate whether or not there would have been war had McLeod been executed is useless. The most that can be said is that the British government formulated no definite policy in advance, other

38. *Ibid.*, Seward to Moulton, September 24.
39. *Ibid.*, Scott to Secretary of War, September 21.
40. *G*, CCXXVII, 613–625. Fox to Aberdeen, October 12, Confidential; also Fox to Sir Richard Jackson, October 2, Secret and Confidential.
41. *G.B. Despatches from*, XLVIII, Stevenson to Webster, April 19.

than to make certain minor naval and military preparations, while the United States government was clearly anxious to avoid war at all costs and made no move to prepare for an immediate war. Public opinion, on the other hand, might have forced both nations into a senseless and fruitless war. At any rate, when McLeod was acquitted and left the United States, it seemed as if the impending threat had been lightly and happily removed.

CHAPTER X

NATIONAL DEFENSE

THE growing number and complexity of the disputes between Great Britain and the United States, for example, those over the destruction of the *Caroline*, the northeastern boundary, and the McLeod case increased both the difficulty of preserving friendly relations and the likelihood of war. This was especially true of the years 1840–42 during which plans were drawn up for the defense of the border—by the British as a matter of imperial policy, and by the United States as a matter of national policy. But before we can examine the military and naval plans of these years we shall have to retrace our steps somewhat to observe the extent to which attention had previously been paid to safeguarding the border against attack from either side.

Three facts stand out in sharp relief. Ever since the Treaty of Ghent, which was regarded as providing anything but a definitive peace, it had been taken for granted that war was the one final method of settling the multitudinous disputes which had developed between the United States and Great Britain. Nor was it anticipated anywhere that the United States could remain neutral in the event of war on a large scale in Europe. It therefore behooved both the British and the Americans to look to the defense of borders which were vulnerable to attack. Indeed, it was this question of vulnerability which determined, in the end, the extent to which both governments prepared to guard the Canadian-American frontier against the contingency of war.[1]

As in other postwar periods, after 1814 there was, in the United States and Canada, a sharp reduction in the military forces. This was particularly true in the United States where, when the army had been reduced for a second time in 1821 (from 10,000 to 6,183), few if any regulars were stationed at Plattsburg, Sackett's Harbor, and Niagara, and Detroit alone continued to have a small garrison.[2] The rapid disintegration of the St. Lawrence defenses can be explained,

1. A study by C. P. Stacey of military and naval relations of the United States and Canada is to be published in the Carnegie Endowment series.
2. E. B. Wesley, *Guarding the Frontier: A Study of Frontier Defense*

to a considerable extent, by the belief expressed by John C. Calhoun when he was Secretary of War in 1819 that the defense of the St. Lawrence–Great Lakes frontier was best served by the extraordinary increase of the population immediately to the south of the border. Again, in 1831, this view was expressed in Congress when a proposal was introduced to survey the northern end of Lake Champlain with a view to building a fort at that point to offset the fort at Rouses Point which had been found to lie north of the forty-fifth parallel of latitude. It was "preposterous," said Ambrose Spencer of New York, to anticipate attack from a weaker power. The United States could not be invaded successfully from the north.[3]

Other matters also distracted the attention of the United States government from the defense of the northern border. Among these were its absorption in the westward movement with the accompanying Indian problems, its interest in the defense of the Atlantic seaboard, the unimpeded control of communications within its own borders, the successful conclusion of the Rush Bagot agreement, and likewise the absence of a military tradition. The defense of the northern border accordingly became of distinctly secondary importance in any general plan of defense.

It was not so with Great Britain. Prior to the 1860's there was no westward movement in British North America comparable to that in the United States; there never was a comparable Indian problem, and there were no costly and long-drawn-out Indian wars. The Atlantic seaboard was safeguarded by the British Navy. On the other hand, the War of 1812 had proven conclusively that the St. Lawrence–Great Lakes region could be attacked with comparative ease and success. Montreal could be cut off from the interior. The defense of this area became therefore of primary importance for the retention of British authority in North America.

The belief that this area could be defended and that it ought to be protected gives us the clue to the military policy followed by the British government after 1815. In the first place, although it was confident that it could achieve command on Lake Ontario, it was in no mood to enter into competitive building on the Lakes, so it concluded

from 1815–1825 (Minneapolis, 1935); and H. P. Beers, *The Western Military Frontier, 1815–1846* (Philadelphia, 1935).

3. *Register of Debates*, VII, 747 ff.

the Rush Bagot agreement in 1817.[4] On the other hand, it was believed that the vulnerability of the military frontier could be overcome by building adequate fortifications and maintaining forces of regulars at strategic centers.[5] But the cost, as estimated by a military commission appointed by the Duke of Wellington in 1825, was prohibitive, and prior to 1837 comparatively little was done, except the construction of the Rideau Canal. This canal would assist the Canadas to withstand the shock of war by providing an alternate route to the head of Lake Ontario.[6]

When the border difficulties began in 1837, the British found themselves relatively unprepared to cope with filibustering or with widespread rebellion, to offset which, as has already been shown, they strengthened their naval and military position in the Canadas during 1838 and 1839. The continuing threat of war, however, forced the British to give attention to defense, not merely against filibustering groups but against the military forces of the United States. In the Canadas this problem was continuously in the minds of the governors. With his weather eye always open to detect bad faith on the part of Washington, Sir George Arthur was, in April, 1838, the first to insist upon the need of carrying into effect the recommendations of the Military Commission of 1825.[7] Now, if ever, he said, was the time favorable for action of this sort, "that under other circumstances, might excite the jealousy" of the United States.[8] By March, 1839, Colborne became convinced "that no time should be lost in making . . . arrangements for the permanent defence of the Colony."[9]

Colborne's plan of March, 1839, envisaged the establishment of a

4. H. and M. Sprout, *The Rise of American Naval Power* (Princeton, 1939), pp. 88–91.

5. *Copy of a Report to His Grace the Duke of Wellington, Master General of His Majesty's Ordnance, &c., &c., &c., Relative to His Majesty's North American Provinces by a commission of which M. General Sir George Carmichael Smyth was president, Lieut. Colonel Sir George Hoste, Captain Harris members.* London, 1825. The commission recommended for canals, £239,-000; for the defense of the Canadas, £1,141,218; and for coastal defenses for Nova Scotia, £266,000.

6. *Q*, CCLXXI, 189–193.

7. *G*, CLXXXIV, 4–8. Arthur to the Colonial Secretary, April 24, 1838.

8. *G*, CLXXXIV, 13–19. Same to same, May 30, 1838.

9. *Q*, CCLVIII, 23–31. Colborne to Glenelg, March 18, 1839, Confiden-

strong line of posts at the points most exposed to attack along the border, together with a force of regulars sufficient to meet any emergency which might arise out of attacks by filibusters from the United States. This plan proved to be unacceptable to Lord John Russell, the Colonial Secretary, who, in September, informed Charles Poulett Thomson, the new governor of Lower Canada, that the government proposed to establish a number of military settlements on the frontier "as at once the most effective and the most economical plan of defence which could be pursued."[10] But the proposal never materialized. In fact, in December Colborne, now Lord Seaton, was called into consultation in London where he impressed Russell so strongly with the need of additional frontier posts[11] that the latter requested the War Office to take Colborne's proposals into consideration and finally to determine the actual defense needs of the Canadas.[12]

Lieutenant General Sir Richard D. Jackson, Colborne's successor as commander of the forces in British North America, had different ideas. Coming for the first time to Montreal in the winter of 1839, his concern was less with the protection of the Canadas against American Patriots than against the United States itself. Pointing to the recent recommendations of the Secretary of War[13] which would have provided for the erection of three new forts on and near Lake Champlain, four additional stations for the concentration of troops, and an increase of the militia, Jackson proposed in March, 1840, that Montreal, as the key to Canadian defense, should be surrounded by a series of forts at an immediate expense of £45,047.[14] The War Office had, however, accepted Colborne's point of view that adequate

tial; CDXVII, 409–410. Arthur to Normanby, June 8, 1839, again urging "good fortifications."

10. *Q,* CCLXIX C, 153–156. September 7, 1839.

11. *Q,* CCLX, 457–459, 460–464. Seaton to Russell, December 30, and "Memoranda respecting the defence of U. Canada with reference to the present state of the Province and the Hostility of the American Patriots."

12. *Q,* CCLX, 465–466. (Writer unknown) to R. Byham, January 13, 1840.

13. 26 Cong. 1 Sess., *House Doc.,* No. 2, November 30, 1839.

14. *Q,* CCLXXI, 171–185. "Memorandum upon Montreal and its Immediate Frontier," March 24, 1840.

defense of the Canadas involved covering the frontier "by good works" at the chief strategic and most exposed points.[15]

Jackson was dissatisfied with this plan. He secured revised estimates of costs of construction[16] and in November, 1840, submitted a lengthy memorandum which stands as the most important Canadian military document of the 1840's. Profiting by a further study of United States military policy as proposed by the Secretary of War on May 12, 1840, in the "Report upon the National Defences and National Boundaries," Jackson found that the key to American policy was twofold: control of Lake Champlain and its outlet, and control of the whole northern frontier "not only for defense . . . but to act offensively with decisive effect in the event of" war with Great Britain.[17] Jackson thereupon urged, even more strongly than Colborne, the completion of all fortifications recommended by the Commission of 1825, the careful guarding of communications with the West, or, failing the completion of fortifications, the maintenance of a large standing army. Disparity in strength between the Canadas and the United States would require the building of "defensive works" even if a treaty should, at any time, proscribe fortifications.[18]

Under such pressure by Colborne, Russell, and Jackson, and again by Sydenham, who insisted upon the safeguarding of the St. Lawrence from Montreal to the Atlantic,[19] the British government took cognizance of its expanding responsibilities[20] and decided to build a number of permanent works and to maintain a large force of regulars in the Canadas—some twenty thousand in all. The price they were willing to pay for the defense of a vulnerable frontier was £100,000 a year in addition to the regular military estimates.[21]

15. Q, CCLXXI, 189–193. R. Byham to Stephen, May 4, 1840.

16. Q, CCLXXIV, 269–271. Lieut. Col. J. Oldfield to Jackson, November 14, 1840. In 1825, the Military Commission had estimated the cost of fortifications at £1,141,218. Oldfield's estimate (after some work had been done at Quebec and Kingston) was £2,306,679.

17. 26 Cong. 2 Sess., House Doc., No. 206.

18. Q, CCLXXIV, 213–268. "Memorandum upon the Canadian frontier," November, 1840.

19. Q, CCLXXIV, 202–204. Sydenham to Russell, December 24, 1840.

20. Q, CCLXXIV, 205–208. Russell to Lord Hill, February 22, 1841.

21. This was reported in the Jour. of Com., July 27, 1841, as well as in several other papers.

In contrast with the generally accepted view that the Canadas could be attacked successfully from the south, it was generally recognized in military circles in Washington in the 1830's that the United States was not vulnerable to attack from Canada. In fact, by 1836, the problem of the defense of the St. Lawrence and the Great Lakes frontier had narrowed down, in the opinion of the War Department, to securing control of the northern end of Lake Champlain.[22] Until 1838, almost no attention was given to fortifying the remainder of the northern border. In that year, owing to the beginning of Patriot troubles, a small appropriation of $3,000 was set aside for repairs for Fort Niagara. In 1839, appropriations were provided for repairs in the Niagara, Oswego, and Plattsburg areas. Not yet was Congress ready to appropriate more than the pittance necessary to discourage Patriot attacks upon the Canadas and protect the border from retaliation by Canadians.

In 1840 this situation had begun to change. The British had then twenty thousand troops in North America. They were repairing military posts and building barracks. The northeastern boundary dispute had not been settled, nor for that matter had the dispute over the slave trade. The heightening tension in Congress in March, 1840, called forth the first serious demand for adequate defense of the northern frontier. The British government, said Senator Norvell of Michigan, "was amusing us with negotiations" at a time when "it was making quiet and steady progress in preparing for offensive and defensive operations, at all important points near the entire frontier of the United States from Maine to Lake Superior." This showed clearly that "spirit of aggrandizement" which animated Great Britain "in all her policy."[23]

The reply to Norvell's outburst appeared in a detailed memorandum drawn up by Major General Scott.[24] It pointed out that construction work was under way on a number of minor posts and on occasional major fortifications from Windsor to Montreal. Moreover, the British military forces were so distributed that practically the whole

22. *A.S.P., Military Affairs,* VI, 390–391.
23. *Congr. Globe,* VII, 262–263. March 12, 1840.
24. 26 Cong. 1 Sess., *Senate Doc.,* No. 346, March 28, 1840. Scott's Memorandum was widely copied in the press under the heading *British Preparations.*

strength of the twenty thousand men in question could be concentrated at these strategic frontier points within a very few days.

This memorandum was designed to arouse in the country and in Congress a demand for an adequate system of defense for the northern frontier; and it had the desired effect. In answer to a resolution passed by the House on April 9, the War Department laid before it the extensive plan of May 12 which had been the basis for Sir Richard Jackson's recommendations to the War Office in the following November. In the face, however, of a particularly bitter presidential campaign year, in Congress few matters of national importance had a chance of being considered upon their merits. But neither the press nor the War Department was satisfied with the attention paid to national defense; and this remained true until March, 1841.

Meanwhile tension between the United States and Great Britain had been stepped up by the arrest, detention, and proposed trial of McLeod. War became a distinct possibility after the Supreme Court of New York had held, in June, that McLeod was triable by ordinary judicial process. From the whole of the border, but from New York State particularly, came growing demands for the improvement of frontier defenses and for increasing armaments on the Lakes where it was said that the British were disregarding the agreement of 1817.

However peacefully inclined the Tyler administration may have been, neither Tyler nor Webster could disregard the clear warnings of the danger of war. A fortification bill was therefore introduced in the special session of Congress on July 7.[25] There might have been some disposition to discuss the bill on its merits had it not been that Tyler, a Southern Democrat, had already run foul of the Whig party which controlled both houses of Congress. To political asperities were added the sharp clashes of rampant sectionalism. For the most part the northern and seaboard members of the House and Senate approved of coastal fortifications as the first and most important lines of defense, and of posts along the northern frontier as only a secondary line, because of the generally accepted belief in the invulnerability of that area. Western members bargained for additional posts to protect their territory from Indian attacks. Still others in-

25. *Congr. Globe*, X, 60.

sisted that there was no danger of war and that expenditures on defense would simply be a waste of money.

At length, on September 4, the bill was passed.[26] Out of a total appropriation of $2,226,401 which was about three times as large as the average annual military appropriation for the previous ten years, there was provided $15,000 for Fort Ontario at Oswego, $20,-000 for Fort Niagara, $50,000 for barracks and defensive works at Buffalo, $75,000 for a fort at the outlet of Lake Champlain, and $100,000 for armed steamers on Lake Erie to offset the two which the British were reported to have on it. No additional sums were set aside for the Detroit area because surplus funds held by the War Department were regarded as sufficient to provide for the moderate needs of the western country. These modest appropriations appeared, therefore, to represent the beginning of competitive building on the northern frontier.

It will be recalled that, in 1838, in an exchange of notes between Forsyth and Fox concerning an alleged British violation of the Rush Bagot agreement, Forsyth accepted Fox's assurances that the British government would take additional ships out of commission as soon as conditions on the frontier warranted it. Throughout the following year no questions or issues arose in or out of Congress over the application of the naval agreement. But in May, 1840, investigations disclosed that a ship of five hundred tons was to be launched at Chippewa in Upper Canada in June, and that the construction of a second ship was to be begun at once thereafter.[27] This appeared to represent a British bid for the control of Lake Erie as well as a total disregard of the provisions of the 1817 agreement.

The fact was that when navigation opened in the spring of 1840 the British, like the United States, had no ships fit for active service on the Lakes. To make up for this deficiency they had building at Chippewa the *Minos* to which reference has just been made. Increased interest in the defense of the Canadas led Sydenham to propose to Russell in October, in response to Russell's inquiry, that there be built a second ship, one that could be used in the narrow channels of the Detroit and St. Clair rivers. For Lake Ontario he recommended

26. *Ibid.*, X, 429.

27. *D.S. Misc. Letters,* John Norvell to Van Buren, May 24, 1840, enclosing a letter to him from Lieut. James T. Homans, U.S.N., April 13.

the construction of an additional steamship, since the *Traveller* was not at the moment fit for active service.[28] In other words, Sydenham was proposing to double the number of ships and more than double the tonnage and armament allowed by the agreement. As a matter of policy, he was anxious to secure control of Lake Ontario, but recognized the impossibility of gaining supremacy on Lake Erie.[29] American observers had good reason for suspecting the British of having intentions to disregard the terms of the Rush Bagot agreement.

Suspicion showed itself in Congress in February, 1841, when Millard Fillmore of New York tried unsuccessfully to get the House Committee on Military Affairs to agree to competitive building on the Lakes.[30] In August, Silas Wright, also of New York, was more successful. He secured the assent of the Senate to add to the fortification bill $50,000 for works at Buffalo and $100,000 for two additional steamers on Lakes Erie and Ontario.[31]

Diplomatically the subject did not come to a head until September. By then the air was thick with rumors of the likelihood of rebellion in the Canadas, of the Hunters' preparations for the invasion of Upper Canada, and of attempts to kidnap McLeod. A partially successful attempt was made to blow up one of the locks of the Welland Canal, and the British armed ships *Minos* and *Toronto* were fired upon from the American shore. Under these circumstances Governor Seward of New York wrote at length to Webster on September 17 and again five days later.[32] He pointed out that the *Minos* and *Toronto*, both alike ships of five hundred tons, capable of mounting eighteen guns and a 68-pounder, actually had on board muskets, hatchets, boarding pikes, and cutlasses, and each was manned by seventy-five men. Seward assured Webster that the people along the border were becoming restive and disturbed by this increase of armaments by the British. He urged immediate reinforcements, both mili-

28. *Q*, CCLXXIII-III, 428–431. Sydenham to Russell, October 9, 1840.

29. P. Knaplund, ed., *Letters from Lord Sydenham, Governor-General of Canada, 1839–1841 to Lord John Russell* (London, 1931), p. 97. In this private note Sydenham asked for immediate authorization to build a second ship for Lake Ontario, saying: "We could hold that Lake—not so Lake Erie, out of which the Yankees would drive us at once."

30. *Fillmore Papers*, I, 165.   31. *Congr. Globe*, X, 292–294.

32. Both letters are in *D.S. Misc. Letters*.

tary and naval. He wanted to know if the British government had shown any inclination officially to annul the 1817 agreement. In the existing state of American defenses on the Lakes this was a matter of importance, for the United States had no naval ordinance of any sort on them, and there was none available nearer than New York.[33]

Seward's communications set off a train of correspondence between the United States and British governments. Webster wrote Fox immediately reminding him of assurances given on November 25, 1838, that the increase of naval armaments was designed specifically to meet a temporary emergency. He reminded Fox that the total armaments on the Lakes in 1841 greatly exceeded what had been agreed upon. Instead of demanding a return to the limits established in 1817, Webster asked for "explicit assurances" that if it were found necessary to use the additional vessels at all, their use would be "confined to the sole and precise purpose of guarding" the Canadas against attack.[34] Fox, to whom the letter had been shown by Webster prior to its formal presentation, suggested that with the McLeod trial in the offing it was an inopportune moment to be lodging a protest. Webster thereupon agreed to defer sending the letter officially until after he had left Washington, but he did not agree to this until Fox had explained that assurances given in 1838 applied to the present moment as well.[35]

When therefore McLeod was acquitted in October and the frontier began to settle down for a peaceful winter, Webster took up the issue again in language which foreshadowed the demands he was later to make of Lord Ashburton when he attempted to secure an apology for the destruction of the *Caroline*. He wrote Fox that a rigid compliance with the terms of the naval agreement could alone accomplish the purposes for which it was intended. Neither side could acquiesce in the other's building or equipping ships "upon the ground of a vague and indefinite apprehension of future danger." The United States could not "consent to any inequality in regard to the strictness with which the Convention of 1817 [was] to be ob-

33. *Ibid.*, F. D. Simms, acting Secretary of the Navy, to Webster, September 23, 1841.

34. *D.S. Br. Legation, Notes to,* VI, 219–221. September 25, 1841.

35. *G,* CCXXVIII, 11–28. Fox to Aberdeen, December 5.

served by the Parties, whether with respect to the amount of naval forces, or the time of its preparation or equipment."[36] Fox's reply stated that the Canadas were still threatened with invasion. It had been "found by experience," he said, "that the efforts of the United States Government, though directed in good faith to suppress those unlawful combinations," had not been "attended with the wished-for success." Consequently the two vessels had had to be equipped to guard the Canadas against attack; and that was their sole purpose.[37]

Informed by Fox on December 5 of the United States protest, Aberdeen let the matter rest until March 31, 1842, by which time negotiations for a settlement of the northeastern boundary were about to get under way. Then he wrote a courteous and friendly letter,[38] pointing out that Webster himself had given warning in the previous September of intended Patriot attacks against British ships, and that he had repeated the warning in December. Four years of filibustering had made necessary the increase of naval strength for the protection of the Canadas. But what of the present and of the future? Aberdeen believed that it was necessary to continue to violate the letter of the agreement, though not its spirit. It would be with the "utmost reluctance" that Great Britain would give notice of termination because the agreement formed, in the estimation of the British government, the cornerstone upon which peace depended in North America, and "which Her Majesty's Government have it so much at heart to maintain unimpaired." Yet it was necessary to keep the enlarged naval force a little longer. He hoped most sincerely that the United States government would see the matter in the same light.

Aberdeen's explanation apparently satisfied the opponents of

36. *D.S. Br. Legation, Notes to,* VI, 223–224. Webster to Fox, November 29. Webster's note to Fox was designed to forestall the recommendations of John C. Spencer, Secretary of War, whose report was presented to Congress on December 1. Said Spencer: "The defenses of the northern frontier . . . must be designed for protection against a powerful enemy, possessing the means of warfare, along a distance of more than 2000 miles. Naval forces on the lakes undoubtedly afford our chief reliance for defense and offense." Harbors should therefore be enlarged and made accessible. Harbors and the "most important of the straits and rivers connecting the lakes should be fortified."

37. *D.S. Br. Legation, Notes from,* XX. Fox to Webster, November 30.

38. *G,* CCXXVIII, 3–10. Aberdeen to Fox.

Tyler and Webster, as well as the President and Secretary of State themselves. At any rate, Fox reported[39] that the United States would probably make no further objections. That country was "extremely anxious that the Convention of 1817 should not be formally renounced or cancelled. . . ." Cancellation would force the United States to enter into competitive building, the expense of which they wished to be spared. Another significant reason was that Lord Ashburton was expected to arrive before long to negotiate a friendly agreement which would settle the northeastern boundary and other outstanding questions. The $100,000 appropriation of the previous September had never actually to be used for the purpose for which it was intended.

As 1842 passed, interest in defense began to lag on both sides of the border. The expansion of the United States military defenses in 1841 to include Lakes Erie and Ontario in addition to Lake Champlain, an equivalent move by the British in the same year, and competitive building of armed ships without abrogation of the Rush Bagot agreement did not materialize. The satisfactory conclusion of the McLeod case, and the northeastern-boundary settlement achieved some months later by Webster and Ashburton, removed the necessity of military and naval preparedness along the border. Toward the end of 1842 the United States Army was reduced to 7,590; British soldiers began to be withdrawn from the Canadas; repairs already begun on frontier posts were not all completed, and within four years many of the posts ceased to be kept in repair.

39. *G*, CCXXVIII, 1–2. Fox to Bagot, April 20, 1842.

CHAPTER XI

THE WEBSTER ASHBURTON TREATY

BOUNDARIES

BY 1842 a comprehensive settlement of outstanding disputes between Great Britain and the United States was badly needed. Since 1783 it had been impossible for the two countries to come to an agreement over the northeastern boundary, which included not only the boundary between Maine and New Brunswick but also the line from the head of the Connecticut River to the St. Lawrence. Navigation rights on the St. Lawrence had not been determined in the case of all parts of the river where it formed the international boundary. The line from Lake Superior to the Lake of the Woods had never been agreed upon. Since 1807 there had been no means of securing a mutual extradition of criminals. The diplomatic impasse over the *Caroline* had never been resolved. There had developed a sharp controversy over the African slave trade, over visit and search, and over impressment. The status of the Oregon territory from thirty-two degrees to fifty-four degrees forty minutes remained to be settled.

By one of those fortuitous circumstances, relatively infrequent in the history of modern national states, in 1841, there came into power in both Washington and London governments which were kindly disposed toward liquidating by agreement all sources of conflict between them. The faltering Melbourne and the truculent Palmerston gave way to the more energetic Peel and the conciliatory Aberdeen, while the cautious Van Buren and the Anglophobe Forsyth were replaced by the more forceful Tyler and the Anglophile Webster. Under these circumstances, on December 27 Edward Everett, who had replaced the inept Andrew Stevenson as minister at the Court of St. James, was informed by Aberdeen that Alexander Baring, Viscount Ashburton, would proceed to Washington in the spring to enter into negotiations, unhampered by minute and restrictive instructions, for the settlement of all controversies between the two countries. The following month Webster wrote that Ashburton would meet with a

similar gesture of good will from the United States government.[1]
The way was thus opened for negotiations.

A few days after his arrival in Washington, Ashburton confided to
Sir Charles Bagot, the governor general of Canada, the principles
upon which he expected to act in negotiating a treaty. He said:

> With respect to this question of Boundaries, I need hardly observe that
> my task here is not an easy one. I have to deal with a critical & jealous
> public and I hold it to be important on this and all other objects of my
> negotiations here to make such a settlement as shall satisfy the honor-
> able and reasonable portion of it. . . . No slight advantages to be de-
> rived from contrivance & cunning can for a moment be placed in com-
> parison with those to be derived from having as a result of my negotia-
> tions a reciprocal feeling of respect & harmony. But at the same time
> that I venture to recommend this to be kept in mind in determining all
> pretentions & claims, you may rely on my zealous defense of all the
> really important interests of our Country. It is indeed for the purpose
> of satisfying myself as to what is really important in the matters con-
> nected with your Government that I am induced to trouble you with this
> letter.[2]

To discover how Lord Ashburton actually defended "all the really
important interests" of Great Britain, it is necessary first to discover
what these interests were considered to be. Ever since the St. Lawrence area had begun to supersede the Maritime Provinces in importance, the British government had for military reasons placed increasing emphasis upon keeping open communications between the
Atlantic seaboard and Montreal at all times of the year. To achieve
that purpose it appeared to be a matter of military necessity to control the northern and western part of the territory in dispute between Maine and New Brunswick. This became a cardinal point in
the British program for the defense of Canada, a point, moreover,
which was well understood in the United States.[3]

The defense of Canada itself, as has been shown, brought to light

1. C. A. Duniway, "Daniel Webster," S. F. Bemis, ed., *The American
Secretaries of State and Their Diplomacy* (New York, 1928), V, 18, n. 33.

2. *Bagot Papers*, II, Pt. 1, 169–179. April 16, 1842.

3. *Stevenson Papers*, XIV, 28452–28454. Benjamin C. Howard to Andrew
Stevenson, May 30, 1839.

two conflicting plans, one to concentrate upon the defense of Montreal by building a series of fortifications around it and by controlling the northern end of Lake Champlain, and the other to distribute
posts and troops from Montreal to Niagara with subsidiary units
west of that point. Acceptance of the second plan by the War Office
in 1841 definitely reduced the importance of attempting to control
Lake Champlain. By 1842 it was admitted that the defense of Canada
did not depend upon the security of Montreal alone, but rather upon
the defense of a number of strategically situated points in addition
to Montreal. From the military point of view therefore—and this
was the most important single consideration involved in the settlement of the northeastern boundary—a British-built road through
the disputed territory, safeguarded by its distance from the United
States, promised to be a more significant factor in the defense of
Canada than control of the Lake Champlain approach.

The United States, on the contrary, had no interest in the disputed territory between Maine and New Brunswick for military purposes, but it did have an increasingly strong interest in retaining
control over the northern end of Lake Champlain from which point
the way to Montreal would lie open.[4] Here, as has been said, at
Rouses Point, north of the forty-fifth parallel, it had erected a fort
at a cost of about $1,000,000.[5] Since it was universally conceded that
Rouses Point was a strategic center of the first importance, the
United States government became acutely interested in retaining
control of that point.

The dispute over Rouses Point need never have occurred had it
not been that between 1771 and 1774 the line of forty-five degrees
from the Connecticut River to the St. Lawrence had been incorrectly
surveyed by the official surveyors, Valentine and Collins. Again to
repeat, upon a resurvey in 1818 by British and American surveyors
acting under the commission appointed according to the terms of the

4. *The Works of Daniel Webster* (Boston, 1853), V, 109–113. These
opinions were expressed in Webster's speech in the Senate, in 1846, in defense of the treaty.

5. *Treaties and Other International Acts of the United States of America,*
ed. by Hunter Miller, IV, 382. By the treaty of 1783 it was agreed that the
forty-fifth parallel should form the boundary from the northwesternmost
head of the Connecticut River to the St. Lawrence.

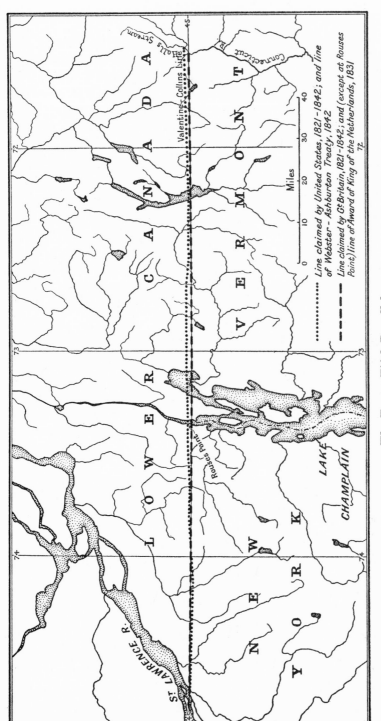

Miles

Line claimed by United States, 1821–1842; and line
········ of Webster–Ashburton Treaty, 1842

Line claimed by G.ᵗBritain, 1821–1842; and (except at Rouses
─ ─ ─ Point) line of Award of King of the Netherlands, 1831

The Forty-Fifth Parallel

Treaty of Ghent, the true line was found to be almost wholly to the south of the old "Valentine and Collins line." Meanwhile settlers had occupied land and lived under the respective jurisdictions of Great Britain and the United States; and the United States had erected the fort at Rouses Point about a quarter of a mile north of the correct line. Altogether some sixty-one square miles were in dispute in this area.

Immediately to the east, controversy developed over what was known as the Indian Stream country or the Connecticut Settlements. The treaty of 1783 had provided that the boundary should be the Connecticut River from its "northwesternmost head" to the forty-fifth parallel. The determination of this depended upon the choice of one of several heads as the proper source of the Connecticut. The United States claimed that Hall's Stream, the most westerly branch which joined the main river somewhat below the forty-fifth parallel, was the one intended by the treaty, whereas the British claimed that a more easterly branch, or Indian Stream, was the stipulated source of the river. Between Hall's and Indian Stream lay an area of some 150 square miles over which, from time to time, there had been jurisdictional disputes.[6]

When Ashburton sailed from England he carried with him instructions that left him a comparatively free hand in his negotiations with Webster.[7] From the tenor of his instructions and his early correspondence with Bagot, it is clear that he was authorized to bargain for a reasonable settlement of the Maine–New Brunswick boundary on the basis of the award of the King of the Netherlands in 1831 or some similar line. The consideration he was enabled to offer included the Indian Stream country and the Valentine and Collins line. Instructions dated March 31, which he received some time after his arrival in Washington, tended to limit his discretionary powers with respect to the Maine–New Brunswick line but provided him definitely with bargaining power.[8]

6. For the dispute of 1835, see *G*, CCXXIII; *Q*, CCXXIII and CCXXVI, and lengthy correspondence in the Archives of the Department of State.

7. E. D. Adams, "Lord Ashburton and the Treaty of Washington," *American Historical Review*, XVII (July, 1912), 768.

8. *Ibid.*, pp. 768–770, which gives these instructions in full. By the award of the King of the Netherlands, Indian Stream was taken to be the source of

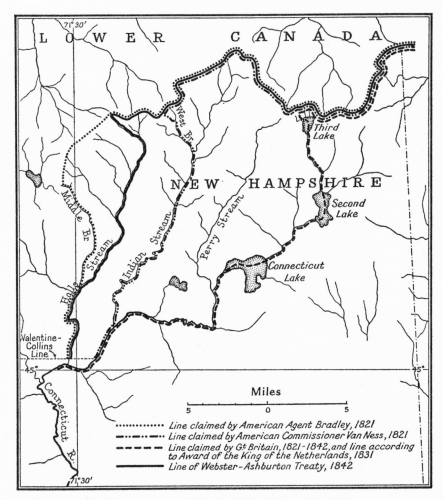

Northwesternmost Head of the Connecticut River

To be certain of the value of the territories which it was proposed to use for bargaining purposes and to be certain of the official Cana-

the Connecticut River. The true 45th parallel was admitted as the boundary, but as a compromise measure Rouses Point was granted to the United States. Though Great Britain and the United States both refused to accept the award, the fact that it had been favorable to the British contentions in these two cases established a presumption in favor of Great Britain and increased the value of these areas for bargaining purposes. So Ashburton believed.

dian attitude toward the propriety of giving up these areas or the necessity of retaining them, Ashburton asked Bagot on April 16 whether recognition of British claims should be insisted upon because of the intrinsic importance of the areas to Canada or whether they might not "be more usefully used as a make weight in other parts of our settlement." Continuing, he remarked,

I presume the land is appropriated & settled. If the occupiers have been there for a length of time, have always considered themselves as belonging to the States, and that from habit, connexions and interest they have a preference to that Jurisdiction I can see no advantage in endeavouring forcibly to acquire for Her Majesty, however good may be her strict title to them, a number of reluctant subjects who would only contribute to swell the number of the disaffected.

Should the case "be a simple one an answer will sufficiently serve my purpose, but should the facts and interests connected with them prove complicated you may perhaps be able to send me here some person with proper maps & plans for my instruction."[9]

Bagot was by no means loath to assist Ashburton to turn the negotiations to the British advantage in New Brunswick. In reply he dispatched a copy of a printed report on the Indian Stream area as well as a copy of a memorandum on the forty-fifth parallel drawn up by one A. Wells, a British deputy surveyor, who had been one of the surveyors officially employed by the Commission in 1818. From Wells's report it appeared that many American settlers were now living immediately to the north of the true line. Bagot therefore concluded that they would not be happy to become British subjects "and they would certainly add very little to the strength or security of our possessions in that part of Canada. But their very reluctance would give us a better chance of turning the concession of our extreme rights on this point to advantage in the negotiation of other points which would require a concession of extreme rights from the Americans."[10]

Ashburton found this information insufficient for his purposes in

9. *Bagot Papers,* II, Pt. 1, 169–179.
10. *Ibid.,* IV, 175–182. Bagot to Ashburton, May 5. For Bagot's correspondence with the quartermaster general's department, see *C,* DCLXXV, 259–260, 261.

view of the fact that the United States government not only had better information but could also call upon its surveyors for advice. He therefore asked Bagot to send Wells to Washington with maps, reports, and other relevant information. He particularly hoped that Wells would arrive in Washington before the end of May, because if the remainder of the treaty were ready for signature by that time he might "find it necessary to conclude while my adversary is in the mood, and while Congress is still sitting, without waiting for all the detailed information which under other circumstances I should require."[11] But owing to various delays in Canada, Wells could not get away until June 5.[12]

Negotiations over the Maine–New Brunswick boundary had meanwhile bogged down because of the necessity with which Webster was faced of securing the consent of Maine to a compromise settlement. This delay gave Ashburton an opportunity to consult Wells before formally proposing a definite boundary to Webster in his note of June 21.[13] In return for a line which would safeguard British military communications in the east, Ashburton was willing to agree to free navigation of the St. John River for all American forest products, to accept Hall's Stream as the source of the Connecticut River, and to agree to the Valentine and Collins line from the Connecticut to the St. Lawrence.

These were by no means the only concessions which Ashburton made. Two weeks before the treaty was signed he confided to Bagot:[14]

I tried hard but in vain for the boundary of the Upper St. John & the object of the present line, for which I have made greater sacrifices than

11. *Bagot Papers,* II, Pt. 1, 258–264. Ashburton to Bagot, May 11.

12. *Ibid.,* IV, 241–247. Bagot to Ashburton, June 5.

13. Ashburton's first formal note on boundaries was written on June 13. It did not contain any precise proposals. The note on June 21 was written three days after a formal conference between the two negotiators. Miller, *Treaties,* IV, 386. The treaty provided that, starting with the source of the St. Croix River, the boundary between Maine and New Brunswick should run northward to the St. John, thence along that river to the mouth of the St. Francis whence it was to follow a southwesterly direction to the 45th parallel. Of the total area in dispute (about 12,000 square miles), Great Britain received about five twelfths and the United States seven twelfths.

14. *Bagot Papers,* II, Pt. 2, 454–458. Ashburton to Bagot, July 26, Private.

the thing is worth, is to satisfy certain Military Critics by bringing the Americans from off the Crest of the highlands which overlook the valley of the St. Lawrence so as to give us the command of those heights.

For this I give up the right to float the produce of that part of Maine on the tributaries of the St. Johns [*sic*] down that river. I also consent to the *Old* boundary on the 49th [*sic*] Parallel of Latitude & give up the heads of the Connecticut river as also a certain Island in Lake Superior called St. Georges Island[15] and I take a medium line of compromise between Lake Superior and Lac La Pluie [Rainy Lake]. On the other hand I have stipulated for the free passage for our vessels through the American channel in Lake St. Clair and by the long Sault & Barnharte Island in the St. Lawrence. This last point Mr. Wells tells me is of some importance.

In defense of the treaty he remarked: "For my own part what seems most important is that there should be a settlement of some sort, and I do not attach all the importance which some do to the precise terms."

Defense of the treaty both in the United States and England, where it was referred to as "Ashburton's Capitulation," did nevertheless involve a defense of the "precise terms." Granted that the cession of the forty-fifth parallel and the Indian Stream country was "considered [in Canada] as doing no injury whatever to Canada,"[16] and that free navigation of the St. John River for forest and unmanufactured agricultural products was not injurious to New Brunswick, what of the cession of Sugar Island to the United States and what of the treaty line from Lake Superior to the Lake of the Woods?

Of these two, Sugar Island, with an area of forty square miles wholly fertile, was in Ashburton's mind "the only object of any real value in this controversy." This island he was willing to cede providing concessions should be made in turn, concessions which could not be asked for in 1818 or thereafter because Great Britain was unwilling to cede Sugar Island. It was accordingly arranged that the British should enjoy freedom of navigation in the American channels in the St. Clair and Detroit rivers and in the vicinity of Barnhart Island and the Long Sault in the St. Lawrence. Reciprocal freedom

15. The present Sugar Island in St. Marys River between Lake Huron and Lake Superior.

16. *G*, CCXXVIII, 121–150. Ashburton to Aberdeen, August 9.

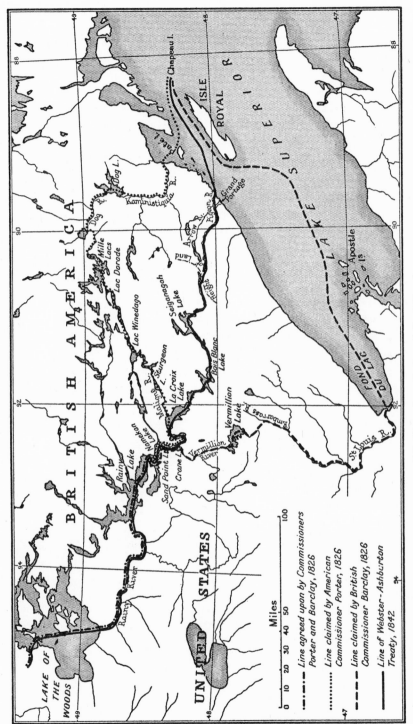

Isle Royal to Lake of the Woods

of navigation in Canadian channels was conceded to the United States.[17]

The determination of the line westward from Lake Superior presumably gave Ashburton less trouble. A compromise line, weighted in favor of the United States, it was one of the few agreements not dependent upon a *quid pro quo*. Ashburton professed to believe that the triangular area of 6,500 square miles, bounded on the north by the Pigeon River and on the south by the line from Fond du Lac up the St. Louis River, was "wild country," that it was of "little importance to either party" how the line should be run from Lake Superior to the Lake of the Woods, but that it was "important that some line should be fixed and determined."[18] This sounds naïve enough when one considers the presidential message[19] written by Webster, which accompanied the treaty to the Senate a few days later. In that document it was expressly stated that this area was "considered valuable as a mineral region," whereas the territory north of the Pigeon River, the boundary agreed upon, was "described by surveyors, and marked on the map, as a region of rock and water." Why Ashburton was led to believe that the Mesabi Range, known to be rich in iron ores, was nothing but waste is a mystery. At any rate, he deliberately chose to accept as the boundary an easily marked compromise line north of the iron region.

From the point of view of Canadian interests, the boundary settlements of the treaty represent a strange paradox. The very region which it was designed to protect more adequately by safeguarding military communications from Halifax to Quebec was the region which was required to pay for that protection through the cession of a strategic point on Lake Champlain and of immensely more valuable iron-ore resources beyond Lake Superior. What was gained in territory in New Brunswick and what was thereby gained in making Canada more defensible was offset by considerable cessions elsewhere. From the point of view of the United States all its essential interests were maintained intact. The retention of less territory in Maine than

17. *Works of Daniel Webster,* VI, 279–282, 282–288. This gives letters from Ashburton to Webster, July 16, and from Webster to Ashburton, July 27.

18. *Ibid.,* VI, 280.

19. Richardson, *Messages,* IV, 160–169.

was anticipated was more than made up for by the grant of free navigation rights on the St. John River, the cession of Indian Stream, and for strategic purposes the cession of Rouses Point.[20] The immense importance of the line from Lake Superior to Rainy Lake and the Lake of the Woods remained to be discovered in the future.

EXTRADITION

Whereas Canada was dragged into the dispute over the northeastern boundary, disputes over the extradition of criminals were centered in the St. Lawrence Valley because of the ease with which fugitives were able to cross the border from one national political jurisdiction to the other. The escape of criminals was rendered easier by the fact that the extradition clause (Article 27) of the Jay Treaty had expired on October 28, 1807. Extradition of fugitives could not after that date be demanded as a right; it could only be requested as a favor. Even though enabling legislation was passed in New York in 1822 and succeeding years and in Upper Canada in 1833, and even though the governor of Lower Canada was regarded as possessing powers inherent in the Crown, jurisdictional disputes effectively prevented mutual extradition by Canadian and United States authorities throughout the 1830's.[21]

That there was urgent need for an extradition treaty after 1830 there is no reason to doubt. Murderers, forgers, deserters, and others frequently fled abroad. Slaves accused of felony also escaped to Canada. The United States and most border-state governments made no provision for giving up fugitives to the British.[22] Although the

20. It was argued with great vehemence by the defenders of the treaty that Rouses Point far outweighed in military importance to the United States any territory ceded to Great Britain. See *Works of Daniel Webster*, V, 109–112.

21. In 1821 Lord Dalhousie, governor of Lower Canada, complied with the request of De Witt Clinton, governor of New York, for the surrender of a forger who had fled into Lower Canada. Shortly after, at Clinton's request, the New York legislature passed a statute which authorized the governor to extradite at the request of a foreign government. The statute was reënacted a number of times. *D.S. Dom. Letters*, XXX, 421–428. Forsyth to J. C. Spencer, August 7, 1839.

22. In 1831, Roger B. Taney, United States Attorney General, gave it as

Canadian and the New York governors had the authority, they commonly based their refusal to extradite on some technical ground. For example, in 1831 Governor Aylmer of Lower Canada refused to give up three persons upon request of Edward Livingston, Secretary of State, because the affidavits accompanying the request did not affirm that the men were American citizens.[23] In the following year Governor Throop of New York refused to give up three deserters charged with felony on the ground that desertion was not recognized as an extraditable offense in the statute under whose authority he exercised discretionary powers.[24]

This particular case was significant because of the many issues which it presented. Recognizing that neither sympathy nor authority existed anywhere in the United States for the extradition of deserters, Aylmer went to great pains to state that the three men would be tried by a civil court for felonies committed. Livingston, through whom the request was transmitted, also went to some pains to suggest that Throop give the men up if it were at all possible to do so under his statutory authority, in the interest of "the cause of justice" and of promoting "the amicable relations, which exist between the United States and Great Britain." In his reply, Throop quoted relevant parts of the New York statute. He pointed out that evidence of guilt accompanying the request was insufficient, that even if it were, the crimes with which the men were charged were "connected with and subordinate to a greater one, desertion," for which the statute did not provide. Furthermore, since the State of New York had no power to negotiate directly with a foreign government, it might, Throop said, "be improper for it to take any pledge" that offenders would be tried only for those offenses for which they were expressly given up. Here Throop was suggesting a *caveat* in case more adequate proof of guilt of felony should be presented at a later time. At this point, Throop entered a complaint and made a suggestion. Since no au-

his opinion that "the President would not be justified in directing the surrender" of accused persons in the absence of a treaty or agreement. *D.S. Misc. Letters,* Taney to Secretary of State, August 4, 1831.

23. *Ibid.,* Aylmer to Livingston, August 26, 1831.

24. For correspondence, see *D.S. Br. Legation, Notes from,* XVI, Bankhead to Livingston, May 31, 1832; *D.S. Dom. Letters,* XXV, Livingston to Throop, June 1 and 15; *D.S. Misc. Letters,* Throop to Livingston, July 3.

thority existed at that moment in the Canadian provinces equivalent to that conferred by statute upon the New York governor, Throop observed that his requests for the extradition of criminals as a matter of courtesy had met with rebuffs. He had accordingly ceased asking favors of the Canadian governors. In view of this highly unsatisfactory situation he urged that "some arrangement" be made for the mutual extradition of criminals.

For the next few years both the Canadian and the United States authorities ceased making requests of each other. But in the years from 1837 to 1842 the confused state of affairs along the frontier brought a new crop of requests for the extradition of criminals. The first of these involved William Lyon Mackenzie who had escaped from Upper Canada to Buffalo, and whose return Sir Francis Bond Head, the lieutenant governor of Upper Canada, requested of Governor Marcy of New York in December, 1837. After due consideration[25] Marcy refused to give Mackenzie up on the ground that "the offences charged against [him], being incidents of the revolt, were merged in the higher crime imputed to him of treason—a political offence, excepted by our laws from those for which fugitives can be surrendered by the Executive."[26] Marcy's refusal was fraught with important consequences. It put an end to requests by the Canadian authorities for the return of political refugees who had found sanctuary in the United States.

To the refusal to give up deserters and political refugees there were added in 1839 refusals to give up any persons for any reasons whatever—and this at a period when incendiarism, destruction of property, and raids by Hunters and others were making it difficult for the Canadian authorities to prevent retaliation against the border states, and against Vermont in particular. Matters came to a head when, in January and February, 1839, Sir John Colborne made three different applications to Governor Jenison of Vermont for the extradition of incendiaries who had attacked the village of Caldwell's Manor on December 30, 1838, of those who had assaulted Abraham Vosburg and his family on February 3, 1839, and of Dr.

25. *Marcy Papers,* III, 32875. Marcy to General P. M. Wetmore, December 22, 1837. "This is a pretty business which requires much time to consider."

26. *Albany Argus,* quoted in *Observer* (New York), December 30, 1837.

George Holmes who had fled to Vermont after murdering Achille Taché.[27] Although Jenison was favorably inclined toward giving up all the persons named, whom he had taken into custody, he decided to ascertain where jurisdiction lay before arriving at a decision.

First, he discovered that the United States government would assume no responsibility. Forsyth's carefully considered statement of January 22 said that since the expiration of Article 27 of the Jay Treaty "the two Governments have uniformly declined complying with the demand repeatedly made by each upon the other for the reciprocal surrender of fugitives; and no authority consequently exists to justify the interference of the United States' Government in such cases." If, however, the case of those who fired Caldwell's Manor involved the violation of United States laws, he would expect Jenison to investigate it.[28] Second, Jenison came to the conclusion that as governor of Vermont he possessed no power, in the absence of statutory authority, to give the men up.[29] In April, he advanced to the position that he could not give up persons accused of crimes committed as a consequence of political disturbances in the Canadas.[30] Finally, in the case of Holmes, who had murdered his paramour's husband, the United States Supreme Court admitted that the governor of Vermont had no authority to order extradition.[31] It was clear at length that the governor of a state, in the absence of a statute, had no right to give up fugitives.

The powers of the President were made equally clear. Forsyth insisted that in the absence of a treaty or agreement the President not only had no obligation but positively had no power whatever to extradite. This position he adhered to most vigorously in the face of a sharp correspondence with Governor Seward of New York, who, with what would seem to have been malice aforethought, sought to bedevil Forsyth and Van Buren with legal niceties concerning the

27. *Q,* CCLVII, 64–66. Enclosure in Colborne to Glenelg, January 15, 1839; *ibid.,* CCLVII, 207–208. Colborne to Jenison, February 4; also correspondence in the Archives of the Department of State. Fox also applied to Forsyth for assistance on February 15 and March 18. *D.S. Br. Legation, Notes from,* XIX.

28. *D.S. Dom. Letters,* XXXI, 134.

29. *D.S. Misc. Letters,* Jenison to Colborne, February 6, 1839.

30. *Q,* CCLIX, 322–324. Jenison to Colborne, April 19, 1839.

31. 14 *Peters* 540–598 (1840).

relative powers of the President and the governor of New York. A request by Sir George Arthur in June, 1839, for the extradition of Benjamin Lett, a murderer, led Seward to inform Forsyth that, while he was anxious to prevent the United States from becoming a refuge for felons, he regarded extradition as coming within the scope of foreign relations, and hence exclusively within the jurisdiction of the national government. Seward refused to exercise the powers conferred upon him by statute until he was ordered by the President to deliver Lett to a Canadian officer. He expected that in this manner "the boundaries between the powers of the Federal Government and those of the States can be maintained, while the laws of this State may be executed, justice may be obtained, and the just demands of a friendly nation fully answered."[32] Correspondence between Seward and Forsyth and between Seward and Van Buren became very lively, until it was terminated by Forsyth who insisted that the President possessed no power to give up fugitives and that further communication on the subject would be fruitless so long as Seward continued to maintain an erroneous position.[33]

Such an impasse, in view of the seriousness of the border situation, clearly required a remedy, and Forsyth was not averse to securing it. Already on March 20 he had acquainted Fox with the willingness of the United States government to open negotiations for an extradition convention. "Under the present pressing circumstances," he said, he anticipated no serious difficulty in coming to an agreement.[34]

Exactly five months went by before Fox communicated the contents of Forsyth's letter to Palmerston. Convinced by that time that there was positively no likelihood of extradition by federal or state authorities of persons claimed by the Canadian governors, and impressed by Sir George Arthur with the need for "some understanding,"[35] Fox reported Forsyth's willingness to negotiate a treaty which would provide for extradition upon the demand of any government, whether provincial, state, or national.[36] But he himself re-

32. *D.S. Misc. Letters*, J. C. Spencer, Secretary of State, of New York, to Forsyth, June 10, 1839.
33. *D.S. Dom. Letters*, XXX, 421–428. Forsyth to Spencer, August 7.
34. *D.S. Br. Legation, Notes to*, VI, 107–109.
35. *G*, CCXLI, 43–44. Arthur to Fox, July 29, 1839.
36. *G*, CCXXV, 286–308. Fox to Palmerston, August 20.

mained unconvinced of the advisability of securing a treaty at a time when border turmoil was continuing, and when the United States was finding it impossible to punish offenders against its own laws. So long as the conflict over jurisdictional rights between the state and federal governments continued, British demands for the extradition of fugitives would not be granted. Any treaty would accordingly be heavily weighted in favor of the United States. Fox also warned against allowing extradition proceedings to be based upon hearings before local magistrates or juries; he warned against possible demands for the persons who destroyed the *Caroline;* and he warned against making any provision for giving up runaway slaves.

If Fox was opposed to securing an agreement with the United States, it was not so with Palmerston who, upon the receipt of Fox's dispatch, immediately set about preparing a draft treaty which could be used as a basis for discussion by the two governments. On two matters Palmerston remained adamant, and so did his successor Aberdeen: they would not agree to the extradition of runaway or criminal slaves, or of those who, like the members of the expedition against the *Caroline,* "acted in execution of orders, from their own Government."[37] Not only did Palmerston take an active part in the preparation of the draft treaty himself—the first was completed on October 29—but he asked for and received Lord John Russell's advice, that of the Attorney General, and the Solicitor General, and John Beverley Robinson, chief justice of Upper Canada, who was attempting to regain his health through a winter's sojourn in England. Robinson was of considerable assistance, for he had grown up in a frontier society and knew and understood the types of crimes which were committed in that kind of community.

When, at length, the final draft[38] was ready to be sent to Fox on April 27, 1840, for presentation to Forsyth, it provided for (1) the mutual extradition of British subjects and United States citizens— but not of "all persons," as had been hoped for in the United States —who were accused of murder, malicious maiming of the person, assault with intent to murder or maim, rape, burglary, arson, burning of boats and vessels of any description, and forgery. Such persons were to be given up on demand of the governors in British North

37. *G,* CVIII, 289–292. Strangways to Stephen, September 12.
38. *G,* CCLII, 95–96. Palmerston to Fox, April 27, 1840.

America or of the United States government. Upon being extradited accused persons were to be tried by ordinary judicial process. (2) Military deserters were to be given up in the same manner. (3) The treaty could be terminated after six months' notice by either party.

In Washington, in the face of Arthur's pressure for a treaty,[39] Fox kept Palmerston's proposals for three months before presenting them to Forsyth, on August 12.[40] He was convinced that so long as the Van Buren administration remained in office, no agreement would be secured which would meet the legitimate demands of both parties.[41]

Informal conversations between minister and Secretary of State elucidated the demands of the United States which Great Britain was unwilling to recognize, namely, the extradition of runaway slaves and of "all persons" regardless of their nationality or citizenship. It is no wonder that the draft convention was laid aside for eighteen months—that is, until Lord Ashburton arrived in the United States.

During these intervening months, as a consequence of a change of administration in Washington, final efforts were made to provide for mutual extradition, without benefit of treaty. The process was facilitated by Sydenham who, in May, 1841, voluntarily gave up Charles F. Mitchell, a forger, on a request from Seward.[42] In August the tables were turned when Sydenham asked Seward for the surrender of one John DeWitt.[43] Seward turned to Webster in Washington.[44] Referring to the Supreme Court decision in the case of Dr. George Holmes, whereby the governor of Vermont was inhibited from turning him over to the governor of Lower Canada, Seward requested presidential authorization to exercise the power conferred upon him by state law. Owing to Seward's importunities, and without waiting for an opinion from the Attorney General, Webster replied that he would be glad to have Seward exercise his statutory powers.[45] Sew-

39. *G,* CCXLI, 66–70. Arthur to Fox, May 5, insisting upon the utter necessity of a treaty, and referring to his letter to Fox on September 27, 1839. This contained a statesmanlike analysis of the situation. *G,* CCXLI, 50–53.

40. *D.S. Br. Legation, Notes from,* XX.

41. *G,* CCXXVI, 527–532. Fox to Thomson, September 10, 1840.

42. *D.S. Misc. Letters,* Sydenham to Seward, May 14, 1841.

43. *Ibid.,* Sydenham to Seward, August 19.

44. *Ibid.,* Seward to Webster, September 6.

45. *D.S. Dom. Letters,* XXXII, 41. Webster to Seward, September 16.

ard thereupon gave DeWitt up. But this arrangement was not a lasting one. The Attorney General advised Webster that neither the federal government nor the states possessed the right to order the delivery of fugitives.[46]

In British North America an impasse was slower in developing, but one came to a head in the spring of 1842. On March 1 there was sent to the colonial governors a circular of instructions which effectively prevented them from exercising any discretion in the matter of giving up fugitives to federal or state authorities. The governors were required to refer each case to the Colonial Office for review and decision.[47] To transfer the authority to London in this manner clearly aggravated the situation, for it would delay considerably, if indeed it would not wholly prevent, the final settlement of cases.

Fortunately a remedy lay not far in the future, for among the matters which Lord Ashburton was authorized to settle, extradition was regarded as important, although of lesser consequence than the northeastern boundary. In the negotiations which followed Webster took the lead by proposing that Article 27 of the Jay Treaty should be revised, and he submitted a revision drawn up by Judge Story.[48] This revised article set forth a large number of extraditable crimes as well as a specific procedure which was designed to prevent disputes between the Executive and the judiciary in the United States concerning their relative spheres of authority in extradition cases.[49]

From Ashburton's point of view the matter of greatest importance was to discover what procedure had been followed in Canada and the United States when requests for extradition had been made, and what crimes should be included in a treaty. As he had relied on Bagot for information concerning the boundary, so he relied on Bagot

46. *D.S. Misc. Letters,* H. S. Legare to Webster, October 11. Legare suggested that Congress be requested to pass an act authorizing individual states to make direct arrangements with foreign states for extradition. Previously Webster had been given some assurance that the Senate would view with favor an attempt to secure a treaty with Great Britain. *Webster Papers,* VI, 16525–16526. William Woodbridge to Webster, June 6, 1841.

47. *Bagot Papers,* VI, 416. Bagot to Stanley, May 28, 1842.

48. *G,* CXIV, 101–107. Ashburton to Aberdeen, April 28, 1842.

49. *G,* CXIV, 108–111.

now.[50] Bagot's reply,[51] based upon a specially prepared memorandum, recommended the inclusion in a revised treaty of just three crimes: murder, attempt to murder, and arson. There could be no objection, he believed, to the inclusion of larceny, forgery, and counterfeiting, all of which, unimportant for Canada, were important for the United States, and likely to be recommended for inclusion by that country. As for military desertion, Bagot urged its inclusion because of the numerous desertions, amounting to 10 per cent of the whole force, which occurred each year. In the matter of procedure, demand should be made only by the federal, state or provincial governments.

In the negotiations[52] which followed, there was no bargaining, no jockeying for position. Both Webster and Ashburton were anxious to secure a reasonable agreement attuned to the everyday needs of both the United States and Canada. Yet, while agreement on the inclusion of crimes such as murder was easily arrived at, they found it impossible to include desertion, runaway slaves, burglary and theft, and mutiny and revolt. Of these four, desertion, like political offenses, was omitted because of the summary method of trial and severe punishment accorded to deserters. The other three revolved around the status of slaves who had escaped into British territory where slavery had been abolished. Not only did Ashburton refuse to include provision for the return of runaway slaves but to make doubly certain that no demands could be made for the return of slaves, charged with theft of the clothes they were wearing at the time of their escape, burglary and theft were omitted also. Mutiny and revolt were likewise stricken out for fear that slaves, like those involved in the case of the *Creole*,[53] would have to be given up. As finally drafted, the agreement provided for the surrender of *all* persons, not merely of

50. *Bagot Papers,* II, Pt. 1, 169–179. Ashburton to Bagot, April 16, 1842, Private.

51. *Ibid.,* IV, 175–182. May, 1842.

52. For correspondence between Ashburton and Aberdeen, see *G,* CXIV, *passim.*

53. On November 7, 1841, slaves who were being transported from Hampton Roads to New Orleans on the American brig *Creole* mutinied, killed one of the owners, and forced the mate to put in at Nassau in the Bahamas. The British colonial authorities hanged the murderers, but admitted that the slaves were free when they reached British soil.

British subjects and United States citizens, who were charged with murder, assault with murderous intent, piracy, arson, forgery, or utterance of forged paper.

Webster's proposal had provided that upon the receipt of a demand for extradition, the determination of the propriety of giving up an accused person should be left to the courts.[54] Judges and magistrates should have the power to issue warrants for the arrest of fugitives, to determine the evidence of criminality in relation to domestic law, and to surrender criminals or to certify to the proper executive authority that the accused person should be given up.

To this proposal Bagot raised strong objections. He contended that to grant extensive discriminatory powers to ordinary magistrates, of the type to be found along the Canadian border, many of whom were illiterate and ill informed, would defeat the purpose of the treaty. Magistrates might arrest and hold accused persons in custody but only the Executive should be clothed with the authority to determine whether they should be given up.[55]

In the United States, however, it appeared essential to avoid reopening the question of the relative jurisdictional rights of the Executive and the judiciary in extradition cases. The procedure, as proposed by Webster, slightly modified to reduce the discretionary powers of magistrates, was accordingly allowed to stand. The British practice of placing discretion in the hands of the Executive was nevertheless maintained by Aberdeen who admitted that he could find no reason why, in actual practice, Canadian governors should not be invested with the sole authority of surrendering criminals upon demand of the United States government.[56]

The significance of this agreement was immense. Delay in putting it into effect, because of the necessity of prior confirmation by Parliament, did not alter the prophetic character of Sir Charles Bagot's

54. In 1797, President John Adams had handed over Thomas Nash, alias Jonathan Robins, to the British authorities. This act provided the Republican party in the election campaign of 1800 with considerable political capital which they turned to good account by accusing Adams of performing an act that lay entirely within the sphere of the judiciary. Cf. A. J. Beveridge, *The Life of John Marshall* (New York, 1916), II, 458–475.

55. *Bagot Papers*, IV, 241–247. Bagot to Ashburton, June 5, 1842; *G,* CXIV, 118–121. Stephen to Addington, June 30.

56. *G,* CXIV, 98–99. Stanley to Bagot, July 7.

words. "If you can succeed," he wrote to Ashburton on July 29, "in making some arrangement by which we may be able reciprocally to give up our own respective delinquents you will have done more for the peace and quiet of These Provinces than I perhaps shall ever be able to do."[57]

The *CAROLINE*

Although the question of boundaries forms the material and most substantial part of the differences which I am expected to settle here, your Lordship is aware that there are other subjects in which the public here take great interest. Of these the case of the Caroline is the principal; it has occupied the public mind for nearly five years, and what is called a *settlement* of it is expected, and indeed without it there is reason to apprehend that there would be a general indisposition to settle anything else.[58] [Ashburton to Aberdeen, July 28, 1842.]

These were no idle words. The failure of the British government to offer an apology or to grant redress for the *Caroline* affair rankled in the minds of Americans and continued to exasperate them. It was substantially for this reason that Alexander McLeod had been arrested, and it was for this reason again that, in March, 1842, J. S. Hogan was arrested twice at Lockport, New York, on charges of murder and arson. Fortunately he had been released each time on technical grounds, a fact which showed that there was a disposition not to press the charges too far. But that Hogan, who had actually been on the *Caroline* expedition, should have, like others, ventured into the United States at all, and that he had been arrested at a time when the federal government remained powerless to intervene, had he been tried, gave Bagot cause for worry. He implored Lord Stanley, the Colonial Secretary, to bring about the settlement of the *Caroline* case without delay, remarking that "so long therefore as the questions involved in this case remain unsettled, it is impossible to say from hour to hour that circumstances may not occur to bring on collision between the two Countries."[59]

57. *Bagot Papers*, V, 36–40.   58. Miller, *Treaties*, IV, 456.
59. *Bagot Papers*, VI, 269–271, 347–349. Bagot to Stanley, March 14 and April 19, 1842. Colonel Allan MacNab, who was honored for giving orders to destroy the *Caroline*, had recently passed through the United States on his way to England, traveling under the name of Colonel Johnstone. Bagot felt

This was the atmosphere in which Webster and Ashburton met. Webster was anxious to secure an unequivocal apology while Ashburton was equally intent upon proving the contention that the British had had, perforce, to act in self-defense. A number of informal conversations took place and correspondence was exchanged until on July 28 Ashburton admitted that,

Looking back to what passed at this distance of time, what is perhaps most to be regretted is that some explanation and apology for this occurrence was not immediately made: this with a frank explanation of the necessity of the case might and probably would have prevented much of the exasperation and of the subsequent complaints and recriminations to which it gave rise.[60]

In Ashburton's view it was even more important to prevent future jurisdictional disputes between federal and state governments in cases similar to McLeod's where the acts of accused aliens were avowed as public acts by their own governments. It became, therefore, of the greatest importance to Ashburton that a Congressional bill should be passed which would provide for the removal of such accused aliens from the jurisdiction of a state court to that of a United States court on a writ of habeas corpus. In fact, he felt so strongly about it that he wrote to Bagot on May 11: "You are aware that this law is indispensable to prevent continued vexatious proceedings against the persons serving their Country in the affair of the *Caroline*, and that there is therefore no possibility of making a settlement of it without it."[61]

It was by no means easy to secure the passage of the bill, particularly in the House where, in addition to considerable opposition to the measure itself, an exceptionally bitter political fight between the President and Congress flared up in the summer of 1842. Fortunately Ashburton was able to assist in speeding up the passage of the bill in an unexpected manner. On the one hand, he held out to

he deserved "to be well scolded for his pains." *Ibid.*, VI, 115–117. Same to same, March 24.

60. Miller, *op. cit.*, IV, 454.

61. *Bagot Papers*, II, Pt. 1, 258–264. Bagot replied that there were few matters concerning which he was more anxious than this bill. He hoped it would be made "as stringent as possible." *Ibid.*, IV, 241–247. June 5.

Congressmen the hope of a satisfactory adjustment of the *Caroline* case. On the other hand, members of Congress who requested Ashburton's intercession with the British government on behalf of the American prisoners who had been transported for life to Van Diemen's Land were met by a firm but determined resistance unless they would push forward the passage of the bill. Ashburton's own statement is most illuminating. Writing to Bagot on the eve of sailing for England, he said:

I had great difficulty in getting this bill to move in the lower house after it passed the Senate but I have the pleasure to tell you that it finally passed by a majority of 9 two days before the session closed [August 29]. I had on several occasions been solicited by members of Congress to intercede about the Van Diemen's Land rebels and I found it convenient to let some of them know that although I could not answer for anything being done, I would not even mention the case unless they passed the McLeod bill, and I believe this course materially determined the passing of the bill.[62]

On August 9 the Webster Ashburton treaty was signed, and eleven days later its ratification was assented to by the Senate by the surprisingly large majority of thirty-nine to nine. In spite of bitter opposition by irreconcilables in Great Britain and the United States,[63] the consequences of the treaty were little short of amazing. As for relations between the United States and Great Britain the removal of certain major sources of irritation made possible that freedom of intercourse in which expression of opinion is not regarded as carping criticism or unwonted "truckling."[64] For British North America, and in particular, for Canada, it meant the cessation of border difficulties, the removal of the danger of war, and an immediate withdrawal of a considerable proportion of the British military forces,

62. *Ibid.*, II, Pt. 2, 252–257. September 3, 1842. Ashburton had been assured before making his "apology" on July 28 that the "McLeod bill" would be passed. Ashburton to Aberdeen, July 28, quoted in Miller, *op. cit.*, IV, 456.

63. For example, Van Buren, Andrew Jackson, and T. H. Benton of Missouri. Cf. *Van Buren Papers*, XLIV, *passim*.

64. *N. Am. Rev.*, LVI (January, 1843), 17–44; and LVI (April, 1843), 412–448.

who were needed for service elsewhere.[65] It meant that naval forces on the Great Lakes would again be reduced to the strength provided for by the Rush Bagot agreement of 1817.[66] It meant that that phase of Canadian-American relations represented by incidents growing out of the Canadian rebellions and of Americans' hope of freeing Canada from Great Britain had definitely come to an end.

65. *G.B. Despatches from,* XLIX, Everett to Webster, September 19, 1842.

66. *G,* CXVI, 135–144. Correspondence between Admiralty, Foreign Office, and Colonial Office in February, 1843, concerning the reduction of armaments on the Great Lakes in accordance with the agreement of 1817.

CONCLUSION

THE year 1842 ended a distinct era in Canadian-American relations. It was an era in which crisis followed crisis in quick succession. Had the American people understood Canadians better, or their form of government and their relations with Great Britain more adequately, it is problematical whether they would have urged the annexation of Canada or have entered so enthusiastically into attempts to free that country from British control. There is no doubt that the British position in North America was at times most distasteful to Americans, for not only did the presence of the British prevent American expansion northward but the presence of British institutions blocked the establishment of the republican form of government in Canada. In fact, this blocking of the northward expansion of both territory and republicanism was, at times, a source of considerable irritation in the United States.

On the other hand, the continuing presence of Britain in North America was highly important for the growth and development of the United States. It contributed to a strengthening of the bonds of union and to the consolidation of the gains made by the westward movement of the American people. Canada stood as a bulwark of the Union in still another sense. As long as it remained British it could not be used as a pawn in the slavery issue. Had it joined the United States it would have thrown out of balance, even more than was already the case, the relations between the free and the slave states. The Missouri Compromise of 1820 might well have been followed some years later by the Canada Compromise.

This is largely speculation. What we do know is that the presence of Britain in North America was immediately responsible for magnifying, as between Canada and the United States, disputes which might never have assumed more than transitory and local significance had Canada been an independent nation. This is particularly true of the period from 1830 to 1842 when, because of Canada's dependence upon Great Britain, controversies between Canada and the United States involved Great Britain and the United States in relations which became tortuous and, in some cases, exceedingly bitter. Thus British-American relations loomed large in the eyes of Americans and their government whereas Canadian-American relations were relegated to a position of secondary importance.

In spite of this trend in the United States a number of circumstances tended to focus the attention of Americans more and more directly upon Canada. This period witnessed a substantial increase in direct negotiation between the public authorities in the two countries. All of the important radical leaders in the two Canadas fled to the United States after the Rebellions and secured there a following which was denied to them at home. Many Canadians began to move by way of the St. Lawrence Valley to the new American West. The very failure of the Patriots to make headway in their several invasions of Canada, together with the obvious intention of Canadians to establish adequate military defenses for protection in the event of war, brought home to Americans the fact that Canada intended to retain its British connections. They also made it clear that Canada intended to pursue an existence independent of the United States.

From this evidence it began to be apparent that if these two nations were to live side by side in North America they must learn to settle their differences by friendly negotiation, and not by war. The discovery and acceptance of this idea at this time by both Canadians and Americans were to be of fundamental importance for the future relations between the two countries. Without such an understanding there could hardly have emerged out of this period of crisis and unrest that substantial foundation upon which the relations between Canada and the United States have endured to the present day.

BIBLIOGRAPHY

I. MANUSCRIPT SOURCES

Public Archives of Canada.
    Series C. Military Papers.
    Series G. Dispatches from the Colonial Office to the Governors.
    Series M. Miscellaneous.
    Series Q. Transcripts from Colonial Office Records.
    Bagot Papers.
    Durham Papers.
Library of Congress.
    John J. Crittenden Papers.
    William L. Marcy Papers.
    Andrew and John W. Stevenson Papers.
    Andrew Stevenson Letterbooks.
    John Tyler Papers.
    Martin Van Buren Papers.
    Daniel Webster Papers.
Department of State.
    Great Britain—Dispatches (from the United States minister in London).
    Great Britain—Instructions (to the United States minister in London).
    Great Britain—Notes (from the British legation).
    Great Britain—Notes to (the British legation).
    Miscellaneous Letters.
    Domestic Letters.
Pennsylvania Historical Society.
    J. R. Poinsett Papers.

II. PRINTED SOURCES

Register of Debates in Congress.
The Congressional Globe.
Journals of the House of Assembly of Upper Canada.
Journals of the House of Assembly of Lower Canada.
Journals of the Legislative Council of Upper Canada.
Journals of the Legislative Assembly of the Province of Canada.
British and Foreign State Papers.
American State Papers.
RICHARDSON, J. D., *comp.* A compilation of the messages and papers of the
    Presidents, 1789–1897. Washington, D.C., 1899. 10 vols.
LINCOLN, C. Z., *ed.* Messages from the governors comprising executive com-
    munications to the legislature and other papers relating to legislation from

the organization of the first colonial assembly in 1683 to and including the
year 1906. Vol. III (1823–42). Albany, N.Y., 1909.

MILLER, HUNTER, ed. Treaties and other international acts of the United
States of America. Washington, D.C., 1931–34. 4 vols.

III. NEWSPAPERS AND PERIODICALS

Albany Argus.
Daily National Intelligencer, Washington, D.C.
The Globe, Washington, D.C.
The New York Journal of Commerce.
New York Commercial Advertiser.
New York Courier and Enquirer.
New York Evening Post (broken files).
New York Observer.
Niles' Weekly Register.
The St. Lawrence Republican, Ogdensburg, N.Y. (rare but nearly complete
  file).
Burlington (Vt.) *Free Press* (rare).
Montpelier (Vt.) *Watchman* (rare).
North Star, Danville, Vt. (rare, broken files).
Vermont Chronicle, Windsor, Vt. (rare, broken files).
Vergennes Vermonter (rare, broken files).
Concord (Vt.) *Freeman* (rare, broken files).
New Hampshire Sentinel, Keene, N.H. (rare, broken files).
The Patriot, Toronto.
The Advocate, Toronto.
Chronicle & Gazette, Kingston.
Montreal Gazette.
Canada Times, Montreal (rare, broken files).
Quebec Gazette.
Cobourg Star (rare, broken files).
Brockville Recorder (rare).
North American Review.
The United States Magazine and Democratic Review.

IV. CONTEMPORARY, NEARLY CONTEMPORARY
WORKS, AND MONOGRAPHS

ADAMS, W. F. Ireland and Irish emigration to the new world from 1815 to
the famine. New Haven, 1923.

BEERS, H. P. The Western military frontier, 1815–1846. Philadelphia, 1935.

BONNEY, Mrs. CATHERINA VAN RENSSELAER, *comp.* A legacy of historical
gleanings. Albany, 1875. 2 vols.

BONNYCASTLE, Sir RICHARD H. Canada, as it was, is, and may be. London, 1852. 2 vols.

CALLAHAN, JAMES MORTON. The Neutrality of the American Lakes and Anglo-American Relations, Johns Hopkins University Studies in Historical and Political Science. Series XVI, Nos. 1–4. Baltimore, 1898.

CHRISTIE, ROBERT. A history of the late province of Lower Canada, parliamentary and political, from the commencement to the close of its existence as a separate province; embracing a period of fifty years, that is to say: from the erection of the province, in 1791, to the extinguishing thereof, in 1841, and its reunion with Upper Canada, by act of the imperial parliament. Quebec, 1848–55. 6 vols.

COWAN, HELEN I. British emigration to British North America, 1783–1837. Toronto, 1928.

CREIGHTON, D. G. The commercial empire of the St. Lawrence, 1760–1850. Toronto and New Haven, 1937.

DENT, JOHN CHARLES. The last forty years. Canada since the Union of 1841. Toronto, 1881. 2 vols.

—— The story of the Upper Canadian Rebellion; largely derived from original sources and documents. Toronto, 1885. 2 vols.

DUNHAM, AILEEN. Political unrest in Upper Canada, 1815–1836. London, 1927.

DUNIWAY, C. A. Daniel Webster. In: American Secretaries of State and their diplomacy, V, 3–67. S. F. Bemis, ed. New York, 1928.

FIDLER, Rev. ISAAC. Observations on professions, literature, manners and emigration in the United States and Canada made during a residence there in 1832. New York, 1833.

FUESS, C. M. Daniel Webster. Boston, 1930. 2 vols.

GUILLET, E. C. The lives and times of the Patriots: an account of the Rebellion in Upper Canada, 1837–38, and the Patriot agitation in the United States, 1837–42. Toronto, 1939.

HEAD, Sir FRANCIS BOND, Bart. A narrative. London, 1839.

HILL, HENRY WAYLAND, ed. Municipality of Buffalo, New York. New York, 1923. 4 vols.

HOUGH, FRANKLIN B. A history of Jefferson County in the state of New York from the earliest period to the present time. Albany, 1854.

—— A history of St. Lawrence and Franklin Counties, New York, from the earliest period to the present time. Albany, 1853.

HUME, G. H. Canada as it is. New York, 1832.

KING, JOHN. The other side of the "Story," being some reviews of Mr. J. C. Dent's first volume of the "Story of the Upper Canadian Rebellion," and the letters in the Mackenzie–Rolph controversy. Also a critique, hitherto unpublished, on "The New Story." Toronto, 1886.

KNAPLUND, PAUL, ed. Letters from Lord Sydenham, Governor-General of Canada, 1839–41, to Lord John Russell. London, 1931.

LINDSEY, CHARLES. The life and times of William Lyon Mackenzie. With an account of the Canadian Rebellion of 1837, and the subsequent frontier disturbances, chiefly from unpublished documents. Toronto, 1862. 2 vols.

LIZARS, ROBINA and KATHLEEN M. Humors of '37 grave, gay and grim. Rebellion times in the Canadas. Toronto, 1897.

MACKENZIE, WILLIAM LYON. Sketches of Canada and the United States. London, 1833.

—— The life and times of Martin Van Buren: the correspondence of his friends, family and pupils; together with brief notices, sketches, and anecdotes. Boston, 1846.

McGRANE, R. C. The panic of 1837. Chicago, 1924.

McLEOD, DONALD. A brief review of the settlement of Upper Canada by the U. E. Loyalists and Scotch Highlanders, in 1783; and of the grievances which compelled the Canadas to have recourse to arms in defense of their rights and liberties, in the years 1837 and 1838; together with a brief sketch of the campaigns of 1812, '13, '14. With an account of the military executions, burnings, sackings of towns and villages by the British, in the Upper and Lower Provinces, during the commotion of 1837 and '38. Cleveland, 1841.

MANSFIELD, EDWARD D. Life and services of General Winfield Scott. New York, 1852.

MARTIN, R. MONTGOMERY. History of Upper and Lower Canada. London, 1836.

MERRITT, J. P. Biography of the Hon. W. H. Merritt, M.P. of Lincoln, district of Niagara, including an account of the origin, progress, and completion of some of the most important public works in Canada. Compiled principally from his original diary and correspondence. St. Catharine's, Ont., 1875.

MOORE, DAVID R. Canada and the United States, 1815–1830. Chicago, 1910.

MURRAY, HUGH. An historical and descriptive account of British America; comprehending Canada, Upper and Lower, Nova Scotia, New Brunswick, Newfoundland, Prince Edward Island, the Bermudas and the fur countries; their history from the earliest settlement; their statistics, topography, commerce, fisheries, etc.; and their social and political condition; as also an account of the manners and present state of the aboriginal tribes. New York, 1840. 2 vols.

NEW, CHESTER W. Lord Durham: A biography of John George Lambton, first Earl of Durham. Oxford, 1929.

PAULLIN, C. O. Atlas of the historical geography of the United States. Wright, J. K., ed. Washington, D.C., 1932.

Peace or war? The question considered with especial reference to the differences existing between the United States of America and Great Britain. By a clergyman of England lately resident in America. London, 1839.

PITKIN, TIMOTHY. A statistical view of the commerce of the United States of

America: including also an account of banks, manufactures, and international trade and improvements: together with that of the revenues and expenditures of the general government: accompanied with numerous tables. New Haven, 1835.

PRESTON, T. R. Three years' residence in Canada, from 1837 to 1839, with notes of a winter voyage to New York, and journey thence to the British possessions: to which is added, a review of the condition of the Canadian people. London, 1840. 2 vols.

ROBINSON, Maj. Gen. C. W. Life of Sir John Beverley Robinson, Bart. Edinburgh, 1914.

—— FAYETTE. An account of the organization of the army of the United States; with biographies of distinguished officers of all grades. Philadelphia, 1848. 2 vols.

ROLPH, THOMAS. A descriptive and statistical account of Canada: showing its great adaptation for British emigration. Preceded by an account of a tour through portions of the West Indies and the United States. 2d ed. London, 1841.

SAINT-PIERRE, TELESPHORE, comp. The Americans and Canada in 1837–38. Authentic documents. Montreal, 1897.

SANSOM, JOSEPH. Sketches of Lower Canada, historical and descriptive; with the author's recollection of the soil, and aspect; the morals, habits, and religious institutions of that isolated country; during a tour to Quebec in the month of July, 1817. New York, 1817.

SAXE-WEIMAR-EISENACH, His Highness BERNHARD, Duke of. Travels through North America, during the years 1825 and 1826. Philadelphia, 1828. 2 vols.

Memoirs of Lieut.-General Scott, LL.D. Written by himself. New York, 1864. 2 vols.

SEVERANCE, FRANK H., ed. Millard Fillmore Papers. In: Buffalo Historical Society Publications, X, XI, 1907.

SHEPARD, EDWARD M. Martin Van Buren. In: American Statesmen, XVIII, John T. Morse, ed. New York, 1899.

SILLIMAN, BENJAMIN. Remarks, made on a tour, between Hartford and Quebec, in the autumn of 1819. New Haven, 1820.

SISSONS, C. B. Egerton Ryerson. His life and letters. Vol. I. Toronto, 1937.

SMITH, G. C. MOORE. The life of John Colborne, Field-Marshal Lord Seaton, compiled from his letters, records of his conversations, and other sources. London, 1903.

SPROUT, HAROLD and MARGARET. The rise of American naval power, 1776–1918. Princeton, 1939.

SWEET, W. W. The story of religions in America. New York, 1930.

THELLER, E. A. Canada in 1837–38, showing by historical facts, the causes of the late attempted revolution, and of its failure; the present condition of the people, and their future prospects, together with personal adventures of the author, and others who were connected with the revolution. Philadelphia, 1841. 2 vols.

TIFFANY, ORRIN EDWARD. The relations of the United States to the Canadian Rebellion of 1837–38. Buffalo Historical Society Publications, VIII (Buffalo, 1905), 1–147.

UPTON, Brevet-Maj. Gen. EMORY. The military policy of the United States. Washington, 1917.

URQUHART, DAVID. Case of Mr. McLeod, in whose person the Crown of Great Britain is arraigned for felony. 3d ed. London, 1841.

The autobiography of Martin Van Buren, John C. Fitzpatrick, ed. In: American Historical Association Annual Report for 1918. Vol. II.

WESLEY, E. B. Guarding the frontier: a study of frontier defense from 1815 to 1825. Minneapolis, 1935.

V. ARTICLES

ADAMS, E. D. Lord Ashburton and the Treaty of Washington, *American Historical Review*, XVII (July, 1912), 764–782.

BONHAM, M. L., JR. Alexander McLeod: Bone of Contention, *New York History*, XVIII (April, 1937), 189–217.

CARON, L'ABBÉ IVANHOE. Une Société Secrète dans le Bas-Canada en 1838: L'Association des Frères Chasseurs. In: Royal Society of Canada, Transactions, 3d series, XX, Section 1 (1926), 17–34.

CREIGHTON, D. G. The Commercial Class in Canadian Politics, 1792–1840. In: Canadian Political Science Association, Papers and Proceedings, V (1933), 43–58.

—— The Economic Background of the Rebellion of Eighteen Thirty-Seven, *Canadian Journal of Economics and Political Science*, III (August, 1937), 322–334.

GARLAND, M. A., ed. From Upper Canada to New York in 1837. Extracts from the Diary of the Rev. William Proudfoot, *Mississippi Valley Historical Review*, XVIII (December, 1931), 378–396.

—— Proudfoot Papers, January 1, 1836 to July 7, 1837. In: Ontario Historical Society, Papers and Records, XXX (1934), 124–142.

HAMILTON, Col. C. F. The Canadian Militia: From 1816 to the Crimean War, *Canadian Defence Quarterly*, V (July, 1928), 462–473.

HAND, A. N. Local Incidents of the Papineau Rebellion, *New York History*, XV (October, 1934), 376–387.

LANDON, FRED. The Duncombe Uprising of 1837 and Some of Its Consequences. In: Royal Society of Canada, Transactions, 3d series, XXV, Section 2 (1931), 83–98.

—— The Common Man in the Era of the Rebellion in Upper Canada. In: Canadian Historical Association, Report, 1937, pp. 79–91.

LONGLEY, R. S. Emigration and the Crisis of 1837 in Upper Canada, *Canadian Historical Review*, XVII (March, 1936), 29–40.

MacDermot, T. W. L., *ed.* Some Opinions of a Tory in the 1830's, *Canadian Historical Review,* XI (September, 1930), 232–237.

Mackay, R. A. The Political Ideals of William Lyon Mackenzie, *Canadian Journal of Economics and Political Science,* III (February, 1937), 1–22.

Mulligan, W. O. Sir Charles Bagot and Canadian Boundary Questions. In: Canadian Historical Association, Report, 1936, 40–52.

New, C. W. The Rebellion of 1837 in its Larger Setting. In: Canadian Historical Association, Report, 1937, 5–17.

Overman, W. D., *ed.* A Sidelight on the Hunters' Lodges of 1838, *Canadian Historical Review,* XIX (June, 1938), 168–172.

Partridge, G. F. A Yankee on the New York Frontier, 1833–1851, *New England Quarterly,* X (December, 1937), 752–772.

Rezneck, Samuel. The Social History of an American Depression, 1837–1843, *American Historical Review,* XL (July, 1935), 662–687.

Riddell, W. R. A Contemporary Account of the Navy Island Episode, 1837. In: Royal Society of Canada, Transactions, 3d series, XIII, Section 2 (1919), 57–76.

Sage, Walter. Sir George Arthur and His Administration of Upper Canada, *Queen's Quarterly,* XXVI (1918), 22–53.

Scott, Ernest. The Canadian and United States Transported Prisoners of 1839. In: Royal Australian Historical Society, Journal and Proceedings, XXI (1935). Reprint, 18 pp.

Shortridge, W. P. The Canadian-American Frontier during the Rebellion of 1837–1838, *Canadian Historical Review,* VII (March, 1926), 13–26.

Stacey, C. P. An American Account of the Prescott Raid of 1838, *Canadian Defence Quarterly,* IX (April, 1932), 393–398.

—— A Private Report of General Winfield Scott on the border situation in 1839, *Canadian Historical Review,* XXI (December, 1940), 407–414.

Stavrianos, L. S. Is the Frontier Theory Applicable to the Canadian Rebellions of 1837–1838? *Michigan History Magazine,* XXII (Summer, 1938), 326–337.

Story, Norah. Papineau in Exile, *Canadian Historical Review,* X (March, 1929), 43–52.

Watt, Alastair. The Case of Alexander McLeod, *Canadian Historical Review,* XII (June, 1931), 145–167.

Way, R. L. The Topographical Aspect of Canadian Defence, *Canadian Defence Quarterly,* XIV (April, 1937), 275–287.

INDEX

78, 96, 108, 114, 115, 116, 117, 125, 127; fears Americanization of Upper Canada, 13; fears consequences of *Caroline* affair, 61–62; use of secret service, 68; organizes defense of Canadas, 68, 104, 105; proclamation of martial law, 68; praised by United States press, 83; plans for defense of Canadas, 103–105, 106, 109, 110; opinion of Hunters, 116; recommends permanent defenses for Canada, 148–150; extradition of refugees in United States, 171–172

Colonial Advocate, 20

Commercial Advertiser (Buffalo), 34, 35, 37

"Committee of 13," 31

Connecticut River, 158, 160; source as boundary, 162, 163–165, 166

Connecticut Settlements, 162

Constitutional Act, 2

Cornwall, Upper Canada, 127

Coté, refugee, 42, 66; judicial proceedings against in United States, 120

Coteau du Lac, 104

Cowell, I. W., 48

Creighton, Ogden, 68

Creole, brig, 177

Crittenden, John J.: trial of McLeod, 134

Croswell, Edwin, 71

Daily National Intelligencer. See *National Intelligencer*

Dalhousie, Lord, 169

Danville, Vermont, 32

Davis, Wingate, 79

Dearborn, Michigan, 75

"Declaration of Independence of the People of Lower Canada," 42

Defense, national, 146–157. *See also* Army, Fortifications, Great Lakes, lakes by name, Militia, Naval policy, Northeastern boundary, Volunteers

Democratic party (United States), 99, 100

Democratic Review, 95; opposed to filibustering, 118; comments on Canadian politics, 119–120

Desertion, military, 170, 177

Detroit, 5, 35, 77, 92, 105, 116, 146, 153; recruiting of Patriot forces, 32; description of, 39; as base for attacks against Upper Canada, 39–40, 75, 80–81, 85; headquarters western frontier district, 62

Detroit Daily Advertiser, 85

Detroit Free Press, 63, 123

Detroit River, 39, 80, 104, 105, 153; freedom of navigation, 166

DeWitt, John, 175, 176

Dodge, W. W., 84

Drew, Commander Andrew: leads attack on *Caroline,* 37–38; commended by Upper Canada Assembly, 38

Duncombe, Dr. Charles, 35, 36, 39, 40

Dundas, Colonel, 98

Durfee, Amos, 37

Durham, Lord, 67, 82, 86, 105, 126; in Canada, 93–99; contribution to peace, 93; American opinion of, 93–94; friendly gestures toward United States, 93–94; Grey's mission to Washington, 96–99, 103; defense of border, 98; informed of Hunters' plans, 106; sails for England via Quebec, 106; defense of the Great Lakes, 109–110; *Report,* 118; treatment of political prisoners, 124, 125; attitude in United States toward treatment of prisoners, 124–125

Eastern Townships, 2

Elizabethtown, New York, 42

Erie, steamboat, 81

Erie Canal, 14

Everett, Edward, 158, 182

Extradition, 158; settled by Webster Ashburton treaty, 169–179; in Jay treaty, 169, 172, 176; conflict over jurisdiction in United States, 170–172

Fairfield, John, Governor of Maine, 114

Family Compact, 25

Fidler, Rev. Isaac, 14

Fighting Island, 40

Filibustering: Navy Island, 34–39; London, Upper Canada, district, 35, 39; Bois Blanc Island, 39–40; Fighting Island and Pelée Island, 40–41; French Creek and Kingston, 41; Lower Canada, 41–42; end of first phase, 43; Short Hills, 72; Windsor, 74–75, 80–81; Prescott, 77–80; opposition to, 82–86; incendiarism, 113–114. *See also* Hunters, Patriot plans, Patriots

Fillmore, Millard: interest in *Caroline* and McLeod case, 132, 133; urges competitive building on lakes, 154

Fond du Lac, 167, 168

Forsyth, John, 38, 40, 48, 69, 96, 97, 116, 120, 121; military protection of the frontier, 46, 98; requires civil officers on frontier to carry out instructions,